THE ONLY SALES PROMOTION TECHNIQUES YOU'LL EVER NEED!

DARTNELL is a publisher serving the world of business with books, manuals, newsletters and bulletins, and training materials for executives, managers, supervisors, salespeople, financial officials, personnel executives, and office employees. Dartnell also produces management and sales training videos and audiocassettes, publishes many useful business forms, and many of its materials and films are available in languages other than English. Dartnell, established in 1917, serves the world's business community. For details, catalogs, and product information, write to:

THE DARTNELL CORPORATION,
4660 N Ravenswood Ave,
Chicago, IL 60640-4595, U.S.A.
or phone (800) 621-5463, in U.S. and Canada.

THE ONLY SALES PROMOTION TECHNIQUES YOU'LL EVER NEED!

Tamara Brezen Block

Excerpted Chapters from *The Dartnell Sales Promotion Handbook, Eighth Edition*, 1994

CONTENTS

FOREWORD

The sales promotion field has grown and changed tremendously, and never so much as in the last decade; yet there is nothing new about it. Sales promotion in all its incarnations has been around for more than a century. The basic sales promotion techniques — couponing, sampling, sweepstakes, premiums, trading stamp continuity programs — are still as viable as ever. What time and technology have accomplished have improved the targeting, the implementation, the understanding, and the effectiveness of these tried and true techniques. Therefore, while sales promotion is not new, a book such as this is more important than ever in this new sales promotion age.

Only a decade ago, many described sales promotion as the "stepchild" of advertising, subordinating its role and its importance to the power of the television commercial or the magazine advertisement. However, anyone who has run a promotion at the end of the year in order to meet his or her annual sales and profit projections knows firsthand the terribly important impact that a coupon drop or a price reduction can have on a brand. Today, it is widely acknowledged that sales promotion is an invaluable part of the marketing mix. Promotion now accounts for two out of every three dollars allocated to the marketing of many consumer products and has become a multi-billion dollar business. Sales promotion has stepped up to its rightful place at the top of the ladder.

What has driven sales promotion to the forefront of the marketing arena, perhaps more than anything else, is our ability to measure and analyze promotion effects. Just as computer technology has allowed the scanning and real-time collection of product sales information, it has also allowed real-time analysis of a promotion's impact — the incremental sales and store traffic generated during the promotional period. By comparing the dollars spent to the incremental dollars earned, the profitability of a promotional program can be calculated. By analyzing the incremental sales over various price points and promotion tactics, a real demand curve can be estimated and used to more accurately predict the outcome of future promotions, thereby assisting the planning process. This kind of accountability and predictability, so lacking in traditional advertising campaigns, has generated the renewed excitement and increased use of sales promotion in recent years.

Of course, the rise and growth of sales promotion can also be attributed to several corollary characteristics and timely environmental factors. In contrast to the runaway cost inflation of the television commercial and the longer approval times, sales promotion can be implemented at a much lower cost and typically in much less production and planning time. Regardless of the product category or the industry, the diversity of available sales promotion tools offers a marketing professional considerable flexibility and undoubtedly a technique with a match to the goals and the targeted audience for the selling situation. Furthermore, today's increasingly cost-conscious customers are more inclined to appreciate, look for, and even wait for promotional deals. A good sales promotion, after all, is predicated on delivering the customer a "deal," and whether it's a BOGO (buy one, get one free), a price-reducing coupon, or a free gift with purchase, the savings and/or value are obvious. Of no less importance is the fact that, time constraints being what they are, today's customer makes most of his or her purchase decisions at the point-of-purchase where consumer and trade sales promotions, rather than advertising, have the distinct advantage.

While sales promotion will continue to evolve with time, it is hard to imagine a time in the future when sales promotion will ever again be relegated to the lower ranks of the marketing mix. The tried and true techniques of old will continue to flourish with renewed vigor and vitality.

THE ORIGINS OF THIS BOOK

Over 50 years ago, Dartnell published its very first sales promotion guide — 30 pages focused primarily on posters and sales letters. From these humble beginnings, the *Sales Promotion Handbook* was born and became an integral part of Dartnell's series of handbooks for business practitioners. In 1994, Dartnell published the eighth edition of this industry bible. That book — all 800+ pages of it — is brimming with information and advice about putting sales promotion into action. The sizable expansion of the book since its inception reflects the ever-expanding role that sales promotion now plays in the marketplace.

The 1994 edition of the *Sales Promotion Handbook* had a broader focus than this present volume: its mission was to be a comprehensive guide to all aspects of sales promotion planning, implementation, and analysis. Entire sections of the book were devoted to the planning stages, with chapters on setting objectives and sales promotion budgets and evaluating promotion results; to special topical issues in promotion such as brand equity, diverting and forward buying, privacy implications, and legal requirements; to sales promotion strategy written from the perspective of practitioners working across a variety of industries such as business-to-business, durables, and food retailing, in addition to chapters on the promotional techniques that make up the field we call sales promotion.

With the success of the *Handbook*, it became clear that there was a special call for an abridgement of the book, focusing simply on the techniques themselves. This volume, *The Only Sales Promotion Techniques You'll Ever Need!*, fills that need. It contains a collection of the chapters from the *Handbook* that delineate the most significant techniques and tools used in the industry today. It provides a convenient manual for readers, at all levels of experience, to use as a reference when creating a new promotion plan.

SALES PROMOTION PLANNING ESSENTIALS

The chapters herein contain valuable information about specific sales promotion techniques; but the promotion planning and evaluation process begins long before a tactical offer is devised, and continues once a given sales promotion ends. While this abridged version of the *Handbook* is intended primarily to highlight the techniques themselves, a quick overview of the essential planning elements is warranted in any sales promotion text.

SALES PROMOTION DEFINED

Sales promotion is difficult to define by its very nature — its diversity. It envelops a great variety of techniques, tools, and activities and is intimately related to many of the traditional arenas of advertising, public relations, direct marketing, and personal selling. The one element that typically differentiates sales promotion activities from these other activities is that they are intended foremost to influence purchasing behavior and induce relatively short-term results rather than create an image over the long term.

The sales promotion arsenal includes techniques such as product samples, coupons, rebates and refunds, premiums, sweepstakes/contests/games, frequency and continuity programs, specialty products, promotions to the trade such as slotting allowances and off-invoice allowances — all targeted at increasing the price/value perception in order to quickly spur the desired action. However different these varied techniques may appear, every promotion attempts to trigger an offer-response-reward sequence that is built upon three key ingredients: 1) the creative concept or offer, 2) the vehicle or system for delivering it, and 3) the fulfillment of the reward promised in the concept or offer.

These three ingredients are not necessarily mutually exclusive or independent. A promotion's creative concept often takes its cue from the way in which the promise is fulfilled. Technology has greatly affected this promotion triangle and given a fresh new presence to what may be categorized as the same old techniques. For instance, couponing is a relatively straightforward, traditional promotion offer; but delivering a product coupon at the check-out counter to a consumer who has just purchased a competitive brand in the category is a whole new promotion concept because of the way it is targeted and delivered.

It is the way in which each of these three areas is applied and implemented in a particular situation that differentiates a successful promotion from one that fails to produce results. Hence, while any good promotion program is founded on a thorough knowledge of the techniques and tools in all their myriad forms, without the essential spark of creativity a promotion program lacks luster and fresh appeal.

Promotion Integration

The blurring of the lines between the marketing activities represented by advertising, public relations, personal selling, direct marketing, and sales promotion has been exacerbated with the ascendence of integrated marketing. It is important to remember that in almost every marketing/selling situation, sales promotion is used in conjunction with the other marketing elements and that each of these, in turn, is used at one time or another to support a sales promotion. The growing discipline of integrated marketing communications simply acknowledges this truth and seeks to promote the harmony and synergy among the many communication components.

Despite the organizational difficulties of integrating these separate marketing functions, the benefits are obvious for brands that achieve integration. Too often, each marketing component is conceived and implemented in isolation of the others without taking note of the the overall aggregate impact on the customer and without considering or capitalizing on the leverage potential that exists among the promotional pieces and parts. In today's cluttered promotional environment, a brand whose marketing activities are truly integrated and in tune with one another can cut through that clutter by creating a powerful, unified campaign (emphasis on campaign) rather than a medley of meaningless or conflicting tactics that never quite connect in the customer's mind for the good of the product.

As evidence of this kind of synergy at work, analysis of retail scanner data for package-goods items show that, while a store price reduction is very effective in generating incremental sales for a product, advertising the price-off and bringing attention to the price reduction in the store via shelf talkers or special end-aisle displays can create a promotional synergy that multiplies sales several times over what might be expected from the aggregation of each advertising and sales promotion technique executed independently.

The integrated approach is gaining much momentum as marketers find that advertising alone, or any other marketing tool by itself, cannot move the sales needle as effectively as a fully integrated promotion campaign. For this reason, when planning the marketing and promotional activities for a product/service, it pays to keep the overall marketing and promotional objectives clearly in sight, considering all the tools available and how they might leverage and support one another most effectively to produce the desired results.

Setting Sales Promotion Objectives and Budgets

Sales promotion can accomplish a great many things. Yet, without a clear understanding of what needs to be accomplished, it will be difficult to plan and implement a successful sales promotion and, indeed, it will never be known whether a promotion has been successful. Clearly stated objectives will aid in the selection of the most appropriate technique(s), will guide the budgetary and executional issues, and should set the criteria for success.

The three components of any good objective, of course, are: 1) an unambiguous, action-oriented statement of one or more measurable goals, 2) a concise and clearly identified audience for the promotion, and 3) a timetable for accomplishing the task.

The goal and the audience are intimately related, in that different actions are appropriate or expected for different audiences. Sales promotion is typically aimed at at least one of three audiences: the consumer, the trade, or a company's own employees or sales force. The action desired from each could be very different. Typical consumer objectives include:

    gaining new product trial,

    encouraging repeat product usage,

    loading the consumer pantry or building consumer inventories,

    increasing usage frequency, or

    trading the consumer up to larger product sizes or more expensive lines.

Goals for the trade would most likely include:

    gaining shelf space or distribution,

    building or reducing in-store inventories, or

    securing trade support for merchandising activity (displays, feature advertising).

Promoting to the sales force or internally to employees might encompass:

    boosting morale, or

    increasing productivity.

While the same technique might be designed to impact more than one audience simultaneously, a sales promotion objective should be targeted for one audience only, with multiple objectives for multiple audiences. Objectives should be quantifiable so that promotion effects can be measured. Sales volume, for instance, can be easily quantified for a promotional period and compared to pre- and post-promotional periods.

The timeframe is the period during which the sales promotion task should be completed and measured. It needs to be thoughtfully set in order to allow enough time to realistically accomplish the goals and not shortchange a promotion's success, but not too long so as to bias the results either favorably or negatively by extending the window beyond the point where promotion can have any incremental influence.

Perhaps as important as setting appropriate promotional objectives is allocating sufficient budget to accomplish the stated goals. The two are not unrelated. The goals and techniques selected to meet those goals are constrained by the monies available, and the allocated budget sets the tone of what can realistically be expected from the sales promotion program. While there are many methods of determining an acceptable, or even optimal, budget, the table that follows aptly summarizes the factors that guide current promotional spending.

Traditional Factors Guiding Promotion Spending for a Brand

	Low Promotion	High Promotion
Consumer Factors		
Price sensitivity	Low	High
Brand loyalty	High	Low
Purchase planning	High	Low
Information needs	High	Low
Perceived risk	High	Low
Brand Factors		
Life-cycle stage	Growth	Maturity
Market position	Dominant	Competitive
Seasonal pattern	Uniform	Seasonal
Category Factors		
Product differentiation	Strong brands	Commodity
Private brands	Limited	Extensive

ANALYZING PROMOTION EFFECTS

To truly analyze a promotion's effectiveness, there needs to be an understanding of how the promotion should work, coupled with an understanding of a brand's demand. In the not-too-distant past, such understanding was sorely lacking. The extent of our knowledge was that sales promotion could and did impact sales. With this limited vision, many sales promotions have been implemented that may have temporarily increased sales volumes, but may not have been profitable in light of the reduced price or the cost to implement the deal. Additionally, promotions have been selected and implemented based on a tradition of what had been done in the past and without regard to what technique or combination of techniques might produce the optimal results.

Retail scanners and powerful computing technology have changed this, opening up opportunities for systematically analyzing sales volume levels before, during, and after sales promotion and enhancing the ability to develop sound promotional principles that can be used to effectively evaluate and plan sales promotions.

With daily sales data available on an item-by-item basis, over time the impact of fluctuating price points and various kinds of promotional activity can be sorted out and understood. A demand curve, which identifies the relationship between price and volume in different promotional conditions, can be generated for a given product UPC. A "baseline," the sales volume for an item at its normal price point without any promotion, can be calculated. With a baseline to use as a standard for comparison, the incremental volume due to a sales promotion can also be calculated for a promotional period. This incremental volume can be further analyzed to determine a promotion's profitability and to understand the relative contribution of each promotional component, along with price, to the sales results.

This kind of quantitative analysis can seem complicated, and it is. However, the facts and information, not to mention the understanding it can give a marketing or sales promotion manager, is invaluable. This whole approach is called Fact-Based Marketing, and it is still relatively in its infancy. Furthermore, the art of baselining and the sales promotion principles learned from analysis of promotion to date are still predominantly package-goods-oriented, because that is presently the area in which the data is readily available. The approach, nevertheless, set the standards for what is possible in the future.

LEGAL CONSIDERATIONS

Every promotion manager ideally should have a working knowledge of the federal, state, and local laws and regulations that govern sales promotion. Without an awareness of the legal risks and issues of running a coupon, sweepstakes, or premium offer, a program may be doomed from the start. Getting into the habit of thinking about the legal review early will avoid many problems later on. Of course, to be safe, any sales promotion should always undergo legal scrutiny from an experienced sales promotion attorney before going to market.

Fundamentally, a sales promotion offer sets up an incentive-reward system in which consumers or another targeted audience are told they are entitled to something, whether it be a discounted price or a chance to win a prize, if they act in the manner specified (i.e., purchase the product or enter the sweepstakes). The sponsor is then legally obligated to fulfill their promise. Generally speaking, the sponsor does not want to leave any room for ambiguity or doubt in the interpretation of the terms and conditions for redemption, winning, or whatnot. The Federal Trade Commission has set guidelines in many areas to help prevent misleading communication; these guidelines should always be followed.

The laws and regulations vary by technique. For instance, the issues for couponing are different from those for a sweepstakes or a premium program; hence, the laws governing each are different. The legal standards and requirements may even vary by industry or audience for a particular technique, as with quick service restaurant premiums and premiums to children, both of which have been deemed to be special classes necessitating special considerations. Many states have different laws governing implementation of sales promotion, meaning that, ultimately, a sales promotion program must be modified on a state-by-state basis before it can be executed nationally.

Almost every aspect of sales promotion can potentially raise a legal issue. And the laws frequently change. Therefore, it is safest to seek and heed the advice of a lawyer during the planning phase of any promotion.

It would be difficult for anyone to claim having *the* most comprehensive and definitive guide to sales promotion. There are, of course, many ways to categorize the various techniques and so many creative ways to combine and reinvent these techniques so as to make any list appear incomplete. In *The Only Sales Promotion Techniques You'll Ever Need!*, you'll find chapters that cover the most basic promotion techniques; and within each chapter, these categories are further delineated to encompass just about every conceivable promotion subtype known. This book contains some of the best chapters anywhere on the tried and true sales promotion techniques such as couponing, sampling, premiums, continuity plans, sweepstakes, and in-store point-of-purchase. It also contains chapters on tools that are often absent from a traditional sales promotion book but which are increasingly lumped into the promotion pool such as direct response, co-op advertising, product licensing and tie-ins, marketing events, and specialty products.

One of the unique characteristics of this book, as with the *Handbook* itself, is that every chapter is written by a different expert and practitioner in the field of sales promotion. Therefore, the book goes beyond the perspective, the experience, and the limitations of any one individual. These contributing authors were handpicked not only because of their knowledge and experience on their chosen topic, but also because they represent some of the most prominent names in the promotion industry today. It is rare to find so much expertise and talent within the pages of just one book. For this reason alone, the book is worth the read.

The mission of this book is to be a comprehensive, yet always practical, guide to learning about the most important sales promotion techniques and how to use them effectively. Whether the reader is an experienced sales promotion user looking for inspiration, or someone just beginning to utilize sales promotion for the first time, the book will become an invaluable addition to any sales promotion library.

To familiarize you with the contents of this book, what follows is an overview of each of the thirteen chapters selected for inclusion.

The book begins with Dr. Dan Ailloni-Charas' chapter on sampling. Ailloni-Charas actually wrote his own book years back on the planning, strategy, and execution of sales promotion; but his current role as president and CEO of Stratmar, providing in-store and out-of-store sampling services for numerous clients, gives him a distinct advantage to writing a chapter such as this. Sampling can be an extremely effective trial device for a new or improved product and is becoming an increasingly effective way to introduce new customers to an established product overlooked by them. The offer is simple — customers can try the product completely risk-free. While the technique would appear to be simple to implement, the chapter points out and summarizes nicely the key issues to consider and questions to ask when planning a sampling program at the point-of-purchase, away from the store, through the mail, or in-home.

Couponing is perhaps the most common form of sales promotion, and has continued to grow and dominate the promotion field. Larry Tucker knows firsthand the positive effects that couponing can have on sales, since his firm has sponsored the nation's largest targeted co-op mailing program for nearly two decades. Because the literature on couponing is large, I have myself assumed the role of academic and assisted in the assembling of material and writing of this chapter. Since the statistics change every year regarding coupon redemption, the chapter instead looks at the broader picture of what couponing can accomplish; how the couponing process works — from budgeting and design to policing for fraud; the variations a coupon offer can take; the diversity of delivery methods; and, in light of all this, the basic truths that are currently known about coupon redemption.

Chapter 3 is entitled "Premiums, Refunds, and Promotional Fulfillment." Premiums, or merchandise incentives as they are also called, are succinctly handled, along with refunding, in Don Roux's chapter. The advantages and disadvantages of each incentive type are covered. Included in this chapter are tools such as direct premiums (in, on, and near packs), reusable container packs, free-in-the-mail premiums, self-liquidating premiums, account openers, business gifts, employee award programs, dealer incentives, and rebates/refunds. All of these require one thing in common — incentive fulfillment. And Roux, as president and CEO of one of the nation's largest fulfillment services, is a leading authority on promotion fulfillment.

Don Jagoda is very well-known in promotion circles as the "guru" of sweepstakes. In Chapter 4, sweepstakes, games and contests are all explained. Jagoda notes the important differences among these three and gives complete illustrated examples of each. Included as well is information on who enters or participates in such promotions; the various formats each can take; a comprehensive checklist for planning a sweepstakes, game, or contest; and guidelines for budgeting.

Today's continuity, frequency, and trading stamp programs are gaining appeal as marketers and retailers vie for customer's loyalty and continued patronage. It is, of course, the loyal customer franchise that most businesses build their business around. It is also more widely acknowledged today than ever before that the cost of retaining one loyal customer is much less than attracting a new customer. James Feldman explains in Chapter 5 the advantages and disadvantages of a continuity promotion designed to encourage repeat patronage or purchase. He also provides a 10-point planning process that will focus sales promotion managers on the key questions and issues to consider when planning such a promotion. Included among his 10 points are such things as when a continuity program is appropriate; how one should structure the program, track sales, and define the rewards; when to use a multi-level awards program; and how to integrate the continuity program with advertising and public relations. One has only to hear Feldman speak in front of a group to realize the power of motivational marketing. Even his role as president of several motivation companies cannot begin to surpass his enthusiasm for this topic.

Probably nothing has received greater attention recently than promotion at the point of sale. While advertising may hope to create an image that allows a brand to stand out in a consumer's mind, it is the point-of-purchase (P-O-P) in the store, at the time the consumer makes the actual purchase decision, that counts most today. In this arena, no one has brought more style and creativity to the point-of-purchase industry than Douglas Leeds. Thomson-Leeds is a leading New York point-of-purchase advertising agency; and Leeds, the agency's president, has had a personal hand in the creation of more award-winning point-of-purchase designs than any other company in the industry. Leeds has also put together a fun, but thoroughly informative, text on this area in Chapter 6. He describes P-O-P in terms of time or duration, location, and function, and conveniently outlines the steps to managing the P-O-P function. His "rules" for developing creative P-O-P concepts are accompanied with relevant and timely examples (and photos) of winning P-O-P designs.

The primary goal of any sales promotion program is to generate immediate sales response. Developing a sales promotion mailing that does just this is the topic of Chapter 7. Larry Tucker, who co-authored the couponing chapter, also lends his hand to this important chapter on direct response. His experience is uncontested; his firm has sponsored the nation's largest targeted co-op mailing program, Jane Tucker's Supermarket of Savings, with an annual mailing to over 150 million households. The chapter subtitle, "Generating Cost-Effective Response or Coupon Redemption with Inserts, Ride-Alongs, and Co-op Mailings," just about summarizes the breadth of this chapter. The text is very hands-on, outlining key tips for better targeting, selecting and featuring products in a mailing, testing pricing strategies, and generally creating a profitable co-op package-insert program, complete with many examples to back up his suggestions.

The whole area of database marketing has exploded relatively recently with the application of technology to customer databases. Sales promotion is not only an excellent vehicle to gain access to and provide information on current customers; as with a sweepstakes entry, the promotion itself becomes all the more effective when "deal-prone" customers can be targeted with the right promotion, the right value, for products/services of interest via database marketing. Connie Kennedy, formerly VP at Targetbase Marketing in Dallas, has organized one of the more comprehensive nuts and bolts chapters on this topic. Chapter 8 begins with the three business strategies which a marketing database can affect, and continues on to checklists for costing, building a database, and evaluating suppliers. In the process, she covers important issues such as customer lifetime value, database formats, sources of external data, and testing a database. The chapter ends with a list of additional resources on the database marketing.

The basic goal of sales promotion is to generate sales and store traffic at the local retail level. Co-op advertising is designed to run at the retail level, identifying products and prices at specific store locations in order to attract customers to those stores. Therefore, while co-op is not traditionally considered one of the promotion techniques, it nevertheless is an important support mechanism for sales promotion. Neil Fraser is a known speaker and writer on the subject of co-op advertising, having published a co-op glossary back in 1984 and having been named one of the six original members of the Co-op Hall of Fame. He has distinguished himself working on co-op advertising programs over the past 30 years for both consumer and industrial marketers. He discusses cooperative advertising from the perspectives of the manufacturer, the retailer, and a wholesaler, and outlines the various kinds of co-op programs as well as the key components of a co-op policy.

Everywhere you turn, you see promotions whose awareness and appeal is accentuated through association with a celebrity or with sports, musical, entertainment, designer, and game properties (to name only a few). Tie-ins can be incredibly lucrative to the property owner and to the licensee alike. Chapter 10, "Product Licensing and Tie-Ins," provides a wonderful primer on the basics of retail licensing and promotional tie-ins. The chapter's author, Karen Raugust, has been the editor of a monthly newsletter on the topic, *The Licensing Letter*, since 1991 and writes, speaks, and consults regularly on licensing. She talks about types of properties, how to select the appropriate licensing and tie-in partners, and lays out the legal responsibilities of both the licensee and licensor.

Paul Stanley likes to say that with event marketing, it's not the event that matters. Rather it's what you leverage with the event that counts. Stanley's company, PS Productions, is the largest entertainment event marketing agency in the country. While he has established his company and his career primarily on music entertainment events, his chapter applies equally to an event of any nature. His chapter illuminates the needs and motivators of the many players involved in the implementation of a successful event, including the manufacturer, the trade, the sales force, the media, the event promoters, the event "property" or celebrity, the consumer, and the important role of publicity.

Specialties, one of the oldest forms of sales incentives, have too often been carelessly characterized as "trinkets and trash." Yet, this $5.5 billion dollar industry obviously occupies an important niche in today's promotion industry. Specialty products are like sales promotion itself, richly diversified and flexible to fit almost any type of business, any size audience or budget, and multiple objectives, from sales to goodwill. In Chapter 12, Richard Ebel from Promotional Products Association International (PPAI) lays out the applications and the strengths and weaknesses of specialties, and gives examples that are sure to motivate its continued use.

The final chapter of the book is on the topic of trade promotion. Because of the importance of the point of sale in purchase, gaining the support and leverage of the "trade" is critical. Trade promotions, including slotting allowances, off-invoice allowances, dating, and free goods may not seem as glamorous as the consumer promotions of the earlier chapters, but together they represent the single largest category of promotional expenditures by marketers, typically surpassing what is spent on either consumer promotions or advertising. These "below-the-line" expenditures, as they are often referred to, have generated increased attention as marketers are feeling trapped and held hostage by the trade promotion practices of the past. James Kunze, of J. Brown Associates of Grey Advertising Agency, takes each trade promotion technique in turn and systematically outlines the key features, objectives, benefits, and disadvantages of each. He lays out the dilemma behind promoting to the trade and suggests a "better way" to approach this technique.

The thirteen chapters in this book should serve to guide and enlighten every marketing and promotion manager who takes the time to read them. Whatever your job title, industry, or need, my best advice is to keep *The Only Sales Promotion Techniques You'll Ever Need!* close at hand. And Happy Promoting!

ABOUT THE EDITOR

Tamara Brezen Block is president of Block Research, Inc., a research firm providing a full range of quantitative and qualitative research services, including sales promotion analysis. She teaches graduate level research methods and sales promotion courses, among others, as a faculty member of the Medill School of Journalism's Integrated Marketing Communications Program at Northwestern University. Before joining the faculty at Northwestern, Block was an instructor in the Advertising Department at Michigan State University and a Visiting Professor at Foote, Cone, and Belding in Chicago.

In addition to co-editing this handbook, Block is co-author of *Business-to-Business Market Research* (Probus). She has been published in several academic journals on topics related to advertising and promotion effects.

Block received a Ph.D. in Mass Media from Michigan State University. Her dissertation on the topic of sales promotion received a national award from the Council of Sales Promotion Agencies. Her Master of Arts degree and Bachelor of Arts, both in Advertising, were also completed at Michigan State.

Dan Ailloni-Charas is Chairman and CEO of Stratmar Systems, Inc., a marketing services company providing sampling, couponing, fulfillment, and other in-store and out-of-store support programs. Prior to his 25 years as CEO of Stratmar, Ailloni-Charas was Marketing Research Manager, New Products Manager, and Manager of International Marketing Services for Cheseborough-Pond's. He also was Director of Consumer and Communications Research at Forbes *magazine.*

He has been an active member of the Promotion Marketing Association of America since 1978, serving on the Board of Directors as Chairman of the Education Committee and Premium Shows Subcommittee, and, for the last five years, has served as Vice President and a member of the Executive Committee. He is past National Vice President of the American Marketing Association (AMA) and past President of the New York AMA chapter. In addition, Ailloni-Charas has served as Editor of Marketing Review *and has been on the Board of Editors for* The Journal of Consumer Marketing *since 1982. He is the author of* Promotion: A Guide to Effective Promotional Planning, Strategies & Executions, *published by John Wiley & Sons (1984).*

Ailloni-Charas has taught marketing as an adjunct or visiting professor at several universities, including Pace University and New York University. He received a Ph.D. from the Graduate School of Business Administration at New York University. He received bachelor's and master's degrees from the University of California.

CHAPTER 1

SAMPLING

It has been said that the fastest way to kill a bad new product is to sample it to potential consumers. Indeed, since sampling is designed to accelerate the adoption process, the quicker consumers know that a new product will not meet their expectations of satisfaction, the quicker its demise.

Consider the following: Trial, or first use, is critical to the adoption of a new product. It is a necessary step the consumer must take before a product can be deemed acceptable for consumption and repeated buying.

Initial purchases of a new product can be brought about through persuasive communications of one sort or another. However, initial purchases all require a potential consumer to "risk" the purchase price, since a new product may or may not live up to its performance promise. Because consumers, under the barrage of an unending stream of new product communications, are slow to take such risks with their money, the nonrisk proposition of sampling serves to accelerate the introduction process.

The introduction of new products has always been an "iffy" proposition. Few products advance from the test-marketing stage to broad-scale commercialization, and, among those that do, many eventually fail. Often, this may be due to a lack of sufficient support over the time frame that is needed for consumers to become aware of a new product, knowledgeable about it, and, finally, interested enough to make that first trial purchase. By then, it may be too late, since the product may have lost its distribution at the retail level.

As manufacturers spend large sums of money to develop and introduce new products and line extensions, R&D costs — coupled with manufacturing, packaging, and front-end loaded advertising and distribution costs — add up quickly. Distribution is critical; unless a product is on the shelf where customers can find it, all is for naught. In recent years, the trade has been exacting increasing levies from manufacturers before accepting their products for distribution at retail. Slotting charges — payments the manufacturer is required to make before the product is accepted by an account for distribution in its stores — further increase the investment required in the launching of a new product.

Today, manufacturers are allowed about three months to prove to the trade that a new product can "make it" in the marketplace. Success is determined by moving an acceptable number of cases of product every week. Should that movement level be achieved, the new product may be allotted a permanent home on the shelf. Should it fail to make it, out it goes, and with it, the sizable investment made to that point. Given more time, that new product might have been successful — but translating "sales in the mind" made through advertising requires time to build up to sufficient levels. Time, however, is a scarce commodity in today's retailing reality; hence, a new product may be delisted before it can make it, and once it is no longer carried by an account, it is virtually impossible, and very costly, to get it back on the shelf.

Enter sampling. By short-circuiting the process through nonrisk trial, we will have accelerated the adoption of the new product — should it meet performance expectations — and enhanced the likelihood of its obtaining a permanent home on the retail shelf. By doing so, sampling helps safeguard the sizable investment made in the new product launch and, most likely, at a fraction of that initial investment.

THE GROWTH OF SAMPLING

Over the years, the sampling "industry" has continued to grow, through good times and bad, and for all the good reasons outlined previously. While no exact figure can be determined regarding the aggregate corporate expenditures spent on sampling, including both costs of product and distribution, it would be safe to assume that hundreds of millions of dollars are spent today by manufacturers throughout the U.S. to jump-start the adoption process.

Since the essence of sampling is the placement of a trial size of a product in the hands of a potential user, there is a continuous proliferation of methods designed to achieve this purpose, from sampling on airplanes, to state and county fairs, to in-home parties. The number of alternative sampling vehicles are many, and new ideas abound. For our purpose, the remainder of this chapter will spotlight the major sampling venues with a clear understanding that the number of potential alternatives is limited only by the creativity and imagination of those active in this area.

SAMPLING AS INSURANCE:
SECURING A TRADE FRANCHISE

Sampling as an insurance policy, representing, in effect, a defensive strategy, is a relatively new idea. For years, offensive objectives were targeted by sampling. The goal was primarily directed to conversions to regular usage (purchases), leading to quicker payouts of total launch investments. While the offensive criteria are still inherent in the accelerating action of sampling, the emphasis today is on faster consumer takeout at retail, which is conducive to regular listing. This, parenthetically, accounts for the literal explosion of in-store sampling activities over the last 10 years or so.

A national study recently published by the National Association of Demonstration Companies (NADC) reports on the growth of this mode of sampling in recent years, as well as anticipated growth through the year 2000. Here are some findings of the survey, which was conducted in mid-1992:

- 70.7 percent of product manufacturers and 100 percent of retailers indicate they are going to increase the use of in-store sampling between now and the year 2000.
- 79.3 percent of shoppers say they will buy a sampled product if they like it and if it is one they need and want.
- Demonstration is the promotional technique shoppers remember the longest, when compared with in-store coupons, end-of-the-aisle displays, or signage on a shelf.
- Shoppers also like sampling because it is "hassle free," that is, they can choose whether or not to participate — and they also like the fact that there is often an "instant discount" associated with the demonstration.

Having reviewed the role of sampling as a trial vehicle conducive to following up full-revenue purchases, we can classify such efforts by positioning them to generate immediate consumer takeout vs. efforts that bring about purchases of the product or services at a later time.

The dividing line here rests with the point of purchase. Sampling a product on the retail floor can be tied to promotional efforts resulting in price featuring, display activities, and incremental pipelining to retail. In effect, we signal to the shopper who samples a product in-store that if the product "experience" was satisfactory, he or she can make a first, full-sized purchase at a promotionally advantaged price. Easing a new user into regular usage of a new product through trial, followed by a discounted first purchase, will usually accelerate the building up of both consumer and trade franchises.

However, it is important to note that not all products can be actually experienced at the actual point of purchase. One can try out a new scent from a tester on a department store counter, taste a few sips of a new beverage, or put a few drops of a new lotion on the back of one's hand to test its level of greasiness. But few people will sample an antacid or laxative while in the store before they decide whether to purchase the product.

A more extreme case is represented by pet foods, which are judged first by their palatability to the pet, their compatibility with the pet's digestive system, and, finally, by their nutritional claims. This trial-and-evaluation process obviously cannot take place at point of purchase.

Additionally, one must also realize that some purchases are made in-store by an adult in his or her role as a purchasing agent, and not by the ultimate consumer who will have the final say regarding the suitability of the sampled product for regular purchase.

SAMPLING AT OR NEAR THE POINT OF PURCHASE

Sampling can be carried out in, near, or away from, the actual point of purchase. This distinction may seem simple, yet it is important. Products that can be "experienced on the spot," at the point of purchase, can be immediately converted into a revenue sale. This allows the sampling effort to be executed as a total "event," fully involving the distribution channel in the process of quickly building up both trade and consumer franchises.

Sampling conducted away from the point of purchase is more akin to the "sale in the mind" effect attributed to advertising. The more time that elapses after sampling the product before the actual opportunity of buying the product in the store presents itself, the more likely the occurrence of "interference" — ranging from competitive efforts to simple forgetfulness — which will negatively impact the initial intent of buying the product sampled.

Further, when an account implements a sampling program in its stores, it is safe to assume that the product is in distribution (in at least the account's stores) facilitating the conversion of customers sampled to actual users/purchasers. This may not be the case when the product is sampled away from the point of purchase where gaps in distribution may have a further negative impact on the customer's intent to buy.

For goods, sampling at the point of purchase, as indicated, is preferable in many ways that can lead to an immediate purchase. However, several caveats must be observed:

1. The product must be in distribution with sufficient stock at retail to satisfy immediate conversion needs. Running out of stock during a sampling period represents a clear case of lost opportunity. It is customary that product is "plussed out" by an account's warehouse in conjunction with a promotional period. Given the number of parallel promotions running every week, one would be remiss in anticipating that sufficient merchandise will automatically be sent out from warehouses to stores. Both quantities and timing must be negotiated and monitored by the manufacturer's sales organization.

2. While trade support of the product through advertised price featuring will help accelerate consumer takeout, manufacturers are advised not to offer label price-off deals on their products during an introductory stage. This would prevent them from establishing a firm value/price reference point for such products in consumers' minds. Price features offered by the trade are acceptable, and even expected. The fact that such price features are based on increased allowances given by manufacturers to the trade so that products may flow through to consumers does not necessarily affect consumers' perceptions of product value.

3. Generally speaking, retail floor displays increase consumer takeout of any product, new or old. Since displays are associat-

ed in consumers' minds with special deals, takeout increases significantly when a product is displayed in one form or another. Given the limited floor space available for displays in the context of the number of items carried by a retail store, manufacturers usually "buy" space for their displays through special allowances. At this point, the retailer must decide how much of this allowance to pass on to his or her shoppers.

Retailers set up their displays at the beginning of the week — usually on Sundays when most of the their advertising is circulated, while sampling is executed Fridays through Sundays, which are considered the best in-store-traffic days. Manufacturers' displays start selling through as soon as they are set up, thus significantly adding to the consumer takeout during the sampling week. In that sense, some of the sampling will take place in the home — after the product is purchased. It is important to note that the placement of a display on the retail floor as part of a sampling event further ensures against potential out-of-stock crises.

4. Securing a spot on an account's promotional calendar is critical and should be accomplished early enough to enable the sampling program to be optimally executed. The program should take into consideration not only the availability of sampling stations on the retail floor (to guard against the possibility of postponement, due to limited floor space), but also potential tie-ins with product advertising schedules, as well as consumer and trade promotions that are planned for later follow-up periods.

One must keep in mind, however, that the complexion of in-store sampling programs has changed radically since the mid-1980s. Pressed for finding new revenue sources to shore up their weakening financial bases, most retailers identified in-store programs as yet another potential profit center.

Under the guise of insisting that they must retain control over activities in their stores, many retailers have set up their own sampling/demonstration units. Alternatively, some retailers have signed exclusive access agreements with one local service or another whose sampling fees often include hefty payments to the trade for such agreements. Where manufacturers are allowed less fettered access to the retail floor through in-store services of their choice, the trade may nevertheless demand significant payments on the premise that giving a manufacturer in-store access to their customer base is valuable and, thus, chargeable. Either way, the costs of in-store sampling have skyrocketed. Nevertheless, sampling as a promotional technique has increased many times over in the last few years, attesting to the growing importance of the point of purchase in manufacturers' marketing plans.

To the trade, individual brands are no longer as important as they once were. Having recognized the commoditization of many of the product classes sold in their stores and consequently noticing the lack of product loyalty and the ease with which consumers switch from brand to brand — retailers have abandoned their commitment to full assortments, concentrating instead on overall product categories. Concerns for specific brands are now left to those manufacturing them. Given that brands cannot survive in the marketplace without adequate distribution at retail, the trade has been able to increase its "take" from manufacturers in many ways — overrides on in-store sampling programs being one.

Still, the key problem is not one of payments, which, however reluctantly, may be disbursed from and calculated in overall marketing plans as part of the cost of doing business. The real problem is one of accountability.

Based on current practices, there can be no doubt that increasing numbers of retailers are using their growing clout over manufacturers to demand more and more money from them as part of their continuing business relationship. At the same time, they are becoming less and less accountable for the performance the money is supposed to buy.

This is certainly true with in-store sampling programs, in which more stringent auditing on the part of manufacturers has helped uncover some of the more glaring performance problems that, lacking proper monitoring, are often papered over.

The pursuit of accountability, then, demands attention to the following:

1. Are all samplers/demonstrators showing up in-store as scheduled? If, for whatever reason, a sampler/demonstrator does not show up at the appointed time, is the sampling service he or she works for alerted to the situation immediately? Does the service have a backup procedure? Will it take immediate action on it?

2. Does the sampling service adhere to the schedules set up by manufacturers to coincide with other promotional and advertising efforts, or does it take it upon itself to change and adjust these schedules to conform to its own considerations and deployment of resources?

3. Are the samplers/demonstrators handling the program assigned to them by strictly one manufacturer, or are they handling additional items at the same time while fees are collected separately from each principal?

4. Are the samplers/demonstrators properly trained, and are they sufficiently knowledgeable about the product, its superiority claims, and its proper preparation — in the case of an actual demonstration — to be able to present it persuasively to shoppers?

5. Often sampling programs require both equipment and supplies. Are these being handled properly and in a timely fashion?

6. More often than not, sampling programs include coupons designed to accelerate immediate purchases, and, in most cases, they are handled separately from the samples themselves. How are they secured? Since coupons are "cash," mishandling of them can be quite costly — potentially exceeding the cost of the sampling effort itself.

7. Is the sampling service ready and willing to conduct program prechecks to ensure that the stores involved are properly alerted to the program and have sufficient stock on hand to meet the ensuing incremental consumer takeout? As previously mentioned, running out of stock during a sampling/demonstration program can seriously hamper the success of such an effort.

8. Will the service provide readings of merchandise sold during the sampling/demonstration period and verification of the number of coupons and samples handed out, as well as information on pricing, display activities, and consumer reactions? Such information is both descriptive (allowing one to judge performance in terms of conversion levels and units moved) and prescriptive (enabling one to fine-tune future efforts using the database accumulated in this and other programs).

9. Does the service carry all applicable liability insurance coverage? Insurance claims follow those with the "deepest pockets," and that may turn out to be the manufacturer whose product is being sampled.

10. Is the service responsive to manufacturers' needs and questions, or is it holding them at arm's length under the premise that its allegiance is to the retailer it is associated with, and not to the manufacturer who is paying the bills?

11. Is the service willing and able to fully document all expenses incurred — particularly the cost of the sampled product, which is often purchased in the store — as it bills for such expenses?

Often, manufacturers (primarily, their local sales organizations) will insist on fielding and managing the execution of in-store sampling programs in their sales areas through services that are available locally. Given the hodgepodge of services operating in each market, and the fact that different accounts or stores will allow access to different services, one can end up using 20 or more in-store sampling companies in one single market.

This makes for the rather formidable task of calling on each local sales office to recruit, train, assign, monitor, and process reports on the work done on each sampling program fielded. Further, one must order supplies and equipment; arrange for their timely delivery and transshipment, where needed; and determine whether the product used in sampling is to be warehoused and delivered to stores, according to schedule, or purchased in-store. The local sales offices also must store and distribute coupons, when they are used, to the individual demonstrators under secure conditions and, finally, provide a paymaster function, carefully evaluating all documentation submitted on both time and expenditures.

Since most in-store sampling programs are still executed locally under the conditions described above, one must query the logic of continuing these practices, given the costs involved. Many argue, with obvious justification, that, in today's competitive environment, salespeople have their hands full properly servicing their own accounts. Diverting their efforts and attention to the handling of sampling programs — a task which, if it is to be done well, is highly time-intensive — is neither desirable nor cost-efficient.

The alternative, assigning in-store sampling programs to national companies that provide top-to-bottom management and performance accountability across the board, is becoming increasingly prevalent. The reasons for this growing shift are many:

1. Employment of national companies frees local sales organizations from responsibilities that, however time-consuming, have no direct bearing on the key account management function with which salespeople are charged. It enables salespeople to target those areas that are, indeed, critical to the success of an in-store sampling program by securing the type of trade support needed to enhance overall performance.

2. Using a national company ensures that the same performance standards will prevail across all markets included in the coverage plan. Allowing each local service in each market to conduct the in-store sampling program according to its own individual procedures can fragment a program to such an extent that no coherent data collection may be possible, thus preventing needed accountability and analytical evaluation.

3. One argument advanced for contracting in-store sampling efforts locally is based on cost. Local assignments cost less money. True, national management has a price. However, studies conducted by some manufacturers have enabled them to conclude that the incremental value inherent in the national management of an in-store sampling program significantly exceeds its cost.

PERSONAL SAMPLING AWAY FROM THE POINT-OF-PURCHASE

Sampling potential users away from the point of purchase can take many forms. These sampling techniques are all commonly designed to accelerate the trial of new products, and the mode chosen to distribute samples hinges on both the nature of the product sampled and its distribution pattern.

Products in high-penetration categories in wide distribution benefit from intensive sampling, reaching large numbers of people as cost-efficiently as possible. Conversely, niche products directed to targeted consumer segments require tailored sampling approaches that are specifically relevant to both usage and purchase of these products.

High-traffic sampling that depends on reaching large numbers of potential consumers over short periods of time is indicated when the product sampled fits in broadly based usage categories, thus minimizing the potential waste inherent in handing out samples to people who are not likely to use them.

Sampling in high-cluster areas (such as shopping centers and commuter stations), and at special events (such as county and state fairs) enables companies to generate immediate, large-scale trial. In years past, cigarette companies used to sample heavily on street corners in downtown locations. Given their shrinking user base, this is less prevalent today. However, companies that manufacture food products (such as candy, beverages, and those that do not require special preparation or storing conditions) continue to include high-traffic sampling in their plans.

The following criteria should be reviewed when high-traffic sampling is being considered:

1. Will the program reach people within the marketing area sampled — thus affecting local takeout patterns at the retail level — or will it target people in the market for short periods of time (such as tourists)? Sampling in San Francisco's Union Square, for example, may be the wrong approach if a product is only being test-marketed in that metropolitan area. Remember that for a sampling program to be successful, it must be translated into actual, full-revenue purchases at retail.

2. Local ordinances and rulings must be reviewed before locking in a sampling plan downtown and in other public locations. While licenses are not usually required, since sampling is not generally viewed as solicitation — no transfer of money is involved — some jurisdictions limit it to certain areas (particularly when public events are scheduled).

3. Litter is of major concern when executing a high-traffic sampling program. This is particularly critical in cases where the sampling effort generates instant discards, such as candy wrappers or cups used in sampling a beverage. Care should be taken to keep the sampling area and its vicinity as litter free as possible by strategically placing garbage cans around the area's perimeter.

4. In order to achieve optimal distribution levels, it is important that sampling be limited to one sample per person. Monitoring this in high-traffic locations is difficult. However, duplication can be significantly reduced if sampling crews in downtown areas or other high-traffic locations are properly spread out to discourage people from walking a little farther or crossing the

street a few times in order to obtain additional samples.

5. The high-traffic sampling plan should allow for the timely resupplying of all sampling stations to prevent "out-of-stock" conditions. Not all samples can (or should) be stacked up in unopened cases next to the sampling station. Some products, such as food samples in need of refrigeration, limit the number that can be handled by samplers at any one time. Also, those products that can be handled in greater numbers are subject to pilferage — one case at a time. Thus, one must build into the plan a good delivery system that is fully cognizant of traffic patterns, particularly when they are affected by the specific event that provided the context for the sampling effort in the first place.

6. Fees may be required, and they usually vary from event to event. While no fees may be levied for sampling in downtown traffic, access to shopping malls, special events, and fairs may require payments based on the number of samplers used and the number of days involved. In the case of fairs, it may require further commitments to staff a booth during the full duration of the fair.

Up to this point, we have talked about in-hand, person-to-person sampling efforts. This form of sampling allows for several levels of selectivity:

- *Locational selectivity* — Sampling is executed selectively in areas that meet the specific potential user profiles, whether classified by area of the country, urban vs. suburban locations, ethnic clusters, and so forth.
- *Visual selectivity* — This allows samplers to visually identify the people who are to be offered the specific samples. (Samplers can visually separate males from females; the young from the old; or bald people from people with hair.)
- *Verbal selectivity* — The ultimate selectivity level in which people can be queried about their likelihood of using the sampled product; that is, their having a dishwasher in their home or owning a dog or cat.

SAMPLING BY MAIL

A great deal of sampling is conducted today by mail. Its ease of execution, coupled with its potential reach of every single dwelling across the country, makes it attractive, although not necessarily economical, particularly in a marketing environment that mandates increasingly narrow targeting.

Much of the sampling by mail goes third class. This is primarily "occupant" mailing that delivers samples to current residents in dwellings in the geographical areas included in the distribution plan. There are no time imperatives to the delivery of samples sent by third-class mail. While first-class mail has overall priority, samples sent third class may linger for a long time in local post offices. When they add up to a lot of undelivered units, the local post office may decide to "lighten the mail" and donate them to a local county hospital, for example, for distribution to its needier patients. That, of course, may not have been the intent of the company whose samples they were.

First-class mailings are often used in preference to third-class mailings when specific recipients have been identified and addressed. By law, the post office must return to the sender mail that cannot be delivered, or forward it if the addressee has moved away and filed a forwarding address. While this is deemed positive, some companies continue to use third class, as they find that the additional benefits inherent in first class do not justify the additional costs involved. These include the incremental cost of buying and processing specific target mailing lists available from various compilers who specialize in this field.

Here are some of the issues that must be considered when mailing samples:

1. How extensive should the sampling program be? Assuming a given conversion level from trial to regular purchases — as indicated by the manufacturer's market research department through earlier product placement and other research efforts — the size of the sampling program should be sufficient to help the new product reach a calculated consumer franchise level. For example, this may call for a 20 percent penetration of households in a specific market. Sampling at twice that level may not be necessary.

2. How good are the mailing lists used? The mobility of households in the U.S. is well documented. "Old" lists — lists that have not been updated for six months or more — will result in a considerable amount of waste. Not only are delivery costs at stake here, but also costs of wasted product add up, as well.

3. How inclusive are the lists used? Do they include single-parent households, a small but growing segment of the market? Do they include buildings with multiple dwellings? High-rises are noted for the way samples, particularly those mailed third class, are left in bulk on tables in mailroom areas to be taken by whoever passes. Do they include ethnic areas, particularly those in midcity?

4. Can the samples be sent out by unsolicited mail? In many states, the mailing of unsolicited samples of health products, for example, is not allowed. This is due partially to the fear that they may be delivered and then consumed by nonadults who may not be sufficiently qualified to understand and follow the cautionary label indications before using these products.

5. As a follow-up to the above point, is the packaging used to mail the samples sufficiently sturdy — not only to protect the

integrity of the product in transit — but also to prevent potential tampering?

To sum up, sampling by mail is widely used and can be quite effective. It must be planned with care and with due consideration of all elements in the process that can optimize its effectiveness, while at the same time avoiding the pitfalls that may, at worst, cause it to fail altogether rather than being just cost-inefficient.

IN-HOME SAMPLING

While mail samples are delivered by the U.S. Postal Service, in-home sampling (often referred to as "door-to-door" sampling) is carried out by special crews who work out of delivery vans.

At one time, door-to-door sampling was quite prevalent, particularly when heavier samples were distributed. In recent years, this form of sampling has declined significantly; only a few companies continue to use it to any substantial degree.

While it enables one to pinpoint distribution to specific clusters of homes, and does not impose the same size limitations that one must keep in mind when sampling by mail, door-to-door sampling raises questions of its own:

1. How is the sample delivered? The "ring-and-leave" approach in which the sample is left — usually in a polybag hung on the doorknob — after the deliverer rings the bell to alert those inside the dwelling, is the way most sampling takes place. It is the least expensive method because the sampling crew can move quickly from house to house. It is also the most prone to mischief, since the samples are left unattended. Remember that in-home deliverers cannot use the mailboxes since legally they are considered to be federal property.

   Conversely, one may choose to "ring, wait, and give." In this case, controls increase considerably because the sample is given by hand to a person actually living in the specific home. Productivity, however, is only a fraction of what it is with the "ring and leave" approach, and, therefore, for the most part, is unaffordable.

2. The safety concerns when samples are distributed by the "ring-and-leave" approach increase significantly, since samples left unattended can be pilfered, tampered with, and misused by minors. Safety requires extra strong and safe packaging be used, and the corresponding costs can be high.

3. The same questions regarding the inclusiveness of the sampling plan, when sampling by mail, apply here, as well. Most door-to-door sampling programs avoid coverage in high-rise areas and limit their reach to single-home dwellings. Given continuing urbanization trends in both city and suburban areas, this method of sampling is quickly losing ground.

SUMMARY

Following is a brief summary of the points and caveats reviewed in this chapter:

1. Sampling is a powerful trial device designed to accelerate the adoption of new products by allowing customers to experience them at no risk.

2. Since the availability of new products at point of purchase is critical to the adoption of the new product (at least for consumer package goods), sampling at or near the stores carrying them, when translated to full revenue purchases, will further ensure the securing of a permanent home at retail.

3. Conducting sampling programs in-store has become increasingly complex as retailers, keen on identifying new income sources to shore up their generally shaky finances, have been exacting increasing fees for giving manufacturers "access" to customers in their stores. Even while paying these fees, manufacturers must insist on full accountability of the moneys spent.

4. Sampling a product that fails to meet a reasonable level of anticipated consumer satisfaction is going to accelerate its demise.

5. Sampling programs should not be executed in a vacuum. They must be supported before, during, and after by other components in the marketing plan. As such, sampling programs should be carefully planned as an integral part of one's marketing strategy.

Tamara Brezen Block is President of Block Research, Inc., a research firm providing a full range of quantitative and qualitative research services, including sales promotion analysis. She teaches graduate level research methods and sales promotion courses, among others, as a faculty member of the Medill School of Journalism's Integrated Marketing Communications Program at Northwestern University. Prior to joining the faculty at Northwestern, Block was an instructor in the Advertising Deparment at Michigan State University and a Visiting Professor at Foote, Cone, & Belding in Chicago.

In addition to co-editing this Handbook, Block is co-author of a soon-to-be-published book on Business-to-Business Research. She has been published in several academic journals on topics related to advertising and promotion effects.

Block received a Ph.D. in Mass Media from Michigan State University. Her dissertation on the topic of sales promotion received a national award from the Council of Sales Promotion Agencies. Her Master of Arts degree and Bachelor of Arts, both in Advertising, were also completed at Michigan State.

Larry Tucker has been prominent in the promotion and direct marketing fields for more than 20 years and is a recognized authority on target marketing, list analysis, promotion, and direct mail. For the past 16 years, his firm, Larry Tucker, Inc., has sponsored the nation's largest targeted co-op mailing program, "Jane Tucker's Supermarket of Savings" — now mailing almost 150 million co-op envelopes annually to growing families, older active adults (50+), and black and Hispanic or Latino families.

An active member of the Direct Marketing Association, the Promotion Marketing Association of America, and many other industry groups, he contributes frequently to industry publications and regularly addresses meetings of marketing executives.

CHAPTER 2

COUPONING

Couponing in the nineties, like other promotional techniques, has begun to reach its mature stage. While the 1980s were boom years for couponing, especially 1982 through 1984, couponing has been increasing at a more modest rate since then. This is due, in part, to the fact that there are very few major product categories that have yet to enter the couponing field. While couponing remains a primary sales promotional tool of grocery and drug manufacturers, its use has extended far beyond the package goods domain. Coupons are used for almost every other kind of product from apparel to toys to airline transportation.

The best sources of coupon information differ on current coupon growth trends, but they do agree on the fact that couponing is still on the rise. Nielsen Clearing House (NCH) estimated that in 1991 manufacturers distriubuted approximately 292 billion coupons, which represented a 4.5 percent growth over 1990. Carolina Manufacturers Service (CMS) reported even larger numbers with 314 billion coupons distributed in 1991, representing a 12 percent increase in numbers of coupons distributed, claiming the state of the American economy in 1991–1992 contributed to the increase in coupon activity.

The two main sources for coupons are manufacturers and retailers. Most manufacturers are generally happy with "direct to the consumer" couponing results but are exploring new avenues and added-value ideas. Retailers are still looking to see how they can make the most of coupons, and are increasing their own in-ad couponing as well.

As couponing matures, manufacturers and couponing service firms alike are viewing this as a time to make the tool more efficient and to generally improve the state of the couponing art.

DEFINITION AND STRATEGIC USE

Coupons, simply stated, are certificates that offer the consumer a stated value, for instance, cents-off or free product, when presented to the appropriate vendor accompanying the appropriate purchase. It is easy to see why coupons, with their obvious immediate value and savings, are the one promotional technique that has dominated the last two decades.

Coupons have many advantages. First, couponing to consumers helps ensure that savings are passed directly to the consumers. Trade allowances paid to the retailer, often to encourage price discounting, may or may not ever filter down into savings to the user. Second, while the consumer receives the benefit of a cost savings, this is perceived as a temporary special offer rather than a price reduction, which would have greater ramifications if removed. Third, coupons can create traffic for retailers, especially when retailers capitalize on this promotional device by doubling or tripling the coupon redemption value at their own expense.

Couponing is not, of course, without problems. Foremost, couponing has become so popular and widespread that the enormous number of coupons in circulation create "coupon clutter," resulting in falling coupon redemption rates. This coupon clutter also increases the potential for misuse and abuse through coupon fraud and misredemption. Furthermore, some allege that couponing is often used as a life support mechanism for weaker brands, while redemption for established brands occurs primarily from loyal users and thus rarely generates incremental business from new users, as it was intended.

Because coupons can be distributed via many different avenues, from mass distribution with free-standing inserts (FSIs) in newspapers or magazine advertising to more targeted delivery via the package itself or through direct mailings to the home, coupons offer flexibility in accomplishing a variety of common promotional goals. The most common objectives for using couponing follow.

Couponing for Trial and Awareness. Coupons are particularly efficient at generating trial of new products or line extensions of current brands. By offering significant savings on a first purchase, coupons reduce the risk to the consumer of trying something new. Alternatively, coupons can be exchanged for free product, almost as a sampling device, to completely eliminate any risk to the consumer at all. In these cases, the free product is often a special "trial size" package, just large enough to give the consumer sufficient trial to entice repeat purchase.

Almost any of the delivery methods mentioned earlier (and detailed more thoroughly later in this chapter) could be used to encourage trial if targeted at potential users. Print advertising, whether in magazines, Sunday magazines, newspaper FSIs, or runs of press (ROPs), can announce the benefits of the product with an accompanying coupon. In-store delivery, whether it's on the pack, on the shelf, on a display, or with a product demonstration, can alert the consumer to the new product in the store. Cross-item trial can also be generated by including a coupon for the new product in or on the package of another product bought by a similar user base.

Because coupons are typically delivered with accompanying sell copy as in an advertising environment, regardless of whether the coupon is redeemed, they can create awareness among the delivered audience of the new or improved brand.

Couponing for Repeat Purchase. While trial is often a first goal of couponing, converting trial users to regular users is also a key couponing task. When a consumer is faced with the decision of which brand to buy, a cents-off discount on an acceptable or superior brand may tilt the balance toward the couponed brand. That is why in-pack samples are almost always accompanied with a cents-off coupon and why in- or on-pack couponing is quite effective. In fact, in-pack or on-pack couponing is a way to cost-effectively reward existing users and encourage repeat purchase or loyal use.

Couponing to Trade Consumers Up. The specific terms of a coupon deal can be designed to manipulate users into buying larger quantities of a product or particular brand flavors, sizes, or forms if that is the goal. For instance, rather than offering cents-off on one unit of the product, the coupon terms might dictate that multiple units must be purchased for redemption, with the possible effect of increasing consumption. This is often the case with quickly consumed items having a short purchase cycle, such as cat food. In the same way, a coupon might be offered for a larger, and usually more expensive, package (for example, cents-off a 32-ounce container of catsup) or a different or more "deluxe" form of a brand (for example, brownie mix with nuts vs. the same mix without nuts). In these examples, the coupon promotion is specifically geared to trade consumers "up" in their purchasing behavior.

Couponing for Competitive Pressure. Couponing can be used with respect to the competition as either a defensive tactic or as an offensive move. By discounting one brand to users of competing brands, coupons entice those competitive users to buy the couponed brand instead. The obvious goal is to encourage continued patronage. But this kind of "switching" behavior can result in increased sales and profits in the short term, even if those consumers switch only for the sake of the temporary deal.

As a defensive price/value tactic, couponing can defend a brand against competition in the same way. By offering current users coupons toward continued purchase or "loading" current users up with product through a cents-off promotion for multiple brand purchases, coupons keep current users using and ward off competitive switching.

Couponing to Encourage Retail Distribution and Support. Couponing, as with any promotion, demonstrates support for a brand. However, if coupons are distributed locally through newspapers or direct mail, this shows local support and impact for retailers. Since manufacturers' coupons are paid for and distributed by the manufacturer in most cases and must be redeemed within a retail store, couponing benefits the retailer with very little out-of-pocket cost. This can help to gain trade support and secure product distribution. Manufacturers can win extra in-store support through increased brand shelf facings or off-shelf displays with the promise of a coupon drop which will further leverage the promotion for both parties. In fact, many retailers will dovetail their own promotion with that of the manufacturer by doubling or tripling the face value for consumers who redeem in their stores, boosting store traffic along with redemptions. Co-op couponing arrangements between the manufacturer and retailer are another way of gaining that ever-so-important retail support.

Couponing to Move Out-of-Balance Inventories. Discounting a brand through couponing can increase sales considerably, thereby moving product out of the store relatively quickly and within a certain time frame. When inventories are at higher-than-desired levels, by either manufacturer or retailer terms, couponing can act as a catalyst to trigger interest and pull the product through the distribution channels. This is especially effective for seasonal products or products with strong seasonal cycles, such as cold remedies or suntan lotions. This can also be a solution when a manufacturer is preparing to introduce a newer version of the brand and wants to clear out the inventory of the old brand in order to maximize profit and minimize cannibalization.

Couponing to Target Different Markets. Coupons can be strategically placed within particular media aimed at key audiences or targeted directly to particular consumers on a list. When there is little overlap between the various delivery mechanisms, effectively different deals can be offered to different consumers. For instance, with a knowledge of who the current users, competitive users, or nonusers are, greater incentives can be targeted to the competitive or nonusers to rally them to switch (or buy), while somewhat smaller savings can be offered as a reward to current consumers who might likely buy anyway.

The same strategy works when differentiating between markets. For example, greater incentives might be needed in a market where the promoted brand has a small market share than in markets where the brand dominates the category.

Couponing to Cushion Price Increases. Price increases are a fact of business but can deter sales in the short term if consumers become aware of the price change. Coupons offering enough of a discount to offset the increase in price can temporarily cushion the sting of the higher price until the time when consumers become accustomed to the higher price levels.

Couponing as an Add-On to Other Promotional Efforts. In a world where both the trade and consumers expect and demand promotion, using more than one promotional technique can leverage the results further by creating more awareness of the brand/promotion and greater sales synergies. Often, couponing will be used in conjunction with refunds or sweepstakes to increase participation (and purchase). As an example, coupons might encourage multiple and continued purchases of baby food, while the product labels and/or sales receipts can be exchanged for additional savings in the form of a refund. A coupon can serve a double purpose if a consumer writes in his or her name and address on the coupon when redeeming so that the coupon then becomes a means of entry into a sweepstakes promotion.

Sometimes coupons can be designed to work with in-store elements to encourage trade support and consumer involvement. An instance of this might be where the face value of the coupon can only be deciphered if brought into the store and held up to a special display or to the product package itself.

TACTICAL VARIATIONS OF A COUPON DEAL

A coupon promotion can be designed to offer deals or savings in many different forms. In reality, most coupon offers exhibit a combination of the following characteristics and can become quite complex and thereby difficult to classify.

1. **Cents-Off.** The product to be purchased is offered at a certain cents or dollar amount off the regular price for a specified time frame. This is probably the most common notion of couponing.

2. **Free.** A free product is given upon redemption. This is essentially an efficient means of sampling interested consumers since it avoids the waste and expense of sampling everyone.

3. **Buy One, Get One Free (BOGO).** With the purchase of a product at the regular price, a second is given free. This encourages multiple purchases and is a good way of rewarding regular users. As with everything else in an inflationary economy, today's BOGO is often inflated to where it is necessary to buy three or five to get one free!

4. **Time Release.** Several cents-off coupons are positioned together with different expiration dates. The objective is obviously to encourage repeat usage over time, aligning the expiration dates with typical usage/purchase cycles. Another variation on this might be when a manufacturer or service distributes coupons via a calendar, where a different deal is available each month.

5. **Multiple Purchase.** The coupon offer applies only when more than one unit of the product is purchased. The goal here is to load up the consumers with product, taking them out of the market for a period of time or with the hope of increasing consumption in the short term.

6. **Self-Destruct.** Two or more coupons are printed over each other in an overlap manner so that in order to redeem one, the other is destroyed. This is a way of offering different deals, perhaps to different types of consumers, without the clutter of multiple deals. Often, a self-destruct coupon is used in combination with time release, whereby greater savings are offered if it is redeemed sooner as opposed to later in an attempt to encourage quick redemption. It is common to see self-destructs used for the purpose of trading consumers up by offering the better deal on the larger size or deluxe form of the brand.

7. **Personalized.** The coupon is personalized by geographic location or store and is redeemable accordingly. This can be effective when used as a sales tool to elicit trade support.

8. **Cross-Ruff.** A coupon for one product is obtained with the purchase of another, unrelated product. When the user base of one

product overlaps substantially with the users of another product, it makes sense to coupon one to the other. Usually cross-ruffs are delivered via the package of a carrier brand.

9. **Related Sale.** A coupon received from the purchase of one product applies to another product, which is related in some way to the purchased product. This is a variation on the notion of a cross-ruff, wherein the couponed brand is connected in some way to the carrier brand, such as when hotdog and mustard coupons are delivered in hotdog bun packaging. The intent is often to encourage consumers to buy add-on items from the same manufacturer, but it can also be coordinated as a co-op between two manufacturers.

10. **Sweepstakes Entry.** The redeemed coupon becomes an entry into a sweepstakes promotion. Overlays of contests or sweepstakes may improve the impact and redemption rates of coupon promotions.

COUPON DISTRIBUTION METHODS

FSI couponing accounted for 77 percent of all coupons distributed in 1991, while all other distribution channels combined account for less than one in four coupons delivered. Given the sheer absolute numbers of coupons, every distribution channel contributes substantially to couponing's success and some, like targeted direct mail couponing, are becoming more popular.

The diverse distribution vehicles can be categorized into five basic distribution modes. That there are so many ways to deliver a coupon obviously adds to the flexibility of this promotional tactic. Each delivery mode has its own distinct advantages depending on the goals, target audience, and budget of the user. This section will briefly discuss each distribution method in detail.

Direct Mail. Direct mail distribution uses the U.S. Postal Service to deliver coupons to mailboxes of consumers. The coupons can be selectively delivered to households by name or more broadly targeted to the "resident" or "occupant" of a dwelling. In this latter case, the desire might be to distribute coupons to all households in a given zip code area.

Direct mail couponing achieves the highest redemption rates of any media or mailed couponing, primarily due to its more targeted distribution. It can offer many options for the user. Through careful selection of lists and demographic breaks, it offers the most selectivity. Through zip code saturation, it also potentially offers the highest coverage. As a result, direct mail is often used by retailers. Compared to other media delivery methods, mailing directly to consumers results in less misredemption. However, compared to most print media delivery methods, it is more expensive.

Couponing that is mailed can be either solo or co-op. A solo coupon promotion would consist of coupon(s) for a single company or brand. Solo mailings usually receive higher redemptions because of the exclusive selling environment for the brand or company. In fact, in combination with a sample, solo mail coupons can be used very effectively for new product introductions.

A co-op coupon promotion includes coupons for a combination of brands usually from different companies. Clearly the co-op route is more efficient and cost effective but there are some limitations to co-ops in terms of their potential pinpoint delivery to very specific list criteria or competitive users. Generally the most used co-ops are either mass broad-reach mailings to 30 million households or more, or demographically selective co-ops to specific target audiences such as households with babies, preschoolers, senior citizens, or specific ethnic groups. Because of the nonexclusive nature of a co-op promotion, there is less opportunity for selling any one brand; therefore, this mode is less desirable for new products.

In-Store or Central Location. Coupons are often distributed in the store where the items can be purchased or in high-traffic locations such as malls, shopping centers, and street corners. Coupons can be handed out personally in combination with or separate from a product demonstration, available for dispensing in a kiosk or display somewhere in the store, or automatically dispensed via a battery or electronic device usually placed near the product itself. Recently, several methods of automatically dispensed and electronic in-store couponing have been developed or are currently in the testing stage.

One such recently introduced distribution device is a battery-controlled coupon dispenser positioned at the point-of-sale on the shelf where the product is stocked. Another notable unique in-store distribution method involves dispensing coupons at the checkout counter, triggered by the scanning of a purchased product's UPC code. This kind of checkout, computer-controlled delivery method allows a brand to strategically target nonusers or competitive users, for example, by distributing coupons for Brand A coffee to those who purchase Brand B coffee.

In cases in which retail participation is a key objective, in-store couponing can be very effective. Additionally, in-store, mall, or shopping center couponing might be especially appropriate if it is part of some other promotional event.

In-store or central location handout couponing gives you some valuable flexibility and options. For instance, product samples and/or demonstrations of the product's use can accompany coupon handouts. Handout couponing also allows for a certain amount of selectivity regarding to whom the coupons are distributed. The people who are sampling or demonstrating or simply handing out coupon packages can screen consumers by asking if they have a dog or cat at home and then handing out the appropriate pet food coupon.

There are some disadvantages to in-store couponing, such as the logistics involved when distributing coupons across a large number of stores. If a number of different outlets in a geographic area are couponing, it is also possible for waste to occur because multiple coupons may be dispensed to the same consumer.

Print Media Delivered Coupons. Print media represent the dominant method of coupon delivery today. Advertising in newspapers with run-of-press (ROP) coupons or free-standing inserts (FSIs) and including coupons in magazine advertising constitute the primary print media used for delivery. Also in this category are print ads that offer consumers coupons if they send in their name and address or call an 800 or 900 number. In this case, the offer is delivered in the print medium and the coupon is delivered by mail.

FSIs comprise over three-fourths of all coupons distributed because of their good color reproduction and ability to efficiently reach a large circulation (50 million) in one day. They are printed in four color on high-quality paper stock and mechanically inserted into the newspaper, usually Sunday newspapers. They have the flexibility to provide special printing options such as rub-offs or scratch-and-sniff coupons.

Although traditional black and white ROP couponing is used much less today, it still has the advantage of very short closing dates, usually less than those for FSIs even, in cases where there is some need to react quickly to a marketing problem or opportunity. Color in ROPs is generally not used because of its poor quality color reproduction. Newspaper delivery shows local support for a brand and can be a sales tool for the trade.

Magazines are used less as a delivery mode for coupons today primarily because of their high costs, lower redemptions, and general inefficiency with respect to targeting. However, depending on the product and how narrowly defined the target market is, some magazine coupons may be a good idea. For instance, in the case of cosmetics or beauty products targeted toward young women, *Seventeen* might effectively deliver coupons to teenagers and *Cosmopolitan* might be appropriate for young working women.

Magazine delivery is of two forms: on-page and tip-in coupons. On-page coupons are usually integrated into a magagzine advertisement that provides both advertising and promotion value for a brand. The quality color reproduction and ad copy provide a good promotional environment, while the presence of a coupon can often increase readership of the advertisement. The ad space is purchased in full-page, half-page, or two-page spread increments, as with any other print advertising. Tip-in or pop-up coupons are typically printed on a heavier weight card stock and are bound in the magazine alongside a brand advertisement. When the magazine is opened, the coupons "pop up." Tip-ins cost more to deliver but almost always redeem at a higher rate than on-page coupons because of their ease in removing (no cutting is required) without destroying the magazine. A variation of the tip-in is the gatefold insert coupon whereby the coupons are printed as an extension of the advertisement and folded over the ad to provide a pop-up effect. Most magazine vehicles allow only a limited number of gatefolds per issue. While this method is more expensive, co-op opportunities can offer a savings.

In-Pack and On-Pack Coupons. In-pack coupons are preprinted and packed inside the product or another product's package. In the case of in-pack coupons, the carrier package inevitably features additional package graphics or copy, for example, a caption that announces "25¢ coupon inside." On-pack coupons are printed on a product's packaging or product label. Instant coupons, another form of on-pack couponing, are affixed to the outside of the package for easy removal and immediate redemption.

In- or on-pack couponing is an ideal strategy for encouraging repeat purchase of a given brand and holding current users. It is a relatively inexpensive distribution method in comparison to other methods, without the same misredemption potential of media delivered coupons. Even though in- and on-pack couponing may not have the same broad coverage of mail or media delivery, and it often delays redemption until the product is gone, redemptions tend to be high. Instant couponing offers the consumer immediate in-store access and redemption for the current purchase of a product and, as a result, receives the highest redemption of this genre and of all couponing delivery methods.

Cross-ruff couponing (in which coupons for one product are carried in or on another product) can be effective for generating trial of a related product in a brand line. This kind of cross-ruff couponing offers a dual benefit: the couponing brings trial for the couponing brand as well as visual point-of-purchase impact and added value for the carrier brand. Selecting the right cross-ruff partner can avoid the waste of mass nonselective couponing, for example, a coupon for cat food can be strategically placed in cat litter. In many instances, co-op cross-ruffs can generate greater consumer interest because of the greater promotion value.

Retailer In-Ad Coupons. In-ad coupons are manufacturers' coupons that are distributed via retailers' advertising and/or mailings. Recently, their use has increased greatly. In fact, according to CMS, in-ad coupon distribution increased from 7 billion coupons in 1990 to more than 23 billion in 1991, a 231 percent increase! Some manufacturers are already seeking ways to reduce their use. Yet, they do gain prominent space and attention in a retailer's ads and/or circulars, and they represent a form of quality "featuring" for a brand name that is hard to resist.

In-ad coupons can be for a single or multiple purchase. They are generally very limited in time, with typical expiration dates of one or two weeks. The average face value for in-ads also tends to be much higher than that for other coupon methods. In-ad coupons are, in a way, another form of trade promotion because they stimulate product sales for a specific retail account. In most cases both the face value and handling charges are paid by the manufacturer, while the media or mailing costs are borne by the retailer. In some cases, manufacturers have agreed to a trade allowance that compensates retailers for inclusion of their brand in in-ad coupons, and those coupons are thereby destroyed by the retailers and not sent to the clearinghouse for reimbursement by the manufacturer in the normal way.

COUPON REDEMPTION RATES

Through the later half of the 1980s and into the 1990s, redemption rates have declined and flattened. This is probably due in part to the clutter of more coupons across more product categories, along with the increasing saturation of competitive couponing within a given product category.

Redemption rates vary depending on a number of product and coupon characteristics, including face value, product category and competitive activity within the category, area of the country, coupon delivery method, audience characteristics such as brand loyalty, and the design and appeal of the coupon advertising itself. Listed in Table 2.1 are average redemption rates in 1990 and 1991 for the overall grocery category by delivery method, provided through NCH Promotion Services.

As discussed in the previous section, the highest redemption rates occur for in- and on-pack delivery methods in which coupons are selectively targeted to users of the product in conjunction with purchase or use of the product. In-store handout couponing and direct mail delivery offer relatively high redemptions as well. The lowest redemptions occur for print media delivery, which usually requires more effort on the part of consumers to cut or clip the coupon.

TABLE 2.1
AVERAGE COUPON REDEMPTION RATES

Delivery Method	1990	1991
Instant on-pack	35.0%	32.5%
In-pack	12.5	12.3
On-pack	10.8	9.2
Cross-ruff on-pack	4.1	4.9
Cross-ruff in-pack	3.1	3.4
Handout couponing	4.1	4.9
Direct mail	4.7	4.3
FSI	2.5	2.4
Sunday magazine supplements	1.5	1.6
Newspaper ROP	1.5	1.5
Magazine tip-in	1.5	1.3
Magazine on-page	1.2	1.2

COUPON FACE VALUE

Traditionally, the face value of a coupon has been set at about 15 percent of the product's retail price. Therefore, average face value varies across product category and is a relative variable. It should be noted that for new products the face value is usually higher to entice first-time purchase and trial.

In general, redemption rates increase as face value increases but not proportionately over the whole range. At some level, redemption rates begin to plateau, and higher face values bring in less or no incremental redemption. Some research has shown that redemptions for regular or frequent buyers are typically higher on average across all face values, while higher-valued coupons are more effective in soliciting redemption among infrequent or nonbuyers of a brand.

Based on when coupons are submitted for reimbursement at the clearinghouse, an average profile of the financial liability for a manufacturer develops over time. This pattern does vary by coupon distribution method to some degree. As might be expected, redemptions for FSI coupons, direct mail, and newspaper-delivered coupons tend to peak more quickly and drop off rather quickly in comparison to magazine-delivered coupons. In- or on-pack couponing redeems the most slowly of all because it is tied to the usage of the product. A timing chart such as this can assist in managing, budgeting, and evaluating coupon promotions.

THE COUPONING PROCESS

Coupon redemption can be a complex process because it involves handling by many different individuals across several stages. The entire cycle is usually completed in approximately 60 to 90 days.

The couponing process begins, of course, when a manufacturer decides to run a coupon promotion. The promotion is planned and coupons are printed and sent to the appropriate distribution points for dissemination to the public. A consumer then redeems the coupon at the store and receives the given cents-off on the appropriate product. Depending on the size and type of the retail operation, a store may forward its coupons to the chain headquarters. From there, the store or chain will send the coupons to one of three places: a retailers' clearinghouse, a redemption agency, or directly to the manufacturer. Because there are so many manufacturers, most retailers use clearinghouses.

Clearinghouses work for and are paid by the retailers. A clearinghouse is responsible for sorting the redeemed coupons and invoicing the manufacturer or the manufacturer's redemption agency. The manufacturer's redemption agency will sort any coupons sent to it and send an invoice and a report to the manufacturer. Payments are then made to retailers to reimburse the total face value of the redemptions plus a handling fee per coupon. The retailer then pays the clearinghouse for handling the process.

The preceding process applies only to manufacturer-originated coupon programs. There are also retailer or store coupons for which the retailer would have the responsibility for printing and distribution, as well as any financial liability. Sometimes a cooperative agreement may be in force between the manufacturer and retailer in which the manufacturer pays either directly for some part of the cost of the promotion or indirectly through trade promotional allowances.

Basic Couponing Costs. The basic costs to the manufacturer for couponing can be summarized as follows:

- Media costs for distribution
- Printing costs (if separate from media costs, for example FSIs)
- Face value of the redeemed coupons
- Handling charge for the retailers, currently $.08 per redemption
- Redemption house or in-house clearing and reporting costs
- Creative/art/photography/production costs

THE COUPON PAYOFF

There are many ways to plan and evaluate the effectiveness and "payout" of a couponing program. However, establishing the effectiveness criteria in advance, along with a preplanned program to evaluate the payout, is essential in any coupon promotion. For example, payout could be measured as (1) increased trial among new users, (2) the best efficiency as measured by the lowest cost per coupon redeemed, (3) incremental volume during a given promotion period, or even (4) increased market share.

Table 2.2 shows figures for calculating the cost and efficiency of

TABLE 2.2
SAMPLE COUPON COST-EFFICIENCY TABLE

($.25 COUPON*/1991 COSTS & RATES)	FSI	Direct Mail	Magazines
Distribution	50 million	30 million	20 million
Cost/M (incl. print)	$7.00	$18.00	$17.00
Cost/media ($000)	$350	$540	$340
Redemption rate	2.4%	4.3%	1.2%
Total redeemers	1,200,000	1,290,000	240,000
Misredemption estimate	25%	—	—
Total valid redeemers	900,000	1,290,000	240,000
Redemption costs ($000)	$420	$451	$84
Grand total costs	$770	$991	$424
Costs per valid redemption	$.85	$.77	$1.76

* $.25 face value plus $.08 handling plus $.02 redemption costs equals $.35

Source: NCH 1991

a coupon promotion. This analysis includes a factor for misredemption. Given a 25 percent misredemption, for example, for FSIs distributed to 50 million consumers as shown in the first column below, only 900,000 coupons would be considered "valid." Consequently, the cost per valid redeemed coupon for FSIs would be approximately $.85.

DESIGNING THE COUPON

While coupons vary widely in the specifics of their "deal," their design, and their placement or distribution method, all coupons look essentially similar.

The following are some guidelines to use in designing the coupon:

- A coupon should look like a coupon — funny shaped coupons are logistically impractical. Consumers expect them to be squares or rectangles, which are easier to clip and store, and the retailers need to fit them in cash register drawers.
- The face value and expiration date should be prominently displayed where they are plainly visible.
- Both the UPC code and manufacturer's coupon code should be included.
- The use of a package shot is preferable if the design allows. This can aid consumers in redemption and cut down on misredemption at the checkout. If it is a multiple-purchase coupon — for example, 10¢ off on two boxes of tissue — showing two packages on the coupon can deter misredemption.
- Burying coupons in complicated graphics within an ad or mailing is discouraged.
- Grocery Manufacturers of America (GMA) standards for coupon size and other specifications should be followed.

COUPON MISREDEMPTION AND COUPON FRAUD

Misredemption is a term used to describe the misuse of a coupon or the redemption of coupons without proper purchase of the specified product. The actual extent of misredemption is unknown, but most manufacturers plan for it and factor it in as a cost of doing business.

Often innocent consumer misredemption occurs when a coupon is redeemed (1) after its expiration date, (2) without the proper brand specifications (the proper quantity or size restrictions), or (3) when the product is not purchased at all. In out-of-stock situations, consumers will knowingly substitute other brands for the unavailable couponed brand. By informing retailers of a coupon promotion in advance or by couponing only brands with sufficient retail distribution, much of this deliberate consumer misuse can be avoided. Furthermore, printing expiration dates so that they are easily noticed and printing a picture of the brand itself in the quantity required for redemption on the coupon front can alleviate problems.

Misredemption that occurs outside the normal customer-retailer in-store transaction constitutes fraud. Most coupon fraud would be difficult without some level of retailer involvement because manufacturers only reimburse coupon submissions received from supposedly legitimate retailers. Therefore, fraud is often committed by "rings" of retailers cooperating and participating with coupon criminals for some of the profit or by criminals who organize phony storefronts or clearinghouses, which mass-clip coupons for submission. This kind of trade misuse is much more serious than consumer misredemption. Criminal redemption can result in massive losses. While estimates vary, NCH has estimated that coupon fraud costs manufacturers at least $250 million annually. Some estimates are as high as $700 million per year.

The situation for trade misredemption is complicated in that abuse can happen at any stage in the coupon process — printing and production, distribution, or redemption. For instance, during the production phase, coupons can be fraudulently printed in deliberate overruns, or the printing plate can be stolen and used to reprint coupons strictly for fraudulent redemption. When coupons are shipped to distribution points, as is the case with FSIs for example, theft can occur even before distributors retrieve them. It is generally accepted that FSIs experience a higher level of misredemption than direct mail or magazine-delivered coupons simply because of this ease of theft and the efficiency with which they can be collected and clipped in mass. Typically in this situation, coupon criminals organize people to cut, clip, and sort the coupons for a percentage of the actual face value. Coupons are then submitted for the full face value. Cashiers, store owners, and managers and retailer clearinghouses may commit fraud to a lesser degree by "salting" coupon submissions (adding fraudulent coupons to the legitimate claims).

Over the years, there have been several cases of mass misredemption that have been brought to trial resulting in criminal convictions. Because coupons are usually redeemed through the mail, or the redemption check is mailed back through the postal system, coupon fraud falls under federal jurisdiction through the U.S. postal codes. The federal government is becoming more actively involved in the surveillance and prosecution of criminal coupon fraud.

Manufacturers can protect themselves from coupon fraud to some extent by selecting the coupon delivery system carefully, with an understanding of the potential for misredemption. In fact, in some cases coupons can be sequentially numbered or specially coded so that mass submissions are more easily detected. This is possible with FSIs, direct mail, and magazine tip-in coupons. Today, many manufacturers and clearinghouses routinely inspect coupon redemption patterns in order to detect suspicious submissions. New coupon scanning equipment is being tested in stores that electronically reads the UPC codes on coupons and verifies redemption at the point-of-sale. This is also expected to assist in cutting costly misredemption.

The following are some suggestions on how to avoid or detect excessive misredemption:

- Excessively high face values should be avoided because higher values are more likely to attract misredemption.
- The number of coupons amassed in one vehicle should be limited. Large groupings of coupons not only result in higher total coupon value but also in more efficient mass clipping for misredemption purposes. Therefore, multiple coupons per magazine page or per mailing are to be discouraged. Again, FSIs, because of their coupon masses, attract misredemption more than other delivery modes. Where appropriate, self-destruct or overlapping coupons could be used in order to limit the actual number of usable coupons.
- Designating a fixed face value per coupon rather than offering free product (shelf value coupons) is preferable to alleviate the temptation to the trade to artificially inflate shelf values for increased reimbursement.
- Coupon expiration dates should be coordinated with product purchase cycles to minimize the time period for redemption. Also, a trade reimbursement policy should be established that allows payment to retailers only within a specified time period after the coupon expires, such as 60 days following the coupon expiration date.
- Retaining a reliable printing firm is an important step toward reducing fraud. Print overruns should be eliminated, and printing plates should be destroyed or retrieved back from the printer after printing.
- One should monitor, or at least be aware of, possible misuse through the distribution channels: for instance, (1) the number of deliverable mail coupons can be estimated based on the mailing lists used, (2) returns on any undeliverable direct mail coupons can be specified in advance, and (3) policies for newsstand returns of magazines and newspapers should always be known.
- A record should be kept of those retailers who do not stock the product being couponed so that illegitimate coupon submissions for the product can be detected.
- Establishing and enforcing a strict policy on coupon misredemption is a must if one is to reduce coupon misuse. For instance, in markets where misredemption is very high or among retailers for which misredemption has been previously detected at high levels, couponing should be avoided.

COUPONING INTERNATIONALLY

Other than Canada and the United Kingdom, most countries represent a relatively small factor in the world of couponing. Couponing in South America has been limited by the fact that newspapers do not have the coverage they do in the United States or Canada and because of the poor mailing systems in those countries. There is also limited distribution of coupons in Australia, Italy, France, Belgium, Spain, and other countries. Recently, however, the Japanese Trade Commission reversed a previous policy, allowing couponing in that country. Japanese couponing has been tested in small booklets distributed by mail and in both newspaper ROPs and FSIs.

Table 2.3 shows distribution numbers (in millions) for 1990 and 1991 in four countries tracked by NCH internationally. As can be seen by these numbers, couponing is substantially more prevalent in the U.S., given that 292 billion coupons were distributed in the states in 1991.

TABLE 2.3
COUPON DISTRIBUTION IN FOUR COUNTRIES

	Distribution (in millions)	
	1990	**1991**
Canada	23,400	26,000
United Kingdom	5,000	8,000
Italy	421	582
Spain	171	141

COUPONING TRENDS

While trends come and go, there are several current trends in couponing that are worth mentioning. The first is that coupons are increasingly being used as a way to selectively target specific consumer groups. Coupon programs that deliver particular demographic audiences have become increasingly popular because of their efficiency and effectiveness compared to other promotions.

More group promotions are appearing that combine several products or brands in one coupon display, often with related products or a family of brands. Along the same lines, promotions combining couponing with other promotional tactics are on the rise. In other words, couponing is increasingly becoming just one component of a multifaceted promotional program. Also increasing is the use of couponing overlaps or tie-ins, especially with sports and charities.

Today more than in the past, more attention is being paid to the creative element in a coupon promotion deal in an effort to increase the appeal and efficiency of the technique. To further leverage coupon effectiveness, more attention is also being given to designing coupon promotions with an eye to how the retailer is benefited. Since the front line of the battle field is in the retail outlet, developing better retailer relationships is of critical importance to manufacturers.

A final trend in couponing is that promoters are more aware of the problem of misredemption and the impact coupon fraud has on the bottom line. Better controls are being implemented across the board to reduce this threat.

Don Roux is President and CEO for Roux Marketing Services, Inc., which provides consulting services to packaged goods manufacturers on promotion concepts, services, fulfillment, and chance and skill promotion handling and judging. Roux has spent the last 30 years in the promotion marketing industry and is one of the leading authorities on promotion fulfillment, collateral material warehousing and distribution, and sweepstakes and contest program handling, judging, seeding, and fulfillment. He has won many awards, including two Reggies and the Association of Incentive Marketing's CIP Man of the Year.

Previously Roux was President and CEO of the Carlson Marketing Division of Carlson Marketing Group, Inc; President and CEO of Spotts International, Inc., one of the nation's largest fulfillment services; and Vice President of the Western Division at Revere Copper and Brass, Inc., working with promotions and product sales.

He is Director and former Chairman of the Board for the Promotion Marketing Association of America. He is also a former director and past president of the Association of Incentive Marketing (AIM) and a founding member and past president of the Minnesota Incentive Organization. He is a frequent speaker and author on marketing and sales promotion subjects.

CHAPTER 3

PREMIUMS, REFUNDS, AND PROMOTION FULFILLMENT

PREMIUMS AND MERCHANDISE INCENTIVES

The usage of merchandise incentives (premiums) dates back to the mid-1800s when B. T. Babbitt began using lithographed prints as an inducement to consumers to purchase Babbitt's soap products and promoted the offer by using the Barnum Bandwagon, which traveled throughout the country.

In recent years, the words *premium* and *merchandise incentives* in sales promotion have become interchangeable. Merchandise incentives are used in numerous promotional techniques. Account openers, business gifts, container packs, continuity and coupon plans, dealer and sales rewards, on-packs and in-packs, free-in-the-mail, frequent user plans, and self-liquidation offers are some of the more common usages for merchandise incentives.

The most concise definition of the term *incentive marketing* appeared in *Incentives in Marketing* written by George Meredith and Robert P. Fried and published by the Association of Incentive Marketing (formerly National Premium Sales Executives, Inc.). Fried and Meredith describe incentive marketing as "a promotional device that induces purchase or performance on the part of a consumer, salesperson, or dealer through the offer of tangible reward in the form of merchandise or travel." The only addition to this definition in today's marketplace would be to include "employees" to the list of those induced.

Incentive, one of the industry's leading publications, reported that consumer promotion sales totaled $59.4 billion in 1991, with $6.5 billion spent on consumer premiums. Another $115.3 billion was spent on trade promotions with $2.03 billion allocated to dealer incentives. Sales incentives totaled $17 billion, which included $4.4 billion for merchandise incentives, for a total estimated merchandise incentive sales volume of almost $13 billion in 1991.

Premiums and merchandise incentives are used for the following objectives:

Consumer incentives:
- Attract attention at the point-of-sale
- Sample new users
- Boost repeat sales
- Enhance consumer goodwill
- Obtain higher advertising readership
- Provide sales with a talking point
- Encourage store display usage
- Increase overall sales volume

Trade and sales incentives:
- Introduce new or improved products
- Pull slow-moving or line extensions through the system
- Increase the customer base
- Reinforce consumer promotions
- Offset competitive promotions/introductions
- Boost sale/dealer morale
- Obtain sales display
- Increase productivity
- Increase overall sales volume/market share

Premium/merchandise incentives cannot make up for a product that is inferior in quality or does not do what it has been advertised to do. Nor can these incentives substitute for inadequate advertising or a poorly trained or inferior sales staff, or change negative consumer attitudes. Consumers can be motivated to buy and try a new product or service or to retry an improved version of the product or service, but if that product does not perform as advertised or the "new, improved" version is not really improved, no amount of incentive promotion will induce consumers to continued purchases.

Each type of merchandise incentive promotion has its advantages and disadvantages. When planning promotions involving merchandise, the advantages and disadvantages must be weighed carefully. For planning purposes, the following is a recap of these plus/minus elements for the major incentive promotion types.

Mail-in Premiums — Self-Liquidators, Partial Self-Liquidators, and Free-in-the-Mail Offers. Oftentimes, premiums are acquired through the mail. The premium may be offered free to the consumer responding to the promotion, or it may be purchased by the consumer — usually at less than the expected retail price. A self-liquidating premium is one for which any direct cost associated with the premium, including mailing or handling charges, is paid up front by the respondent. For instance, the incentive to the consumer consists of receiving a desirable premium item at the same low wholesale price at which the promoter can buy it. Therefore, the consumer receives a good value at very little cost to the promoter. A partial self-liquidator, then, is a promotion for which at least some of the cost is paid by the respondent.

Advantages of mail-in premiums:
- Can be easily targeted to the promoted product or to a specific advertising theme
- Can be selected to encourage future use of the promoted product or group of products
- Attract brand switchers
- Increase product consumption
- Are relatively inexpensive
- Encourage on- and off-shelf display

- Create consumer goodwill
- Leave a long-lasting recall of the product or service

Disadvantages of mail-in premiums:

- Difficult to measure true sales results
- Require long lead times and require a dedicated product resource
- Product liability insurance coverage and a legal contract with supplier must be implemented
- It is always difficult to forecast merchandise needs, and this could lead to the added expense of sending "delay notices" or selling excess inventories at a loss.

Frequent Buyer/User and Continuity Plans. Frequent user programs have been in existence for many years and fall into a number of categories. A differentiating factor here is that, in order to encourage continuity of use/purchase, customers must save up to acquire a premium. By redeeming product proofs of purchase, game pieces, or savings stamps the consumer can "buy" a premium, often selecting from a variety of options offered at different price levels.

One of the longest-running programs has been the Brown and Williamson Tobacco Companies' Raleigh-Belaire coupon program. Coupons are packed in each individual pack of Raleigh and Belaire cigarettes and are redeemable for a wide array of merchandise that is presented in a beautiful four-color catalog. The catalog is redone regularly to keep up with new merchandise trends and prices.

Savings stamps that were widely used by the petroleum retailers and supermarkets in the 1950s, 1960s, and 1970s suffered serious setbacks in the United States during the recession and inflationary times of the late 1970s. This rapid decline in the popularity of trading stamps was the result of the grocery industry's attempt to reduce or maintain price levels by reducing costs. In reality, while prices were reduced by as much as the 2 percent that grocery chains claimed the stamps were costing, prices soon returned to original prices and the cost savings went to the bottom line. Today, services such as hotel chains and airlines, consumable products manufacturers of frequently purchased items, or multiple-line manufacturers use this type of frequency promotion most often.

Another type of frequency program is the "save-a-tape" programs run by supermarkets. These plans ask the consumer to save a predetermined dollar value of cash register tapes that are redeemable for merchandise (usually encyclopedias, cookware, flatware, or dinnerware). These programs usually require a cash payment in addition to the tapes, which makes the program self-liquidating.

Advantages of frequency programs:

- Gain good retailer support
- Attractive to consumers
- Create heavy user involvement

- Encourage continuity of purchase habit
- Keep customers from taking advantage of competitors' short-term promotion/couponing efforts
- Can be easily targeted
- May promote slippage

Disadvantages of frequency programs:
- Expensive to promote
- Require a long-term commitment
- Can require substantial back-up inventories
- Requires dedicated suppliers
- Difficult to cut off

Direct Premiums — In-Pack, On-Pack, and Near-Packs. Direct premiums are those directly received by the consumer upon purchase of a product by virtue of being packaged or sold with the premium. In-pack and on-pack incentives are either packaged in or on the product being promoted. The most widely recognized in-pack offer is the one that has been used to promote the sale of Cracker Jacks for more than 50 years. Cereal companies are major users of in-pack offers.

A near-pack incentive is usually shipped separately from the product being promoted and is displayed directly adjacent to the product. Fast-food restaurants also use this type of promotion to promote add-on sales — for example, buy a burger and a carbonated beverage and get a special, decorated glass free. These promotions usually have a number of differently designed glasses to encourage continuity of purchase.

While the previously described incentive programs require mailing in for the premium or saving toward a premium, direct premium offers provide instant gratification and create a "warm, fuzzy" feeling with consumers. Users can repeat such programs in a predetermined time slot year after year to further the continuity of the offer.

Advantages of direct premiums:
- Promote off-shelf display in grocery outlets
- Generate trial
- Encourage continuity of purchase
- Provide instant gratification
- Can tie directly to the promoted product or service
- Eliminate the need to pack and mail to consumers
- Cost per premium used can be closely controlled
- Differentiates the promoted product from the clutter
- Can be used in conjunction with a tie-in partner to help control promotion cost

Disadvantages of direct premiums:
- Heavy breakage of fragile merchandise
- High employee pilferage rate
- On-packs may require special packaging
- Retailers may refuse to purchase/display on-packs and near-

packs because of the additional space required
- Pretesting is expensive and alerts the competition
- Not appropriate for all products or services

Container Pack Incentives. Specialty container packs have been used for many years. One of the most successful container pack promotions was offered by General Foods on their Maxwell House coffee brand. Maxwell House packed its coffee in a decorated glass coffee carafe, which was given to consumers at no additional cost. This program generated tremendous sales increases in Maxwell House coffee and provided consumers with an ongoing reminder of the brand. Glassware incentives have also been used for years on jam and jelly products.

Advantages of container packs:
- Encourage future consumption of sponsor's product
- Can be inexpensive when normal container cost is deducted
- Provide instant gratification to consumers

Disadvantages of container packs:
- May be refused by retailers if a new stock keeping unit (SKU) is required or special container takes too much shelf space
- Cost to produce, package, or distribute may be prohibitive

Account Openers. Account openers have been used by many companies to encourage their current and new consumers to purchase an item on time or, in the case of financial institutions, to open a new type of account or to secure a loan or certificate of deposit. The direct mail industry utilizes these incentives to encourage consumers to purchase or try an item of merchandise of much greater value. In the event the consumer wishes to return the trial item for credit or refund, the incentive item may be retained as a reward for the trial.

Advantages of account openers:
- Encourage trial of service or product
- Control rewarding current users
- Costs can easily be controlled
- Instant gratification

Disadvantages of account openers:
- Some consumers partake of an offer for the incentive only with no intent to try or purchase the item or service
- Can encourage account switching just to take advantage of the incentive

Business Gifts. Business gifts are rewards given to stockholders, customers, business friends, and employees as an expression of appreciation for performance, loyalty, or friendship. The federal government limits the dollar amount that can be paid for such rewards. While there are some minor advantages and disadvantages to this type of incentive, the major purpose is a gesture of friendship.

Employee Awards. Incentives used to reward employees for safety, quality control, attendance, productivity performance, longevity, or suggestions fall into the employee awards category. Most employers use one or more of the motivational techniques to reward employees for predetermined performance levels. There have been substantiated reports of employee lost-time accidents being reduced by more than 50 percent as a result of safety award programs. It is a normal practice to present these incentive awards at special luncheons and dinners to honor those who have achieved the level of excellence required to earn an award. This recognition can also encourage teamwork and is an employee morale builder.

Advantages of employee award programs:
- Loyalty builders
- Create employee goodwill
- Are very cost-effective
- Easy to implement
- Result in higher profits
- Can reduce total employees because of absentee reduction

Disadvantages of employee award programs:
- Require long-term management commitment
- Management training is required at all levels

Dealer Incentives. Dealer incentive merchandise sales accounted for more than $2 billion of the almost $13 billion of incentive sales in 1991. Dealer or trade incentive programs are structured to reward these customers for purchasing, displaying, and selling products and services. The program can be a "short-term" offer built around a single item — for example, purchase a predetermined quantity of product, put up a display detailing the consumer offer, and keep the consumer incentive item affixed to the display when the program is completed. Alternatively, these programs could be very detailed "long-term" offers promoting continuity of purchase and requiring accumulation of points redeemable for high-cost merchandise and/or travel displayed in very high-quality, four-color, comprehensive catalogs with custom-designed covers and promotional literature. There are also "step" catalogs offering a variety of items at various point levels that are used for this type of incentive, as well as offering executive gifts.

Advantages of dealer incentive programs:
- Costs can be structured to fit even the most austere budget
- Encourage display
- Increase off-shelf display
- "Load" merchandise into customers, keeping the competition out
- Recall of incentive source is very high

Disadvantages of dealer incentive programs:
- Load dealers with merchandise that can cause sales dip following promotion
- If used in standard cycles, can result in dealers delaying purchases while awaiting the incentive offer
- Delays in fulfilling dealer incentive awards can cause negative reactions

Sales Incentives. Sales incentives provide a reward for achievement performance of a predetermined sales goal during a defined time period. The length of the program varies from very short-term events, often referred to as "spurt" programs, to programs that last the entire year. These programs can be designed to motivate a salesperson to sell a particular product or service, a product line, or multiple lines or services.

Many believe that a salary or commission should be sufficient motivation to perform to the utmost ability, but the use of sales incentives has proven that sales forces can be motivated to achieve sales goals far in excess of forecasted levels. The drive to make the extra sales call or push the promoted line or service to "win" the sales contest or award has resulted in sales increases of more than 100 percent of the projected goal.

Cash, merchandise, and travel are the most popular awards. Some sales incentive programs offer a wide selection of gifts, and this merchandise is pictured in a catalog from which winners may select awards based on the points or credits they have earned as a result of their sales efforts. Other programs offer exotic travel destinations for all winners who have achieved or surpassed their sales goal. Successful sales incentive programs are structured so that even the top goals are within reach of all participants. If goals are set at levels that are not achievable, a negative reaction could result.

Advantages of sales incentives:
- Motivate the sales force to achieve sales levels beyond budgeted levels
- Reward sales personnel for "going that extra mile"
- "Load" customers to take competition out of the market
- Move a slower-selling product or service
- Can be structured to fit any reasonable budget

Disadvantages of sales incentive programs:
- Can reward the sales staff for doing the job they are being paid to do
- Sales support staff personnel can become disgruntled if they do not have some type of incentive program to reward them for their added workload
- Sales following the program may decline because of inventory buildup resulting from the extra sales effort during the program
- Long-range programs require continual updates and progress reports

FULFILLMENT

The incentive promotion is not completed until all awards, incentives, and premiums have been delivered to the recipient in perfect condition. Failure to complete the fulfillment process on time, properly packaged, and in good condition can turn a successful program into a disaster. The fulfillment process must be carefully planned to assure that this critical delivery cycle is handled efficiently.

Fulfillment of consumer incentives and rebate offers, because of the high volume of response and control, is usually handled by professionals who specialize in the high-volume, low-cost, fast turnaround of incoming mail responses. These fulfillment houses have the electronic data processing software programs that are capable of eliminating duplicate requests, producing zip sorting labels, and making checks to take advantage of the best postal and United Parcel Service (UPS) rates. They also have database management systems and specialized packaging equipment to provide low-cost, safe packaging to assure that merchandise and materials arrive in good condition.

The cost for this service is based upon volume of mail that is processed and the amount and quality of service that is provided. The companies offering fulfillment services must also have the capability of providing on-line consumer service to assure that any consumer inquiry is handled quickly and efficiently to avoid any dissatisfaction.

To provide marketing data, each medium used to promote the offer to consumers is usually provided a separate post office box or specific media code so that responses to the different media can be carefully evaluated for future advertising consideration.

When an incentive merchandise order has been processed, shipment of the merchandise can be made directly from the fulfillment house, or labels can be forwarded to the incentive supplier or their designate for drop-shipment. The processing of orders through the mail is closely regulated by the Federal Trade Commission (FTC) and must be shipped to the respondent within the time specified in the offer, or a delay notice must be sent to respondents advising them of the delay and offering them an opportunity to cancel their request and receive a full refund if they elect not to accept the delay.

Dealer and sales incentive merchandise or travel award mailings are usually handled by professional incentive merchandise suppliers who keep running totals of how each participant is progressing toward his or her goal. They also send updates on this progress to the participants and motivate them to work harder to assure they qualify for their desired award. Mailings are also made to the participants' spouses asking for their help in motivating their spouse to achieve the goal.

In some instances, large, multiple-line consumer product companies have their own fulfillment centers. These companies must have sufficient mail volume to be cost effective. For instance, General Foods Corporation, R. J. Reynolds, and Scott Paper Company have set up their own fulfillment operations.

One of the most damaging occurrences in any incentive program is the lack of merchandise necessary to fulfill requests in a timely manner. This normally is the result of poor planning/forecasting or unanticipated response levels. It is imperative that a contingency plan be incorporated into every promotion plan to assure that merchandise of equal or better value is available should requests surpass projections.

REFUNDS/REBATES

Cash and coupon refunds are the second leading promotional incentive behind manufacturers' store-redeemable coupons. Refunds/rebates are very easily implemented and can be set up to combat a competitive promotional effort in a very short period of time.

Unlike merchandise incentives, cash refunds require no inventories and can be advertised to consumers at point-of-sale, in best-food-day advertisements, on a regional or specific market basis, nationally in FSIs, magazines, or Sunday supplements without a great deal of time required to put the promotional effort together.

Refunds/rebates may be paid in cash or in store-redeemable coupons. Consumers are required to purchase the product or service and submit a specified "proof-of-purchase" by mail to receive their refund. Most often, refund programs set specific limits on the total number of rebates a single consumer may obtain, and strict legal copy explains precisely what these limits are.

To prevent rules violations, computer programs are set up to eliminate duplicate responses or requests for refunds that exceed the specified dollar amount allowable. To request, receive, and cash a duplicate refund check or to redeem a coupon in excess of the limits of the offer constitutes a violation of the United States mail fraud statutes (18 USC sections 1341 and 1342). This crime is punishable by a fine of as much as $1,000 and imprisonment for as long as five years.

Prior to the mid-1970s, most refund offers were fulfilled with cash because the cost to key respondents' names and addresses on checks was prohibitive. In the mid to late 1970s, the advent of mini-computers and microcomputers and laser scanning technology made it possible to send impact-printed check refunds, usually containing a personalized "thank you" note. Check stock had to be ordered in advance and could be expensive if a special check was required on a lower-volume promotion. Check and coupon stock had to be stored in high-security storage areas or vaults because checks were preprinted with the dollar amount and were signed. Preprinted coupons could be easily redeemed for merchandise or sold illegally to retailers who could redeem them for cash.

The introduction of high-speed laser printing technology has advanced refunding to the 21st century. The requirement of having large quantities of blank, presigned checks in stock, which creates a major security problem, is no longer a necessity. Today, check or coupon stock, printed with only a pantograph background, is all that is required to laser-produce checks. Company or brand name logos and check authorization signatures can be electronically digitized and laser printed on the check along with the payee's name, dollar amount, the required OCR (Optical Character Recognition) numbers, and any personalized message. Messages may be changed and dollar amounts varied to correspond with the item the consumer purchased or the quantity of proofs-of-purchase submitted.

Coupon refunds can also be laser printed and personalized to a particular consumer, retailer, or both. The personalization of coupons helps to reduce consumer fraud and misredemption. It also eliminates the possibility of theft of preprinted coupons. The flexibility of laser printing on high-speed equipment has revolutionized the cash and coupon refund business. Cash and coupon refunds are structured in many ways:

- **Buy one, get one free.** Consumers purchase the promoted product, mail in the required proof-of-purchase, and receive a coupon good for free product.
- **Multiple-purchase coupon refunds.** These are structured similarly to the "buy one, get one free" offer, except that multiple purchases are required (for example, consumers purchase two products and get two free, or make four purchases to receive three free).
- **Refund and coupon combination offers.** These are used in tandem to provide greater incentive value to consumers (for example, purchase a product, submit the required proof-of-purchase, and receive a $1.00 rebate plus a coupon good for $.50 off the next purchase of the same product or, if desired, off a related product, whichever the manufacturer prefers).

The combinations of possible refund scenarios are endless, and "tie-in" promotions with other noncompetitive companies are often set up to add value to the offer and reduce the cost to both companies because they can share the mail processing and mailing costs.

Advantages of refunds/rebates:
- Easy to implement
- No inventories required, except of preprinted store-redeemable coupons
- Encourage trial
- Encourage multiple purchase
- Can be used to counter competitive product introductions and other incentive offers
- Easily used with tie-in partner to share fulfillment costs
- Easy to control budgets

Disadvantages of refunds/rebates:
- Easily countered by the competition
- May delay purchase if used too often; Consumers will delay purchase awaiting another refund offer
- Misredemption or duplicate refunds to same consumer
- Reward regular users

- Mail delays and losses may cause consumer dissatisfaction

It is estimated that more than 75 percent of all households in the U.S. take advantage of at least one refund annually. There are numerous refund publications available for a very low subscription price that list all refunds, rules, expiration dates, and required qualifiers.

Don Jagoda is President and Founder of Don Jagoda Associates, Inc., which he has headed for more than 30 years. As one of the nation's foremost promotion and marketing organizations, specializing in planning and administering promotions, tie-ins, sweepstakes, games, contests, merchandise and travel incentives, and premiums programs, his company may well have given away more money and prizes than any other!

Over the years, Don Jagoda Associates has worked with almost all of the top Fortune 500 companies, including Lever Brothers, General Foods, Coca-Cola, Philip Morris, Showtime Networks, and hundreds of other major corporations that have all used his innovative concepts to promote products.

Jagoda is on the Board of Directors of the Promotion Marketing Association of America, Association of Incentive Marketing, Incentive Federation, and Marketing Communications Executives International. He is a member of the Premium Merchandising Club and the Long Island Advertising Club.

CHAPTER 4

SWEEPSTAKES, GAMES, AND CONTESTS

Sweepstakes, games, and contests are among the hottest sales promotion techniques today. There are several reasons for this popularity. Certainly, one of the best is that a lot of people, in a lot of fields, have learned how to use them effectively.

Let's put this into numbers: Back in 1980, according to industry publication studies, $650 million was spent on sweepstakes. By 1983, this total rose to $732 million. By 1990, the billion-dollar mark was passed, with total sweepstakes spending estimated at $1,135,327,148 — a 74 percent increase in just 10 years.

Sweepstakes are no longer confined simply to packaged products with carefully built-up identities and images. Today, we are seeing sweepstakes utilized by a host of new industries that never before ran any promotions other than basic trade incentives and allowances.

Recent sweepstakes promotions have included instant-winner games for combination locks; a programmed-learning sweepstakes for design engineers with questions on the applications of urethane foams; a sweepstakes for paint contractors requiring pickup of entries at paint stores; a sweepstakes designed to create frame-by-frame involvement with a hot rock-video release; an instant winner game with preselected lucky numbers designed to get farmers into agricultural equipment dealerships in the United States and Canada; a programmed-learning program for cattle ranchers, focusing on a pest insecticide; an instant winner game for beauty salon operators designed to get them into cash-and-carry wholesale locations, supporting a major hair care marketer's professional products; and a qualified-entry sweepstakes designed to encourage bookstore browsing — and purchase — of a line of paperback romances.

Clearly, sweepstakes are growing and are very much in the forefront of people's minds. By "people," we mean marketers, wholesalers, retailers, and, most important, consumers.

It's really ironic, because 30 years ago, when Don Jagoda Associates started in this business, the sweepstakes was often considered a last-gasp promotion. It was something that was used when all else failed and a brand was dying.

Today, sweepstakes have done a complete about-face. Along with games and contests, they've been repositioned as a hard-hitting, sales-generating promotion technique, transformed from a passive promotional technique into an aggressive marketing tool.

It is change that has engineered this 180° turnaround and has made sweepstakes a state-of-the-art promotion. Specifically, change has occurred in four significant areas.

1. **Change in legality**. There's been a definite trend toward easing of federal and state restrictions on lotteries and sweepstakes. And, while this type of program still calls for significant legal as well as promotional expertise, it's not as handcuffed as it used to be. Today, you can run a sweepstakes in all 50 states.

2. **Change in consumer acceptance.** Today, more than half the states are conducting their own lotteries. Every state lottery ad or commercial helps build simultaneous acceptance for sweepstakes and games of all types. This, combined with a general liberalization of consumer attitudes, has been a tremendous help in removing the stigma that used to be attached to sweepstakes.

3. **Change in economic conditions.** The inflation and recession of the 1970s and early 1980s became a one-two punch that devastated a large part of the populace. Today, with the economy mired in recession, anything offering the consumer a chance to become Cinderella or the hope of a better life or something for nothing is warmly welcomed. As a result, cents-off coupons, refunds and rebates, sweepstakes, games, and contests have blossomed.

4. **Change in entry mechanics.** This is the most visible area of change. It has added the whole new dimension of greater involvement — that is, getting the consumer to do more than just write down a name and address. Ways have been developed to make participating more interesting, literally by forcing consumers to study an ad, handle a product, and, yes, even buy a product.

BASIC DEFINITIONS

It is important to understand the terms sweepstakes, games, and contests. A sweepstakes is a prize promotion in which winners are selected by chance. These promotions are regulated primarily by federal and state lottery laws, which declare that a lottery is an illegal promotion. A lottery is any promotion that contains these three elements: prize, chance, and consideration (purchase).

So, how can the states run lotteries? They pass legislation authorizing their own lotteries.

Private-sector marketers avoid the lottery restriction by eliminating the element of consideration. Authorities have agreed to allow sponsors to request proof-of-purchase with sweepstakes entries, as long as consumers are given the alternative of not submitting proof-of-purchase. In most cases, the acceptable alternative is a plain 3" x 5" piece of paper with the brand name handwritten on it.

All forms of sweepstakes, including the instant winner games that utilize some form of concealment device, fall under the same laws and guidelines. All these programs, no matter how complex or how steep the odds, are random-chance events.

A contest, like a sweepstakes or lottery, is a prize promotion. However, in a contest, prizes are awarded not on random chance but on the basis of a test of skill or personal talent. A contest can require a recipe, a photograph, a jingle, or an essay as a test of skill. The winners in such a program are not picked randomly. All contest entries must be opened and screened, and the judging proceeds according to a weighted set of criteria that are made known to all entrants as part of the contest rules.

Because the element of chance is not present in contests, they are not subject to the same restrictions that govern sweepstakes. In a contest, consideration, or purchase of a product, may be required for entry in many categories. Because skill is involved, contests logically generate far fewer entries than sweepstakes. In fact, in terms of entries, industry observers say sweepstakes will generate anywhere from four to 10 times more entries than contests. Because a contest will generate only a fraction of the entries generated by a sweepstakes, many marketers waive any purchase requirement in a contest, even though such a requirement is legal. The idea is to present as few obstacles to entry as possible.

ADVANTAGES OF SWEEPSTAKES, GAMES, AND CONTESTS

Why should marketers use sweepstakes, games, or contests? We see five key advantages.

1. **Fixed budget.** The sweepstakes, game, or contest is one of the few promotions in which you can determine your costs in advance. Because it is not open-ended, like a coupon offer, the sponsor can establish the budget and tightly control expenditures. Regardless of how many entries are received, the sponsor's liability is limited to the budget established in advance.

2. **Excitement.** The sweepstakes carries its own built-in excitement. The basic appeal is to acquisitiveness and the fact that it's human nature that everybody wants something for nothing. There is also something of the thrill of gambling. However, the consumer is really safe because little, if anything, is being risked. The big promise — The Grand Prize, such as a car, a trip, cash, or a variation on these — is always a surefire attention getter. When executed properly, the inherent excitement of the sweepstakes, game, or contest literally magnifies the promotion, making it look much bigger than it actually is.

3. **A sales tool.** Frequently, we'll tell a client his sweepstakes will be a success or failure before the first ad ever appears. Why? Because the primary reason for many prize promotions is simply to give salespeople a selling tool, more ammunition, to enable them to offer the buyer a whole promotion, an event that meets the buyer's need, not merely another price deal.

4. **Generating displays and features.** In packaged products, increased sales invariably occur when a product is featured in an on-or off-shelf display treatment. The inherent drama and excitement of a sweepstakes (which translates into more eye-catching displays) and its potential for increasing store traffic are two of the reasons why many buyers will approve the store displays and support a sweepstakes event.

5. **Greater ad readership.** The magic lure of free prizes draws people into reading sweepstakes, game, and contest ads. Certainly, their readership scores, as shown in the next section, are higher than average. By carefully integrating the brand copy platform into the sweepstakes' theme or mechanics, you can further extend the reach of your advertising and therefore your advertising dollars.

ESTIMATING RESULTS

Two concerns of marketers who are considering using sweepstakes are their appropriateness for the particular target audience and the question of what a sweepstakes can actually do.

It is difficult to gauge the impact of a sweepstakes. The number of entries received bears little or no relationship to sales, since product purchase cannot be required. A sweepstakes that is heavily advertised will naturally generate awareness and recall. Today's generation of instant winner games, matching games, programmed-learning sweepstakes, telemarketing promotions, and the like can increase store traffic; and this will impact on sales, but in a way that cannot be predicted with certainty. Many sweepstakes today are, in fact, geared to development of a database of users or, at least, of aware consumers.

It is probably best to think of a sweepstakes as a dramatic element of a brand's advertising strategy, since a good sweepstakes will have a theme and a prize structure in keeping with the product and its advertising. The advertising will impact on the trade and the consumer. A sweepstakes may or may not be advertised in consumer media. But it must get visibility at the point-of-purchase, even if only on the product package itself.

To the trade, utilizing sweepstakes at the point-of-purchase helps create in-store excitement. Increasingly, trade sweepstakes are held in parallel consumer programs.

The rule of thumb is that sweepstakes should generate entries on the order of 1 to 2 percent of total circulation of the program, including advertising and point-of-purchase materials. As an example, a sweepstakes featured in a national FSI ad (circulation 50MM) and generating a response of 1 percent of the circulation yields 750,000 entries. The real power of sweepstakes advertising lies in the attention paid to it by consumers. The figures in Table 4.1 show readership scores for a recent food product sweepstakes appearing in a major women's magazine.

TABLE 4.1
SWEEPSTAKES READERSHIP SCORES

	Noted	Read Most
Sweepstakes ad	49%	17%
Norm for all food product ads	46	9
Sweepstakes ad index	107	189

While the sweepstakes ad was noted by 3 percent more readers than other food product ads in the same issue of the magazine, the dramatic difference is the extent of intensive readership. The sweepstakes ad's rate of "read most" attention on the part of the readership sample was nearly double that of other food ads in the same issue. The lure of big cash, travel, or merchandise prizes will get people reading and keep them reading.

WHO ENTERS SWEEPSTAKES?

Nearly half of the respondents in a study of 2,000 consumers by a major polling organization reported that they had entered a sweepstakes at least once in their lives, and nearly one-third reported that they had purchased products featured in a sweepstakes ad (see Table 4.2).

Sex, age, working status of female heads of households, and marital status are apparently not major determining factors in sweepstakes entry. What seems to matter most is the existence of children under 18 in the household, the size of the household itself, and family income, along with the region of the country in which the family lives.

Larger households with young children, families with larger incomes, and people living in the West seem to constitute the most active sweepstakes-entering groups. Younger and larger households with higher incomes tend to buy the featured brand more, as part of the overall sweepstakes program.

By and large, the greatest response to a sweepstakes promotion comes from the same audience that is more involved with consumer promotions of all types, consisting of larger, relatively affluent families.

SWEEPSTAKES PROMOTION FORMATS

Few marketers are aware of the many types of sweepstakes, games, and contests. There are no fewer than five sweepstakes formats plus three types of games.

First is the *Standard Sweepstakes* (see Exhibit 4.1), in which a consumer receives an entry in some print media or at the point-of-sale and is instructed to mail it in to a specific post office box or deposit it in a handy ballot box. The drawing to select winners is conducted at some specified later date.

TABLE 4.2
PARTICIPATION IN SWEEPSTAKES

	Percent of each group who purchased products along with sweepstakes offer	Percent of each group who "ever entered
Total Sample	48.2%	28.4%
Sex:		
Men	44.0	28.4
Women	49.1	28.4
Age:		
18 to 34	51.5	32.3
35 to 49	53.3	31.2
50 and over	42.7	23.6
Female head of household:		
Working	50.9	28.6
Not working	47.8	27.2
Marital status:		
Married	51.2	29.0
Single	46.4	33.8
Children under 18 in household:		
One or more	53.3	32.4
None	44.5	25.4
Household size:		
One to two persons	41.8	24.0
Three or more persons	53.9	32.4
Annual income:		
Under $10,000	42.0	23.1
$10,000 to $14,999	50.5	29.3
$15,000 to $24,999	54.1	34.6
$25,000 and over	54.6	34.8
Geography:		
East	42.6	24.6
Midwest	50.3	31.0
South	46.5	27.0
West	55.7	32.1

Yes, this is the old workhorse program we've all known since sweepstakes began. But, given the right product, the right prize structure, and the right advertising support, this type of program can grab attention and deliver readers. It is why so many more marketers are using sweepstakes today.

Second is the *Multiple-Entry Sweepstakes* (see Exhibit 4.2), in which each prize is literally a separate sweepstakes by itself. So, in order to be eligible to win any of the prizes in this type of program, a separate entry is required for each prize. This type of format greatly multiplies consumer involvement in the advertising and, not incidentally, mushrooms the number of entries received.

The multiple-entry sweepstakes is clearly an ideal way to focus on or enhance the importance of a specific number. For Benson & Hedges 100s, which used the format for many years, that number is obviously 100 — 100 individual sweepstakes, supporting a top 100mm brand.

The *Programmed-Learning Sweepstakes* (Exhibit 4.3) uses a technique that's popular in elementary education. It's like an exercise in conditioning. As a prerequisite to entering, we require the consumer to read the ad and give us back key copy points or information.

The *Qualified-Entry Sweepstakes* is similar to programmed learning except that the information needed to qualify the entry is not presented in the advertising: The consumer must guess the answer from clues or solve a puzzle, for example. Involvement here is at a maximum. Increasingly, marketers are using toll-free or 900-number telephone systems to provide clues or information to qualify entries.

One of the hottest sweepstakes techniques today is the *Automatic-Entry* format (Exhibit 4.4), where a store coupon in an ad doubles as a sweepstakes entry. When the consumer redeems the coupon with the name and address information filled in, he or she is automatically entered in the sweepstakes without the need for mailing in the entry or adding extra postage. The result? Incremental entries. In fact, we estimate that automatic-entry coupons will hype coupon redemption rates by as much as 25 percent.

Interactive telephone programs also offer an automatic-entry mechanism for consumers. By calling an 800 or 900 telephone number featured in advertising, consumers may also enter a sweepstakes.

THREE TYPES OF GAMES

Games represent the most powerful sweepstakes formats to create traffic and sales. The *Matching Instant Winner Game* (see Exhibit 4.5) literally steers consumers into stores. That's because one key element of a matching game is an ad that contains a matching symbol the consumer has to take to the store to find out if and what he or she has won. In fact, the headline often says, "You May Have Already Won — ."

EXHIBIT 4.1
STANDARD SWEEPSTAKES FORMAT

EXHIBIT 4.2
MULTIPLE-ENTRY SWEEPSTAKES FORMAT

EXHIBIT 4.3
PROGRAMMED-LEARNING SWEEPSTAKES FORMAT

EXHIBIT 4.4
AUTOMATIC-ENTRY SWEEPSTAKES FORMAT

For a major paint retailer, which at the time was an official NFL licensee, a matching game was developed in which consumers took scrambled color game symbols to participating stores across the country and unscrambled them by placing the symbols behind special acetate screens to reveal the hidden matching symbol. All of the motivating terminology of football, from touchdown to reverse, and exciting football graphics were used to excite the primarily male target audience. The delivery medium was a special eight-page color Sunday tabloid insert, with the sweepstakes getting front-page treatment.

In matching games, where it is difficult to set up displays, the UPC number, which is on every package, may be used as the matching element.

Collect-and-Win Games (see Exhibit 4.6) are often used in conjunction with instant winner games, but they can stand alone, as well. In this format, consumers get a game piece or symbol that represents a piece of a picture or part of a name or phrase. By getting enough game pieces to spell the name or complete the picture, the consumer can win a prize. Generally, one or more of the individual collect-and-win phrases or symbols is a rare game piece, limited to the total number of prizes available.

Instant Winner Games (see Exhibit 4.7) are self-contained and self-judging random-chance promotions. Consumers receive a game card requiring one or more scratch-offs or peel-offs to reveal a prize message, or instructions to enter a "second-chance" random drawing, or to save for a collect-and-win prize. New technologies include interactive games in which cards are scanned by readers with a voice message announcing a win or "Sorry, Try Again" message, or even devices that heat or cool the cards to reveal a hidden message.

CONTESTS FALL INTO BASIC TYPES

A contest requires a demonstration of skill or personal trait on the part of the entrant, who mails the entry to a post office box or deposits it in an on-premise container. The contest, therefore, has remained a basically static type of promotional program. Regardless of the theme, the specific test of skill required, or the prize structure, contest programs, when stripped to the bare essentials, are all pretty much alike (see Exhibit 4.8).

This does not mean that there is no purpose for contest programs. In recipe contests, marketers are trying to appeal to heavy users and tap the creative genius of the American homemaker. Winning recipes may appear on product labels, in printed ads, in TV commercials, or in recipe booklets. In photo contests, winning entries may provide visual elements for a continuing series of advertisements. An essay contest winner may be recruited as a corporate spokesperson for the brand or service.

EXHIBIT 4.5
MATCHING INSTANT WINNER GAME FORMAT

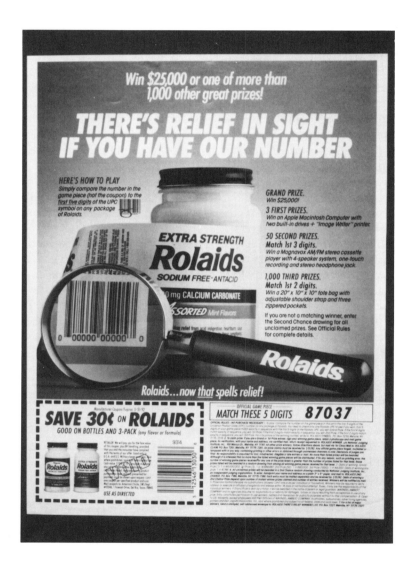

EXHIBIT 4.6
COLLECT-AND-WIN GAME FORMAT

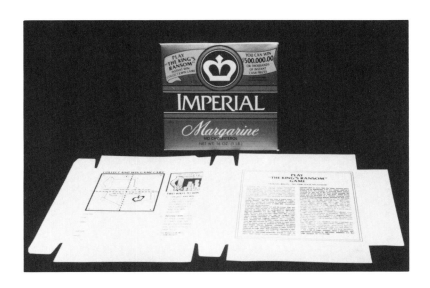

EXHIBIT 4.7
INSTANT WINNER GAME FORMAT

EXHIBIT 4.8
CONTEST FORMAT

Marketers who equate promotion success with sales may select contests over sweepstakes simply because proof-of-purchase can be required. However, contests will generate only a fraction of the entries generated by a sweepstakes. If a sweepstakes entry blank asks for either an actual or a facsimile proof-of-purchase, the number of actual proofs-of-purchase will probably far exceed the number generated by a contest identically exposed and advertised to the target audience, simply because the sweepstakes generates so many more total entries.

PLANNING FOR SWEEPSTAKES, GAMES, AND CONTESTS

1. **Determine the objectives**. Before you can know whether a sweepstakes, game, or contest will do the job, you must analyze the reasons for the promotion and determine what you expect it to achieve. For example, you must decide whether the problem is sales or distribution and whether the promotion is to cover a single product or the full line.

2. **Establish the markets.** The next step is to determine whether the promotion is to be national or regional and to establish the audience at which the sweepstakes will be aimed. Both these factors will affect the ad media and the prizes.

3. **Assign responsibilities**. Decide who will be responsible for each facet of the promotion and who will do the planning and create the sweepstakes idea and mechanics. Specify what your ad agency will be responsible for and who will handle the sweepstakes and post-sweepstakes details. Decide whether to use the services of a sweepstakes planning organization. Sweepstakes specialists can create sweepstakes ideas; develop the mechanics; draft the rules; receive, process, and store entries; judge the winners; arrange for the prizes; and handle all details and correspondence in connection with the prizes, including supervising their delivery. The important thing is to use every available source of assistance to carefully plan and administer the promotion.

4. **Develop the theme**. The sweepstakes idea or theme must be integrated with your objectives so that your product will not suffer from being subordinated to the sweepstakes itself.

   Another approach is to spotlight a specific product feature or benefit and build the sweepstakes theme around it. As noted, Benson & Hedges 100s cigarettes focused on the length of the product in its sweepstakes.

   Another effective way of integrating a sweepstakes and the product is to make the product an integral part of the grand prize, as Sunkist did recently with a "Win a Carload of Oranges" sweepstakes.

5. **Determine the entry mechanics**. Should the promotion be a sweepstakes or a skill contest? If getting a lot of entries is

important, then a sweepstakes is best. On the other hand, if you want to be able to require a proof-of-purchase with every entry, you'll have to go with a skill contest. As we've seen, that doesn't mean you're limited to the old "25-words-or-less" format. There are jingle-writing contests, photography contests, and the ever-popular recipe contests. Bear in mind, too, that a clever entry device can sometimes greatly enhance the promotion.

The entry mechanics should spell out the duration of the promotion and the conditions covering participation and judging. In a skill contest, it's especially important to make certain that you establish measurable, judgeable criteria. Most important, keep the sweepstakes and the rules as simple as possible.

6. **Check the regulations.** Although there's some confusion in this area, sweepstakes are perfectly legal. It's lotteries that are illegal for use in connection with consumer goods and services. There are federal, state, and local lottery laws, as well as Federal Trade Commission regulations, that must be adhered to. And several states now require that sweepstakes be registered and reported. Just make sure that you, your attorney, or your sweepstakes planning firm is up on the latest statutes governing games of chance.

7. **Select the prizes.** The prizes are the heart of any sweepstakes, contest, or game. They should be appropriate for the audience and the time of the year, and they should tie in with the theme. Offer as many prizes as possible so that people will feel they have a better chance of winning. For the supplementary prizes, a variety of merchandise is preferable to cash. Merchandise is more interesting and significant than a small cash award.

8. **Estimate the costs.** Early in the planning stage, firm up estimates of the cost of advertising, production, sales promotion and display materials, prizes, handling, and judging.

9. **Plan the advertising**. If you're going to have a promotion, promote it. Be prepared to devote both print space and airtime to the sweepstakes. Use the same media you have used all along. Keep the layouts simple and feature the prizes prominently; they are the carrots you are dangling before your audience.

10. **Get the sales force fired up**. Whether you have your own sales force or you sell through brokers, jobbers, distributors, or dealers, the task is still the same: to convince them that the sweepstakes is a sales tool designed to make their jobs easier and help them write more business. The sweepstakes gives them a change of pace, another reason for asking for a display or an order.

11. **Sell the trade.** Dealer cooperation is essential. Sometimes it's the reason for the whole promotion. Get dealers excited about

the impact the promotion will have on consumers and the traffic it will pull into their stores. Set up a trade sweepstakes to run simultaneously with the consumer sweepstakes; this will give dealers an added incentive to cooperate.

12. **Plan the publicity**. Back up the advertising with publicity. Frequently, the sweepstakes idea or the fact that you are running a sweepstakes is news. Send trade publications a publicity story spelling out the details. When it's over, send releases to every prizewinner's hometown paper. Then follow up with "how-we-did-it" articles.

13. **Arrange for judging the winners**. Whether you're running a sweepstakes or a skill contest, the safest thing is to have the judging done by a professional organization. You want to make certain that the winners are selected fairly and impartially; so leave the judging to the experts.

14. **Check the major winners**. Conduct a background check on the major prize winners to ascertain that the entries are their own work and that there is no question about their entries or their eligibility as winners. The judging agency usually will handle this for you.

15. **Announce the winners.** Once the sweepstakes is over, see that the judging is done as quickly as possible and that the winners are announced promptly. You must also send a list of winners to anyone who requests it.

16. **Deliver the prizes.** Nothing creates more ill will than a disappointed prize winner. Delivery of the prizes should therefore be handled quickly and smoothly.

17. **Analyze the results.** The most important criteria are as follows: Did the sweepstakes achieve its objectives? How did the sweepstakes affect sales? Did it succeed in getting all the displays you wanted? What did the sales force think of the promotion?

BUDGETING FOR SWEEPSTAKES, GAMES, AND CONTESTS

As has been noted, a critical benefit of a prize promotion is the fixed-cost nature of the event. The fact that there are no major open-ended liabilities in a sweepstakes or contest makes this type of promotion affordable to marketers for whom an elaborate program of coupons, samples, or refund offers may be too costly. At the other end of the spectrum, a sweepstakes may be ideal for brands in product categories with such high volume and purchase frequency that a coupon drop or refund offer will result in a redemption rate so high that the promotion becomes a victim of its own success, blowing budgets through the roof.

Many sweepstakes and contest programs are overlaid with coupon offers for the sponsoring brand. This has the function of encouraging purchase of the product in association with the sweepstakes and of utilizing media delivery of a sweepstakes or contest ad to provide a direct price incentive to the consumer. In such combination programs, the cost of the add-on promotion device must be budgeted separately from the sweepstakes or contest event itself, and the marketer must use all the data available in planning for the coupon response.

The costs of the sweepstakes or contest event can be grouped as follows:

1. Advertising and point-of-purchase production and media costs,
2. Prize costs, and
3. Administration and judging costs.

Advertising and point-of-purchase costs in a prize promotion are no different from those in any other type of promotion, and the result of a greater expenditure on media advertising is also the same. Strong, extensive national advertising and a major drive to get the store materials up will result in a much stronger program, whether it's a coupon drop or a sweepstakes. Television and radio support will also increase awareness of the program and add somewhat to the entry rate, but at an increased cost.

Prizes in a sweepstakes or contest are the great variable. We have long since crossed the $1 million threshold in private-sector prize promotions. The various state lotteries have yielded cash prize jackpots of $50–$60 million or more, and this has had an impact on prize promotion planning.

Depending on the product, the theme of the sweepstakes, and the regionality and nationality of the event, a prize budget as low as $25,000 can still produce an exciting, results-getting promotion.

While cash prizes may be the most universally accepted and desired, they raise a number of problems and questions for the marketer.

1. There is no disputing the impact of a large grand prize of, say, $1,000,000. However, smaller cash prizes may be unexciting, depending on the amounts, the nature of the target audience, and the relevance of a cash prize to the featured product and to the theme of the event. In the case of a sweepstakes aimed at children, for example, cash prizes would be meaningless. Children want to win trips, bicycles, games, and electronic gadgets. A $1,000 cash prize means less to a child than a $500 video game plus game cartridges.
2. A cash prize cannot be discounted or bartered. A $100,000 cash prize costs the marketer $100,000. The same $100,000 expressed as retail value of merchandise prizes may cost the marketer far less. In fact, when advertising exposure to a potential prize supplier is significant — for example, when there is extensive national print advertising, point-of-purchase advertising, or even a special 30-second TV commercial — prizes may

be obtained at little or no cost in exchange for this valuable exposure. It becomes an advertising bargain for the prize supplier and a trade-off for the sponsoring marketer.

3. The tax implications to winners of cash prizes may be considerable. Prizes over $600 must be declared as income. In fact, professional sweepstakes administration and judging organizations report this income directly to the IRS. A cash prize thus may involve a greater tax liability than a merchandise prize.

Administration and judging costs depend on such factors as the complexity of the program mechanics, special printing involved in concealed-device instant winner games, the need to visit printing or packaging plants to supervise the production and distribution of instant winner game cards and packages, prize fulfillment, and special tabular analyses of entrants. For planning purposes, marketers may estimate that the administrative cost of a typical prize promotion, exclusive of any special printing, will range from $7,000 to $25,000.

The total prize promotion package, including administration, judging, prizes, and media and point-of-purchase advertising, could range from $100,000 to $500,000 for a national event.

In budgeting for a prize promotion, the utilization of a professional administration, implementation, and judging organization is probably the least costly element, but it could be the most important one, since independence and objectivity are vital in the proper handling of these programs; a professional service can anticipate problems before they arise, thus helping the marketer avoid them.

For most marketers, a do-it-yourself sweepstakes is entirely possible. But, putting clerical people and legal retainers who are relatively inexperienced in this area to work on the event can prove far more costly and cumbersome than letting the professionals do it in the first place, not to mention creating a potential legal nightmare.

James Feldman is president of several motivation companies, including James Feldman Associates, a full-service marketing services agency; Incentive Travelers Cheque International, Inc., which offers individual travel incentives; Incentive Travel Corporation, providing group incentive travel; and Fulfillment Awards, Ltd., a data-processing and fulfillment house. His companies have provided merchandise, advertising specialties, data processing and fulfillment, and sweep-stakes to clients that include Toyota Motor Sales USA, Apple Computer, Helene Curtis, Frito Lay, MGM/USA, Volkswagen USA, and Clairol, among others.

Feldman is a featured international speaker, trainer, author, and advocate for incentive usage. He has been an active member of the Association of Incentive Marketing (AIM) since 1979 and currently serves on the Board of Directors and as Seminar Director for AIM. He has been a speaker at almost every AIM seminar since 1980. He also has been an active member, board member, and committee chairman for the Society of Incentive Travel Executives (SITE) and a contributor to In-Site, *their quarterly magazine. He has been a member of the Promotion Marketing Association of America since 1981.*

CHAPTER 5

CONTINUITY PROMOTIONS

The excitement and challenge of sales promotion revolves around the fact that motivation is always changing in application — but the central concept seldom changes. This is a people business. The application of motivation planning to tangible products or services is universal whether you represent a small company or a giant corporation.

Sales motivation program results are measured by the company's maintaining or increasing its share of the potential market, as well as improving the overall sales effort within its marketing organization. The selling organization might consist of highly controlled, company-directed, salaried people. In addition, it might include uncontrolled, independent distributors, jobbers, and retailers and their sales employees. In all cases, there is a common element — the end consumer, the person who is the final purchaser, the ultimate user of the product or service. And it is that individual who is the target.

No matter how good the product or service, it must be consumed to keep the system moving. If it remains on the shelf, if the plane seat is empty, or if the hotel room is vacant, the loss of revenue causes a backup in the system. Fewer pilots are needed; fewer and smaller planes are built; there are no new construction of hotels, no refurbishing of existing properties, and no new stores; fewer employees are needed to manage, sell, or service; and the economy becomes sluggish.

Frequency or continuity programs are one of several basic sales promotion techniques that form an integral part of the marketing arsenal available to use in today's marketing mix. These are promotions whereby customers are rewarded in some manner for repeated or frequent purchase or use of a product or service. The parameters of the promotion may vary, but the intent is the same — to encourage purchase loyalty, continuity, and frequency. Today, all indications appear to point to frequent "buyer" programs as one of the most important promotion forms available to consumer marketing.

All three programs — continuity, frequency, and stamps — are considered in this discussion, but for the purposes of simplification, they will all be called frequency programs. The term *frequency marketing* is an arbitrary name for a new but now familiar promotional strategy. It has become a more familiar term through its use in the travel industry in the form of frequent flier, frequent guest, and frequent renter programs.

To continue from a solid conceptual foundation, a definition is needed:

To identify, maintain, and increase yield from the best customers through a long-term, interactive, value-added relationship that encourages our target audience to continually utilize or purchase the services and products we offer.

Millions of business travelers have been conditioned over the past decade to trade brand loyalty for miles and points, for trips, prizes, and special treatment. It has worked so well that major packaged goods manufacturers are energetically launching national frequent shopper programs in the grocery business.

The benefits of frequency programs include the ability to break through the clutter of a crowded marketplace and bring customers in to shop at a store, fly on a particular airline, stay at a given hotel, rent cars, or purchase a branded product or service. Once a customer has purchased a product or service, the programs can also be an effective method of ensuring that the customer stays loyal and that he or she comes back week after week. Perhaps most important, frequency programs can be a powerful defensive strategy to counteract competitive activities — a key benefit in an age of product parity, intensified competition, and eroding brand equities. Frequency programs can go a long way toward building a wall around customers to keep the competition out and customers in.

Exhibit 5.1 is a simplification of how adults learn. In the case of frequency programs, one can easily see that the key target audience falls into an area between 70 percent and 90 percent. By having one's customer make frequent purchases of the product or service, a pattern of buying is created that causes trial, continuity, and reward. It is much the same principle of having a child learn by repetition. Once adults get into a buying pattern, they are often likely to continue that pattern.

Frequency programs all ask the customer to "purchase today, get a reward later." Exhibit 5.2 shows the entire universe of potential prospects.

As one moves up the triangle, notice that prospects may also be former customers who switched brands for a number of reasons. Frequency programs or any other promotion may have the effect of returning them to the promoted brand. While the prospects are not first-time customers, they may have forgotten the brand, the product differentiation, or its positioning in the marketplace. They often are very fickle customers because they switch from brand to brand, depending on the promotion. Therefore, the instant gratification portion of any promotion will have great appeal to this segment of the target audience.

Frequency programs require repeat purchases. Repeat purchases require establishing a buying pattern as shown in Exhibit 5.1 and makes them repeat customers as shown in Exhibit 5.2. This repetition of buying habits is one of the main benefits of any frequency program.

EXHIBIT 5.1

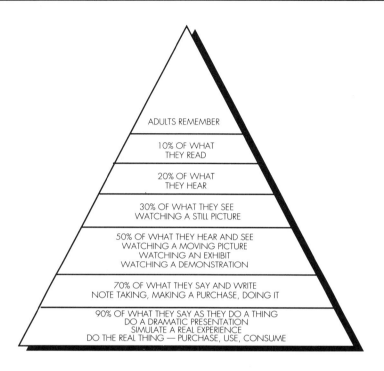

ADULTS REMEMBER

10% OF WHAT
THEY READ

20% OF WHAT
THEY HEAR

30% OF WHAT THEY SEE
WATCHING A STILL PICTURE

50% OF WHAT THEY HEAR AND SEE
WATCHING A MOVING PICTURE
WATCHING AN EXHIBIT
WATCHING A DEMONSTRATION

70% OF WHAT THEY SAY AND WRITE
NOTE TAKING, MAKING A PURCHASE, DOING IT

90% OF WHAT THEY SAY AS THEY DO A THING
DO A DRAMATIC PRESENTATION
SIMULATE A REAL EXPERIENCE
DO THE REAL THING — PURCHASE, USE, CONSUME

EXHIBIT 5.2

BEST CUSTOMERS

REPEAT CUSTOMERS

FIRST-TIME CUSTOMERS

FORMER CUSTOMERS

PROSPECTS

In all cases there are economic issues, implementation problems, and overall effects on the long-term relationship with the consumer and trade (if applicable). Frequency programs can become a curse:

- Who bears the sponsor's cost?
- How does one break through the clutter?
- How does one bring customers to enter the store, stay at a hotel, fly on a given airline, or rent a particular car?
- What is the most effective method of keeping customer loyalty?
- How are customers brought back, week after week?
- How does one counteract competitive activities?

So who bears the sponsor's cost of using this promotional technique? As is well known, marketers operate in a very competitive environment. Properly used, frequency programs increase sales and require loyalty for the duration of the promotion. If the promotion increases sales volume sufficiently, the consumer benefits from the additional rewards and the sponsor offsets the cost of the promotion with greater productivity and greater utilization of resources. If the program is not effective, the cost of the program must be absorbed and used as a historical basis for future promotional evaluations. There has been no research that substantiates some claims that frequency programs raise prices. However, any promotion becomes a cost of doing business that must be covered in the gross margin of the product or service being sold.

TYPES OF FREQUENCY PROGRAMS

The particulars of a frequency program and how it can be structured vary. A brief discussion of continuity, frequency, and stamp programs, and what distinguishes one from the other, follows.

Continuity Programs. A continuity program is a self-liquidating or profit-making plan, most often used by supermarkets, in which a set of related items is offered. For instance, the consumer could get a different item each week for a given time in return for purchase or use. Supermarkets may offer dishes, flatware, cutlery, glasses, or encyclopedias. Today, these types of programs are used by quick-service restaurant establishments as well, where a continuing line of toys is offered each week to be collected. The programs encourage regular repeat visits. Most often the store purchases a completely packaged program, tailored to the specific needs of the sponsor, with a guarantee that the supplier will take back all unsold merchandise. Generally they are not directed to a specific product, but a specific dollar purchase for each visit.

Frequency Programs. A frequency program is a tracking program of purchases by a given consumer of a particular product, with a reward, usually free goods or services of the same nature as what was tracked or purchased. These programs are customized by the sponsor. Frequency programs are most often used by airlines, hotels, and name-brand products, such as canned goods.

The airlines pioneered this concept when industry leaders fought back against regional carriers that were taking away their customers. Frequent flier programs gave customers added value for choosing a specific airline when making reservations. As the airlines attracted new customers and generated passenger loyalty, they enhanced their programs with newsletters that offered additional values and monthly point statements that maintained interest.

The hospitality industry rewarded loyal customers with special amenities and low- or no-cost upgrades in services. Quick service restaurants spawned a flood of games, premiums, and incentives. Alert marketers in every field learned that if there is a way to monitor customers' purchases, it is possible to analyze and act on that information.

The very nature of this huge database tracking system has led to many companies selling their services and/or data to other firms. Examples can be found with airlines such as United's Mileage Plus and American's AAdvantage; hotels such as Hyatt's Gold Passport, Marriott's Honored Guest, and Fairmont's President's Club; and charge cards including Diners Club Premier Rewards and Citibank Dollars. And now a packaged goods program that tracks, through proof-of-purchase, more than 100 brands. The participant clips and saves the proofs-of-purchase and mails them to the processing center. Using preprinted personalized bar code stickers, the travel credits build a bank of air miles to be used for future travel.

Trading Stamp Program. Stamp programs were created long before the term *frequency program* was developed or implemented. In this instance, stamps are collected in conjunction with use or purchase and redeemed for merchandise. Stamp programs were most often used by gas stations and supermarkets because they built strong loyalty for an individual store, bringing the customer back repeatedly. Trading stamp popularity spread usage from store to store until the stamps lost their power to set apart any individual store. Now, due to the popularity of frequency programs in general, trading stamps are enjoying renewed interest as a continuity vehicle.

Trading stamps afford guilt-free shopping for discretionary items. The awards-merchandise for the family, for gifts, or for the home or garden has lasting value. Families enjoy pasting the stamps into books, spending the books, and planning for their free purchases.

Sweepstakes Continuity. This kind of continuity program works by collecting the parts to build a slogan, picture, or other device. Much like a jigsaw puzzle, each game ticket is obtained by making a visit or purchase or writing to the sponsor. Several game tickets are needed to complete the picture that will allow either a winner or an entry into a random-draw sweepstakes. (See Chapter 4 for a detailed explanation.) The premise is the same — buy now and get the reward later. However, in these programs there are often instant winners. These are prizes that keep up the interest of the participants. Upon opening the game ticket, a winning prize is revealed that may be instantly obtained from the sponsor.

For example, an instant prize, as well as the collectible feature, was used by Apple Computer. The top portion can be rubbed off to reveal an instant prize. If the participants wanted to obtain that prize, they could not rub off the bottom section. If they did rub off the bottom section, they forfeited the instant prize. Once the bottom section was revealed, they collected the "points" revealed on each card. If more than one section of the bottom was revealed, the card was void.

The Purpose of Frequency Programs. The differences in the reward structure define the type of frequency program, and it does not matter whether trade channels or consumers are the target. Yet frequency programs all have the same purpose and have one ultimate goal: to get the targeted purchaser to build brand loyalty. This loyalty pattern may mean continued spending, a repeat of using the service, staying at the same hotel chain, flying the same airline, charging on the same credit card, or using the same detergent or cereal. In exchange for that loyalty, the sponsor of the program will provide some form of reward to the purchasers.

ADVANTAGES OF FREQUENCY PROGRAMS

The advantages of using a frequency-type promotion are many. Frequency programs can achieve some or all of the following:
- Increase frequency of purchases of goods or services
- Increase frequency of store visits, where applicable
- Create a purchase habit that continues after the promotion period is over
- Provide a database of participant buying behavior
- Are easy to measure and track effectiveness

One of the side benefits of creating a promotion to induce short-term continuity of purchase is that these programs can also create a purchase habit that continues after the promotion has ended. (See Exhibits 5.1 and 5.2.) Frequency marketing is extremely effective in focusing the loyal customer's attention on the brand over the long term.

A very important advantage of most frequency programs is the extraordinary database that can be obtained. Properly maintained, it contains the buying or usage habits of consumers over time. Information gained from the program can actually become an additional source of revenue through the sale of mailing lists, information, purchasing habits, interests, and other data to providers of noncompetitive services. In many cases they also provide data that can be used to target new products and offer a reason for both former customers, as well as new prospects, to purchase.

As an example, United Airlines rented its list of frequent fliers who had made more than one trip per month to Los Angeles. The local Hyatt in Los Angeles sent a mailing to those fliers in the hope that they could encourage them to stay at a Hyatt instead of some other chain. Hyatt paid United for the list, United customers earned frequent flier points if they stayed at the Hyatt, and United frequent customers were given upgrade certificates for suites if they presented their "Mileage Plus" cards upon check-in. Then Hyatt gave United information about the frequency that each member stayed at Hyatt, and the duration of each stay. United could then check to see if that customer flew into and out of Los Angeles on a United flight. This kind of data exchange can be invaluable to program sponsors in furthering their business among customers and prospects.

One of the most important blessings is that it's relatively easy to measure a frequency program's effectiveness. Consumers' involvement in the program is obvious — if they are collecting their reward, they are participating.

DISADVANTAGES OF FREQUENCY PROGRAMS
The disadvantages of frequency programs are as follows:
- May have a limited appeal
- May have difficulty in getting trade support due to the long-term nature of programs
- Opportunities exist for misredemption, barter, or reselling
- May create an IOU for the sponsor that can have detrimental effects on total dollar allocations (reserves) needed to address the building of obligation to participants
- May be difficult to alter
- May be difficult to terminate
- May be more costly to administer than estimated
- May be easy for competitors to duplicate and improve
- Possible rewards may be given to customers who did not alter their purchase habits, but were rewarded anyway
- Customers may anticipate program and collect proofs-of-purchase before announcement, to hold for later redemption. This is especially effective in label savings' programs such as school computers, for which high levels of collectibility are required.

A frequency program can suffer from limited appeal if the consumer doesn't perceive that the added value of the reward is high enough. It can also be difficult to obtain trade support because, by their nature, frequency programs are long term and there can be a substantial difference between a sponsor's interest and the retailer's. It could be a major mistake to assume that retailers or distributors will participate in the program unless their needs were considered in its development.

Frequency programs can also, unfortunately, have a high potential for abuse. The opportunities for misredemption, bartering, and reselling can be significant. Airline frequent flier programs have found this to be an especially difficult problem to overcome.

The contingent liability of a frequency program is another potential problem. In essence, the program creates an IOU for the sponsor that can have a detrimental effect on the total dollar allocation needed to address the building obligation to participants. In addition, for this reason, frequency programs may be difficult to terminate. It's critical that the sponsor plan an exit strategy to minimize any negative impact on program participants. Just as the program may be difficult to terminate, it may also be difficult to alter. Changing the rules of the game midway through a promotion is likely to create customer relations headaches, not to mention possible legal problems.

When American and United tried to change the points needed for travel redemption, there were groups that threatened to file legal claims against the carriers. To make a smoother transition, both carriers agreed to carry on the old mileage points for several years and for the same travel point redemption requirements. New mileage points could not be used to purchase the old awards, but the old awards could be used to purchase the new travel prizes.

Careful administrative planning is essential to the successful frequency marketing program. Costs can get out of hand if the program grows more quickly than anticipated and there's a poorly designed system in place to handle it.

A FREQUENCY MARKETING EXAMPLE

Most recently a company called Air Miles became a frequency partner with many companies who could not deliver these programs on their own. Products such as charcoal, potato chips, condiments, and other less expensive products all joined with Air Miles to create a collectible program that rewards participants with air miles on certain carriers.

At the same time, American Express created a similar program so that each dollar charged on its credit card would allow the points to be converted to several of the existing airline frequency programs. To experienced participants, this meant that they could earn points for charging on their credit card, earn points for flying on that same airline, and earn additional points by staying at certain hotels, and charging on their credit card. Table 5.1 shows an example of a business trip and the points that could be earned.

Currently a round-trip, coach-class United Airlines ticket is 20,000 points. In Table 5.1, it can be seen that a short trip with normal activities obtained about one-third of the points needed for a coach round-trip ticket and two of the 10 nights for a free weekend stay, and it probably was written off as a business expense. In addition, the cost of the ticket was coach, but the participant flew first class, stayed at the hotel for the corporate rate but obtained an upgrade to a suite, and drove

TABLE 5.1
FLIGHT FROM CHICAGO TO LOS ANGELES

Charge the United flight tickets on Diners Club, earn 2 points for each dollar spent ($1,000.00).	2,000 pts.
Mileage Plus gives me 1,850 miles. If an Executive member, it is doubled and upgraded to first class using flight coupons.	3,700 pts.
Rent a Hertz Rental Car, charge on Diners $50-double points.	500 pts.
Upgraded to luxury sedan using coupons from United.	100 pts.
Stay at the Hyatt LAX one night ($170), Gold Passport Bonus point plan — double points	2 nights
If Diamond member, upgraded to suite. Charge the room on Diners — double points.	240 pts.
Took a client to lunch $100, charged to Diners.	200 pts.
Took client to dinner, charged to Diners. Took client to theater. Had brief meeting, cocktails after theater. Total for above = $350.	700 pts.
Purchased a gift for my children and wife.	150 pts.
TOTAL POINTS EARNED	7,590 pts.

a luxury car for the price of the economy size. Instant rewards were given, as well as long-term point accumulation for future vacation travel.

PLANNING A FREQUENCY PROGRAM

To be effective, frequency programs should address the following marketing issues. Answers to these questions can be used as a template for creating a frequency program.

1. What is the measurable goal of the frequency program? In almost all cases, increasing the frequency by which the participant continues to purchase the product or service is the main goal. Frequency programs want to establish loyalty in the purchase cycle of a product or service.

In order to measure and reward continued purchase and use, behavior must be individually tracked. Since the collection of proof-of-purchase seals or points for each purchase or each stay is the method of earning the reward, the targeted participants want the points to be tracked and participate willingly in the process. They present their account number, collect the proof-of-purchase seals, and fulfill other requirements. In all cases the accumulation of these data is needed to determine the type of reward that participants can earn.

In a 1991 Promotion Marketing Association of America (PMAA) survey of its members, respondents were asked what criteria they used to measure success for their continuity programs. Sales increases, use of displays, redemptions, and market share gains were all cited. The survey showed that:

- 86 percent indicated that an increase in sales was the measure.
- 59 percent indicated an increase in displays.
- 55 percent used redemptions as their criteria.
- 41 percent increased their market share.

2. When is it appropriate to use a frequency program? When the objective is to increase sales, frequency marketing is an obvious choice. In fact, this is the number one reason for any frequency program.

Brand loyalty, however, is important for maintaining sales. Today many products exist that have the same characteristics, price, and awareness. To keep customers from trying other brands, frequency programs offer a reason for the customers to remain loyal. Frequency marketing is very often used, therefore, to maintain sales.

Logistically, it is difficult to turn on and turn off a frequency program; these programs require long-term commitments. For this reason, it is more difficult to use this type of promotion with seasonal items. Likewise, short-term frequency programs do not work with any product that is not consumed or repurchased within a week's time. Most often quick service restaurant operators use short-term frequency programs, and even then they run for several months at a time.

As Table 5.2 shows, there are certain conditions that favor frequency marketing and those that are less favorable. If there is little differentiation between the sponsor's product or service and the competition's, frequency marketing can be beneficial. On the other hand, if the sponsor's product has the best prices in the market, frequency marketing may be a costly strategy with little potential for market share gains.

When the sponsor can absorb extra sales with little extra operating costs, frequency programs can also be useful. If the sponsor is already operating at near capacity, however, the incremental sales generated may not translate into added profits. Sponsors should have the room to make substantial market share gains among the target purchasers before setting up the program. Furthermore, if the sponsor has little competition and already dominates the market, frequency programs aren't likely to increase business.

It's also critical that the prospective customer perceives significant rewards for loyalty to the brand, so that switching to the brand will be worth breaking old purchase habits.

Finally, the customer needs to be able to switch brand loyalty at will and without hindrance. If it's inconvenient for the customer to switch, the frequency program is not likely to help.

TABLE 5.2
FREQUENCY MARKETING

Favorable Conditions	Unfavorable Conditions
Little product differentiation	Distinctive product
Little price differentiation	Best prices in market
Sponsor can absorb extra sales with little extra cost	Operating near capacity
Sponsor can experience substantial gains among target	Little competition dominates market
Prospective customer recognizes significant rewards for loyalty	No incentive to switch; rewards are not incentive
Customer can switch loyalty at will without hindrance	Pricing, proximity, etc.; switching prohibited

3. Determining the proper audience. Some consideration must be given to the audience of the promotional program early on in the planning stages. Who is the purchaser? Can the purchaser buy more as a result of the frequency program? Will purchasers continue to repurchase as a result of the program? Will they willingly do what is necessary to participate by collecting pieces or tracking usage? A program must be structured with the intended audience in mind.

4. Financing and budgeting for a frequency program. Budgeting for a frequency program is similar to budgeting for any promotional program. The key questions are what monies should be allocated to the program and where should these monies come from? A fixed percentage method is often used whereby a certain amount of money from previous product sales or value of services rendered is set aside for developing a frequency marketing program. Decisions such as which department(s) should fund the program are important in the initial planning stages. In many cases, variable allocation is used across several sponsoring brands or services, depending on the profitability of the particular product or service purchased by participant. How this is done depends on the situation, for example:
- Tape plan for grocery stores
- Mileage for airlines
- Per night allocation for hotels
- Percentage of merchandise cost for credit card companies or merchandise retailers

5. How should the frequency program be structured? There are several basic decisions that need to be made that determine the scope and structure of a frequency program. For instance, if the program encourages purchase of, say, a packaged goods product, what purchases qualify for accumulation in the promotion? The product(s) to be honored need to be specified — what brands, what sizes, and the like. Whether a certain number of purchases will constitute "winning," or whether a dollar volume instead will be the determinator, needs to be decided.

Once this basic parameter is set, a key question to ask is what will be used as the "proof-of-purchase"? Often, packaged goods products have the convenience and opportunity to use package labels or the UPC codes from the label, box, or bag as the proof-of-purchase. Where labels are not easily removed or collectible, or where other specifications — such as time of purchase or dollar amount — require more than a label can provide, grocery store receipts are an acceptable alternative. These can be saved and presented as purchase proof, especially when an identifier is printed on the receipt as with grocery store scanners. Sometimes both the receipt and a label are necessary to claim that a purchase was made, and this should be clearly stated for the consumer.

Where the product is a service, some "unit" of use needs to be determined for the frequency program. With airline travel, specifics regarding what constitutes a ticket must be decided in advance. Either the distance flown or the dollar value of a ticket could be used in accumulating toward a reward, but most airlines today use the miles. For hotels, there is sometimes a minimum room rate in place or a minimum number of nights required for qualification in a frequency program. If dollars spent at a hotel (as an indication of length of stay) are to be used as the unit, some rules need to be set regarding whether other room charges will count toward the reward. Everything must be anticipated and written into the program in order for it to run smoothly and successfully.

A last structural detail for frequency programs is the amount of time to be allocated for the program. This is especially important when determining the program liability. Some programs are meant to increase or at least sustain purchase or use within a certain time frame, such as a month or a season or a period in association with a holiday or an event, and as such have clear start and stop dates to delineate the time parameter. Any purchases or accumulation before or after those particular dates are then no longer redeemable or no longer qualify for a reward.

Other programs are more long term, perhaps ongoing over an indefinite period. In this case, to limit liability, purchases, usage, or points accumulated expire after a certain length of time. In other words, there is a moving window of eligibility. In this respect, miles flown on an airline, for instance, cannot be counted toward free trips after a certain number of years. The old miles drop off and the new miles continue to accumulate. This encourages consumers to redeem their miles in a regular and timely manner.

6. How should rewards be defined? What is the best way to reward participants in the program — with merchandise, travel, or cash? In each case, of course, the exact nature of the merchandise or travel, and the cash amounts, need to be determined. Sometimes participants can be allowed to self-select their own award from a variety of alternatives.

There is always the alternative of giving away more of the product or service that was sold in the first place. One needs to ask whether doing so will have a positive or negative effect on business. If future business is negatively affected by awarding more product, this may not be desirable. However, where the product or service is perishable, this may be a good way to go. An airline sells seats on an airplane; a hotel sells rooms; a cruise ship sells cabins. In all cases, if those seats/rooms/cabins are empty on a given flight/day/cruise, the profits from them are lost. In this case, it makes economic sense for the marketer to fill those vacancies with program winners at no extra cost. In many cases, the seats awarded are in addition to normal traveling requirements and do not diminish future sales.

7. Should a multilevel awards program be created? It is possible to create a multilevel program where what the participants are awarded or are eligible to win is scaled to fit the level of use or purchase. Participants may be inclined to purchase more or use a service more often over a competitor's if the increased benefits of attaining and maintaining higher levels of participation within the program are valuable to them. Programs such as Hyatt's Gold Passport Program — with its Gold Passport, Platinum Passport, and Diamond Passport tiers — have successfully applied this concept to reward different levels of usage and loyalty to visitors staying at the hotel chain. While many applications of multitiered programs have developed within the services categories, a multilevel structure can also be used by packaged goods companies to create special incentives and increase frequency.

Of course, if multilevel awards are developed within the general structure of a frequency program, the criteria for maintenance at a particular level need to be decided. Once participants have achieved a certain level within a program, can they be bumped down a tier if they do not continue to maintain high levels of participation? Criteria regarding how strictly to adhere to the rules established in this regard should also be developed. This can be a sticky problem in a service-oriented category in which frequency programs are attempting to generate participant loyalty and goodwill, as well as their increased usage.

8. The frequency program database. As mentioned earlier, one of the side benefits of using a frequency marketing program is the ability to build a list of current users that can be leveraged for future promotions and/or tracked in terms of future sales. If capturing a database of participants is a goal, however, what information should be gathered and maintained for the frequency program database? While a listing of names and addresses can be convenient for targeted mailings of promotions in the future, much more has probably been learned about these customers, which should also be kept. Not only the level of usage, but also the specifics of what, when, and how might be important information to retain.

9. Forecasting response. In any promotion, some thought must be given to what the demands of the promotion will be so that a sponsor can be ready to fulfill those demands. Anticipating response and participation levels is an important step in determining how much product to have on hand during the promotion period, or how to handle the increased traffic and loads in a service-oriented industry. Where suppliers are involved, contracts may need special provisions to accommodate promotion demands. In some cases, most likely in service areas, safety provisions need to be considered.

If rewards are to be given, forecasting these demands is also critical. Poor word-of-mouth can result when rewards remain unfulfilled as promised. Lead times and delivery issues are a constraint to be reckoned with. If a company is purchasing merchandise instead of rewarding participants with its own products, the goal is to properly plan for maximum sales with minimum leftover merchandise.

Estimating program participation and resulting needs is obviously integral to creating a budget and pro forma statement for the program.

10. Integration of frequency programs with advertising and public relations. How can a frequency program be integrated into an advertising or public relations program? Frequency programs often become an advertising tool that overshadows normal advertising messages. The goal is to integrate and best use the natural strengths of both to attain the objectives set for the brand or sponsor.

Many frequency programs have come under attack because the realization of the reward is not anticipated, creating public relations problems. For instance, upgrades for car rentals, hotel rooms (to suites), or airline tickets (to first class) may not be readily available for redemption by participants. Another problem situation that results when a loyal consumer becomes a winner, based on consumption or usage, is that service seems to be less effective than when the participant was in the purchase cycle.

What can be done to correct this condition? Most companies should remember that they encouraged purchase of their product or services. Once winners want to redeem, they are still purchasers and should not be treated in less than a "first-class" manner. Many participants have been treated so badly once they redeemed their prize, they switched to other suppliers in the hopes that they would be treated better. This obviously negates the progress toward the objective set in the first place — to encourage loyalty and continued purchasing.

DIFFICULTIES IN IMPLEMENTING FREQUENCY PROGRAMS

One of the key reasons for using frequency programs is to attract incremental sales. However, it is not always easy to fine-tune the promotion strategy so that it has the desired effect of building business. Sometimes, customers who don't alter their purchase habits are also rewarded. Additionally, most industries have seasonal shifts in usage that can have an impact on program response patterns. The trick is in finding a way to reduce nonrevenue participation during peak selling seasons and drive redemption to off seasons — not an easy task.

The other problem that has not been discussed is the customer who anticipates the program and collects proofs-of-purchase to be redeemed before the program has been announced. Salem brand cigarettes once offered free Hyatt weekend stays for proofs-of-purchase from their cigarettes. Hundreds of redemptions took place within days of the initial announcement of the event. This kind of redemption would have required a consumer participating in the program to have "smoked" hundreds of packs of cigarettes — not possible within the time frame for the promotion. This example is only one of many problems encountered by both packaged goods companies, as well as those with proofs-of-purchase that are easy to remove or collect. This can be a particular problem where high levels of collectibility are required such as the Apples for Students program or the Campbell Soup program in which labels were used as points for purchase of computers or athletic equipment for schools.

A last thing to consider when implementing a frequency promotion is whether consumers view frequency programs as adding "additional cost" or creating additional benefits. What is the consumer's attitude toward these programs? Anticipating trade response, too, is advisable. In most cases, the trade likes frequency programs because they encourage more purchasing.

In general, the primary roadblock to implementing a successful frequency program is managing the program over its duration and understanding the investment required to support and sustain the program. The right mix of support must be available to field a successful program.

CONCLUSIONS

In the 1991 PMAA survey mentioned earlier, association members were asked about their experiences with continuity programs. The survey found that, of those responding:

- 51 percent indicated that they conducted a continuity program in the last year
- Nearly four programs (an average of 3.8) were run by those members surveyed
- The average duration of the continuity program was 16 weeks
- The average cost of these programs was $147,800 — although

the range was from $28,000 to $31 million
- 100 percent stated that the program was successful

The fact that no one claimed his or her program to be a failure is noteworthy. Either frequency programs are creating much success, or marketers were in the process of justifying their budgets for next year when the survey was taken! In many instances, respondents reported overlaying other types of promotional techniques with the frequency programs. For instance, 58 percent used rebates and 58 percent used coupons with purchase.

Given all the positives, it appears that frequency programs are here to stay. They offer increases in sales, displays, and brand loyalty. Frequency programs are a way of gaining the attention of the purchaser when basic services or goods are quite similar in the eyes of customers and whenever there is excess capacity. In industries such as airlines, hotels, or canned goods, the product may have a unique life cycle or buying pattern. The differentiating power of frequency programs is that the reward can be unique to the purchaser. Free hotel rooms, airline tickets, and upgrades have a perceived value that is significantly higher than the actual cost to the supplier. Further, with these rewards, the customer is once again retained in the exclusive franchise and prohibited from discovering the competition.

To the sponsor, frequency programs give more information about their customers' habits than ever before available. Airlines know when and where customers fly, they know how far in advance tickets are purchased, in what seats they reserve, and what special meals are ordered. This marketing information alone could make the frequency program cost-effective.

Clearly, under many conditions, frequency programs will be a blessing. Whenever a product or service is similar, the value of the frequency program is evident. Frequent customer buying increases turnover in inventory, assists in research information, and allows the sponsor to target promotions more effectively.

Douglas B. Leeds joined Thomson-Leeds, a leading New York point-of-purchase advertising agency, as account executive in 1977 and became its president in 1988. His agency has won more awards for creativity and innovation than any other company in the industry, creating displays for a broad range of clients, including AT&T, Bausch & Lomb, CBS Records, Ford, Kellogg's, Lever Brothers, Nike, Philip Morris, and Sony.

A frequent speaker at industry conferences in the U.S. and abroad, Leeds is currently on the Board of Directors of the Point-of-Purchase Advertising Institute (POPAI) and was formerly chairman of POPAI's Educational Relations Committee and POPAI's Annual Industry Conference and Marketplace Show. Leeds is a trustee of the Whitney Museum of American Art, a director of The American Theatre Wing, The Checkerboard (film) Foundation, and Ronald McDonald House Associates. During the last six years, he has produced two Broadway shows.

Leeds is a graduate and past trustee of Babson College in Wellesley, Massachusetts.

Chapter 6

POINT-OF-PURCHASE

If dollars spent is the measure, marketing's battleground clearly has moved from the TV set to the retail store. A research study by Veronis, Suhler & Associates, published in *P-O-P Times*, an industry trade publication, reported that spending on promotional advertising media outweighed that of measured media (television, radio, magazines, newspapers) by $108 billion to $80 billion in 1990, the end of a five-year reporting period. Promotional spending was further projected to lead measured spending by up to $46 billion a year over the next five years, reaching $153 billion to measured media's $108 billion by 1995.

The Veronis, Suhler study measured expenditures on point-of-purchase (P-O-P) advertising, meanwhile, at nearly $20 billion in 1990, making P-O-P the fastest growing segment of all promotional advertising categories. Allocations to point-of-purchase advertising and displays, the study predicted, will reach $30.2 billion by 1995 and account for 19.8 percent of all promotional outlays. In short, promotional media budgets continue to outpace those of measured media advertising, and P-O-P leads the promotional advertising pack in spending growth.

What is Point-of-Purchasing Advertising?

How does one define point-of-purchase advertising? As the name itself suggests, point-of-purchase is advertising where the sales transactions occur. Point-of-purchase advertising dominates the moment at which all the elements of a sale converge — namely, the buyer, the seller, the money, and the product. Point-of-purchase advertising assumes countless forms and employs myriad materials, but it always is directed toward one very important objective: to communicate sales and marketing messages at the moment purchasing decisions are being made.

Why Is P-O-P Growing in Importance?

Point-of-purchase advertising is and always has been a highly efficient and effective way to influence consumer behavior at the moment buying decisions are being made. P-O-P's long-held and well-documented ability to target, inform, persuade, enhance, and sell have lately positioned the medium as a more pivotal element of the marketing mix. Following are 10 reasons point-of-purchase advertising has grown to become so important:

1. **Retail support is declining**. The level of sales personnel at retail has declined steadily, creating a selling environment in which products must speak for themselves. The reasons for sales personnel reduction are many, ranging from cost-cutting

measures to changes in store formats. P-O-P has stepped in to fill this salesclerk void, providing product information and a measure of persuasion to help consumers make purchasing decisions.

2. **Consumers respond to self-service.** Long gone are the days in which shoppers were attended upon by aproned clerks behind counters. With the advent of the supermarket came a strong consumer preference for helping oneself. The importance of having point-of-purchase materials rose accordingly, particularly for product categories such as pharmaceuticals, food and beverage, do-it-yourself products, and electronics.

3. **Consumers make unplanned purchases.** Often quoted is the statistic that two-thirds of all purchasing decisions are made at the point-of-sale. Few are aware, however, that this phenomenon was first measured in a 1945 study by duPont deNemours & Company, which conducted the research because of its product packaging business. That 1945 study showed that 51.8 percent of all purchasing decisions were made in-store. By 1949, however, the percentage of in-store purchasing decisions had grown to 66.6 percent; and by 1954, duPont found that the figure had ballooned to 70.8 percent!

   Today, the Point-of-Purchase Advertising Institute reports in-store consumer purchasing decisions at the two-thirds figure, which is generally accepted and supported by scanner data. This now-famous statistic has helped confer enhanced status on point-of-purchase advertising, now regarded as a critical element in prompting both unplanned purchases and last-minute brand-switching.

4. **Retailers appreciate P-O-P's value.** Retailers view P-O-P as a way to increase sales and profits, affording manufacturers an opportunity to build mutually beneficial relationships with retailers through strategic P-O-P programs. Retailers welcome with open aisles in-store marketing concepts that will make their profit margins grow, concepts that manufacturers are eminently well qualified to deliver.

5. **The local marketing trend increases.** The shift in attention from a single national marketplace to multiple local markets today often takes yet another step down to specific neighborhoods and individual stores, where P-O-P can pinpoint specific consumer segments. Linked to databases detailing demographics, psychographics, brand preference, and purchasing patterns of shoppers in a particular store's trading area, P-O-P programming can easily be tailored to suit both local marketing conditions and class of trade.

6. **Excitement for mature product categories grows.** Most consumers regard shopping as a form of entertainment, and P-O-P can add fun to the experience. This presents special opportuni-

ties for mature product categories, since P-O-P can draw attention and excitement to products, such as frozen foods, that otherwise would be considered uninteresting and therefore largely ignored.

7. **Comparative CPMs are favorable.** Point-of-purchase advertising is not only a highly effective medium able to target purchase-ready consumers, but it is also relatively inexpensive. The cost-per-thousand of reaching a consumer by P-O-P usually does not exceed 50 cents and is often far less. By comparison, the cost-per-thousand to reach a consumer via a network television commercial ranges to as much as seven or eight dollars.

8. **P-O-P focuses money on consumers, not the trade.** Point-of-purchase advertising has emerged as a key means of bridging retailer and brand objectives. P-O-P serves the retailer's interest in earning healthy profits while meeting the manufacturer's objective of building brand equity. By providing retailers with profit-building displays, manufacturers have an opportunity to reallocate dead-end trade funds to brand-building consumer programs. Such funds otherwise would have gone directly to the trade's bottom line (in the form of off-invoice discounts, slotting fees, etc.), with little or no pass-through to the consumer.

9. **Performance is easy to measure.** Whether the marketing discipline is advertising, promotion, or point-of-purchase, accountability is a central concern. Advertisers need to know that the marketing activity has had a tangible effect on sales. P-O-P has grown in popularity in tandem with the installation of checkout scanners, which can provide up-to-the-minute reporting on the effectiveness of an in-store advertising program.

10. **Brand images are reflected and built.** Point-of-purchase advertising often shares the look of an image advertising campaign, sometimes even bringing to life product mascots such as Kellogg's Tony the Tiger. P-O-P is capable of reinforcing a brand's image while promoting the product's sales. With consumer loyalty to brands reportedly declining, the importance of conveying product personality in-store cannot be underestimated. As an advertising medium, point-of-purchase is uniquely qualified to remind shoppers why they prefer one brand over another, blunting growing perceptions among consumers that all products essentially are the same.

TYPES OF POINT-OF-PURCHASE

Attempts to categorize point-of-purchase advertising can be difficult, because standard P-O-P concepts frequently cross-pollinate to produce new ideas. P-O-P advertising can be as small as a window decal or as large as a self-contained boutique. It can be permanent or temporary and can be used indoors or out. It can hang on a ceiling, sit on a floor, or perch on a counter or cash register. P-O-P can be any and all of the above, combined and recombined to suit specific brand and retailer objectives. The array of display types and how they function truly is infinite.

Perhaps even more important, a virtually unlimited array of potential materials applicable to P-O-P affords the medium an extraordinary capacity to continuously reinvent itself. Because of this executional flexibility, one can easily make the case that no other advertising medium offers as much nonstop creativity as P-O-P.

No other advertising medium can use all materials known to humankind. Point-of-purchase advertising is not confined to a printed page or taped images and sounds, though it can incorporate both. P-O-P can use light, motion, sound, smell, or texture. It can be flat or dimensional. You can touch it. It often uses ostensibly mundane materials such as paper products, plastic, wood, and wire. But it can also employ unlikely elements such as water, rock, or sand, and even the latest in laser or interactive technologies. Such possibilities give P-O-P an unmatched opportunity to communicate brand benefits and sell products.

Timely knowledge of the infinite variety of materials is pivotal to effective development of P-O-P programs. The P-O-P executive who is resourceful and digs deeply into production materials and methods invariably creates more effective and distinctive point-of-purchase advertising.

To develop a manageable working understanding of P-O-P displays, it is useful to categorize them by (1) length of time they are to be used, (2) location in which they are to be used, and (3) their marketing function.

1. **Time.** A P-O-P program is considered permanent if its materials are durable and its intended period of use is six months or longer. Anything less is considered a temporary or semipermanent display. These guidelines were established by the Point-of-Purchase Advertising Institute, which administers an annual awards contest for both permanent and semipermanent displays. Obviously, the type of material used and method of manufacture greatly affects a program's potential for permanence. So development of a P-O-P program requires the planner to determine first the desired length of use.

   A study by Nielsen Marketing Research, reported in *P-O-P Times*, provided an affirmative answer to the question: Are semipermanent displays worth the extra expense? Nielsen conducted research on behalf of a packaged drink manufacturer that supported the argument that higher-quality displays generally are worth the extra associated costs. While both types of displays are of comparable effectiveness, the semipermanents have a bottom-line edge because more retailers accept them and they stay up longer.

2. **Location.** Every square inch of a retail environment represents an opportunity for P-O-P advertising. Just where the advertising ought to be positioned for maximum result is a central issue when planning P-O-P programs, because location tremendously influences performance. Designing P-O-P to fit a specific location can increase its effectiveness. Another Nielsen study, reported by *P-O-P Times*, showed that displays for a snack product located in the front, rear, and lobby of a store generated up to twice the volume of displays in other locations. The manufacturer also discovered that "substantial differences in responsiveness" to specific display locations differed brand by brand and region to region (see Exhibit 6.1).

    The ability of marketers to make informed recommendations to retailers concerning the strongest sales-building display locations for their brands is greatly enhanced by scanner data generated at the checkout counter. Applying such information is

EXHIBIT 6.1
POTENTIAL DISPLAY LOCATIONS

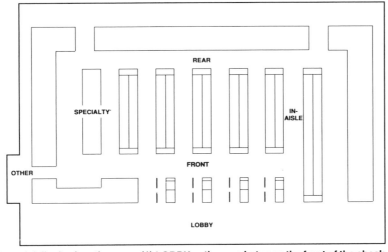

Potential display locations are: (1) **LOBBY** — the area between the front of the check-out counters and the front walls as you enter the store; (2) **FRONT** — the front of the store between check-out counters and the front end-caps; (3) **IN-AISLE** — any of the areas between the two ends of the primary shelving units, i.e., the main shopping aisles of the store; (4) **REAR** — the rear of the store, between the end-caps and the back wall; (5) **SPECIALTY** — any area in the main traffic flow devoted to a specific product, i.e., cheese, wine, flowers, etc., that appears to be a store-within-a-store; (6) **OTHER** — any place out of the main traffic flow that does not fall into one of the other five areas although there may be shelving units and additional displays.

crucial for marketers in today's retail environment, where the trade is increasingly tightfisted about how nationally advertised brands are presented at the point-of-purchase. Marketers must be prepared to prove that a retailer's category-wide profits will improve if their brand is given special exposure in a prime retail location. Some retailers, aware of the ability of displays to increase sales, now design their stores to maximize the potential of display space. Such was not the case 10 or 20 years ago.

3. **Function.** What P-O-P advertising can accomplish at retail falls into a variety of broad categories:

   - *Merchandisers* generally are designed to hold the product being advertised and are meant to create a specific "home" for the product apart from standard store shelving. Examples include permanent racks that hold candy, overhead racks for cigarettes typically found at the checkout counter, and pallet displays. Temporary units known as prepacks consist of the shipping cartons themselves, turned inside-out to become a display unit.

   - *Signage* reinforces a product, company name, or an advertised theme. It can also simply inform the consumer of various product benefits. For example, an outdoor sign might be used to tell a consumer that a certain brand or category of goods or services is available. Indoors, signs can help alert consumers to the availability of a product and influence the sale.

   - *Glorifiers* make the product stand out to the consumer in stark contrast to other products. Glorifiers almost always hold the product in some way, by placing it on a pedestal or otherwise surrounding it with an attention-getting device.

   - *Organizers* help the retailer control inventory or help the consumer make a selection more easily.

   - *Shelf space* has itself become something of a de facto point-of-purchase advertising medium. Faced with decreasingly available space for traditional displays (and only temporary access to such opportunities), many manufacturers are cleverly enhancing the advertising value of the shelf itself through more effective product packaging and merchandising concepts, such as "shelf-talkers" that extend from the shelf without interfering with consumer access to the products.

   - *New media* include shopping-cart "billboards," in-store sound systems, digital signage, interactive video kiosks, and even television sets at checkout lanes.

P-O-P INTEGRATION

"Integrated marketing programs" became a popular concept in the advertising community in the late 1980s and early 1990s. A number of advertising and promotion marketing companies responded by packaging together various promotion and retail marketing groups in hopes of offering advertisers a cohesive resource capable of creating a unified message.

In fact, the idea of making the various marketing disciplines work more effectively together is nothing new. *Advertising at the Point-of-Purchase*, an out-of-print volume edited and compiled by the Point-of-Purchase Advertising Institute (POPAI) and the Association of National Advertisers (McGraw-Hill Book Company, Inc. 1957), devoted an entire chapter to the concept of integrated marketing; within it appeared this prescient passage:

> Because point-of-purchase is present at the place and time goods are bought, it has the opportunity to supply the final nudge — the stimulus or impulse that creates the actual transaction. In doing this job, it ties all advertising together, probably more than any other single medium, by restating the selling theme at the point-of-sale. This tying together is known as "integration."

And later:

> [I]t is important to note that integration includes a good deal more than repeating the campaign theme in copy and pictures. It also takes into consideration timing, geographical considerations as to seasons and regional markets, distribution, publicity, trade advertising, and promotion literature. ... At a POPAI panel discussion, one member advocated that salesmen have some voice in planning since they are in the field and know what material is wanted.

Integrating P-O-P advertising with a brand's image advertising campaign and coordinating the program with both the advertiser's sales supports and the retailer makes fundamental good sense. A recent study by Information Resource, Inc. showed that when P-O-P reinforces an advertising message, sales increase for that product 128.2 percent over P-O-P that does not underscore the ad (see Exhibit 6.2).

Integration, however, should not be considered the end-all and be-all of marketing into the 21st century. Another study, this one by Nielsen Marketing Research conducted exclusively for *P-O-P Times*, showed that displays generated significant sales increases by themselves, without any accompanying promotional or advertising support. The research study analyzed scanner data across 26 product categories in 323 markets over a two-year period, and found that display-only promotions consistently improved sales in every instance. The average percentage increase in sales for stand-alone P-O-P advertisements ranged from 57 percent in Tampa and Miami to 108 percent in Milwaukee, and from 33 percent for salad dressing and beer to 177 percent for dishwasher liquid (see Exhibit 6.3).

EXHIBIT 6.2

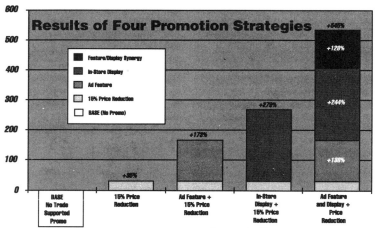

Source: InfoScan® Topical Marketing Report 1988 Data

Although the power of P-O-P is uniformly evident in this research, it is also clear that P-O-P effectiveness can vary by product category and region. This underlines the imperative for marketers today to fully understand the dynamics of P-O-P advertising relative to the specific, market-by-market conditions that affect the fortunes of brands. When developing a P-O-P program, one must also consider the manner of distribution. Will the program be installed by the advertiser's sales force, by independent reps, or by the retailer's own staff? Such considerations must be factored in when designing the program.

The decline of small, "mom and pop" retailers and the consolidation of retail chains throughout the country has given the retailer a strong voice in the in-store marketing environment. P-O-P advertisers must consider whether the retailer will accept a particular P-O-P program — even before thinking about whether a consumer will respond to it. Many retailers today have their own facility planners who dictate the type of display material they will allow in their stores. Displays may be required to conform to customized gondolas and may be restricted in terms of color, height, size, or location.

MANAGING THE P-O-P FUNCTION

The P-O-P industry is comprised of a diverse group of individuals and organizations that design, manufacture, or subcontract P-O-P advertising materials.

EXHIBIT 6.3

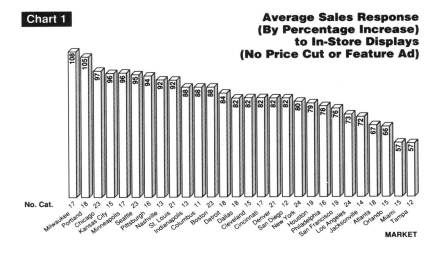

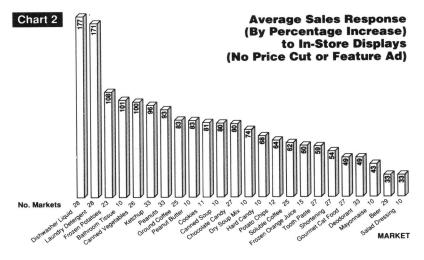

93

Advertisers typically see the industry as comprised of three types of suppliers:

1. Factories that specialize only in production of a specific type of display, such as wire or corrugated;
2. Agency/Factories that specialize in production of one or more of the display's components and subcontract the rest to produce finished displays; and
3. Agencies, that do not own a manufacturing plant but design and then subcontract production of the finished displays.

The category of supplier the advertiser uses obviously depends on the nature of the project at hand. Sometimes an advertiser knows in advance the type of material best suited to produce the planned display and will select a supplier based on its ability to deliver a display constructed of that material. Because of the rapid advance of new materials and technologies, however, advertisers increasingly are keeping options open because a new material or production process might significantly reduce costs or improve the durability of the display.

Advertisers generally review about three potential suppliers to help ensure that a healthy selection of available alternatives is fully explored. Because P-O-P suppliers fall under different categories, it is extremely important that the advertiser provides as much information as possible to ensure comparison of "apples to apples."

Planning is indeed the most important step in the development of a point-of-purchase advertising program. Initial planning will deliver the best possible return on the merchandising investment. Preparing information regarding the following points will help provide the information the advertiser should give its supplier. Again, the more information the advertiser provides, the better the job the supplier can deliver. This point cannot be stressed strongly enough.

- *Objective.* The very first step is to define the display's purpose — for example, introduce a new product, highlight new features, motivate impulse purchases, promote deals, announce special promotions, or link to other products.
- *Brand image.* Integration requires a design consistent with the product's image. The supplier should be given copies of any advertising that expresses the product's advertised image.
- *Other media.* Integration also requires consideration of other media to be used in connection with the display. If the display is to be activated during a television, print, or radio campaign, the supplier should be aware of the intention to integrate.
- *Type of display.*
  — Function. Determine whether the display is intended as a merchandiser, information-provider, product image-maker, or signage.
  — Packaging. Consider the number of packages to be displayed, the size, weight, and variety. Think about the total

weight of the merchandise and whether it is compatible with the type of display you envision. If new package designs are to be incorporated, they should be made available to the supplier at the outset.

— Structure. Establish the type of material you prefer and whether you wish to incorporate motion, light, or other special effects. Decide whether you require a display for the shelf, wall, floor, counter, ceiling, or gondola and if that display will be indoor or outdoor.

- *Competitive research.* As with any marketing program, it is critical that the competition is shadowed, that you identify competitive merchandising efforts, and that your display program factors in your marketplace position relative to that of other brands in the category. Advertisers frequently rely on their P-O-P suppliers to provide original research in this regard, including performance analysis of previously used displays in the category.
- *Quantity.* It is essential that desired production quantities are achievable given the intended delivery schedule.
- *Distribution.* Is this a regional or national program? Are there any warehouse limitations regarding size? Do you intend to ship the displays by truck or air? Is it to be a drop shipment or bulk?
- *Permanency.* The supplier must know whether the display is for short- or long-term use to select appropriate materials and display designs.
- *Placement.* Determine *where* your display is to be set up. This must be considered both in terms of class of trade (drug, food, mass market, service station, hardware) and in-store location (counter, floor, wall). Identify any dimensional limitations for each retail environment, as well as any trade practice limitations.
- *Sell-in.* Winning trade acceptance is mostly a matter of understanding retailer needs as precisely as possible. Retailer objectives vary from chain to chain and even store to store. The advertiser should make suppliers aware of any account-specific element of the display program, which may mean the display should be designed for flexibility in terms of size, style, construction, and function.

The supplier should know if the display is to be used as a sell-in incentive, with its availability linked to purchase quantities. If so, it should be designed for and constructed of especially high-quality materials. Suppliers should also be aware of any intention to develop sell-in materials — such as sales sheets, brochures, special presentations, or videos — and any role they may be assigned in the development of such materials.

Suppliers should also be made aware of the profile of your sales force to ensure it is equipped to implement the pro-

posed display program. The supplier should be told the size of
the force and be apprised of its executional capabilities. If brokers are to be used, the supplier should know this so that the
display is designed (1) to win brokers' undivided attention and
(2) to not burden brokers with complex assembly requirements.

Advertisers should also take care to ensure that the sales
force is adequately compensated with bonus incentives for display placement.

- *Presentation.* Specify the type of presentation you will need to
  select your supplier, and pinpoint a deadline. Establish whether
  you require sketches, models, prototypes, or units for testing
  prior to final production.
- *Budget.* Both advertiser and supplier should be up front about
  costs. A good supplier knows how to design and produce programs that meet an advertiser's budget. If advertisers cannot
  identify a budget, they do a disservice to both themselves and
  the supplier because they are likely to get wildly different solutions, some of which they may not be able to afford.

  With a specific budget, smart suppliers will make several
  options available to an advertiser. Often, suggestions are made
  that are lower, on target, and slightly higher, so that an advertiser has a full range of choices. The skill of a good supplier is to
  give the advertiser the absolute best program for the budget. By
  having a specific budget, it is also easier to judge the creativity
  of one supplier against another.

  It is important to understand that the value of a display to
  the advertiser does not consist exclusively of the cost of its
  components. It is the display's ability to attract consumers to
  the advertiser's product and to motivate a sale. Therefore, its
  value cannot be equated to the cost of materials only.

  Advertisers should also be aware that their suppliers incur
  costs from the moment a project starts in the creative phase.
  Expenses continue through all phases of design, production,
  and shipping of the finished displays. This process often covers
  many months, requiring considerable expenditures. For this reason, it is absolutely imperative that the advertiser select a supplier that is financially stable.
- *Production control.* Producing a complex job often requires
  multiple materials processed in multiple plant operations so that
  the finished display meets the advertiser's needs. This typically
  requires the skills of experienced project managers, whose job
  is to oversee all phases of the work in progress. Often this
  requires daily in-plant inspection to maintain promised delivery
  dates as well as quality.

  The project management function sometimes requires the
  involvement of several people with expertise in various fields,

such as printing, injection molding, or assembly.

Managing the P-O-P function for both agency and supplier is a complex process. The following points summarize the key elements that advertisers should look for and suppliers should provide when planning point-of-purchase advertising:

- *Experience.* a seasoned account team that knows the advertiser's dealers and its product;
- *Creativity.* a wide selection of creative ideas, incorporating the specialized expertise of point-of-purchase, and not stifled by any particular class of material or production process;
- *Cost-effectiveness.* display proposals developed to fit an established budge, and guaranteed for delivery at the promised per-unit price; and
- *Reliability.* a full-time staff of experts prepared to follow up on all phases of production and delivery of the display program.

CREATIVITY AND P-O-P

Creativity in point-of-purchase advertising is *not* a pretty picture. P-O-P creativity is not merely a question of clever design — the truth is, you can be equally effective with cardboard and magic marker as with microchips and cathode-ray tubes. Creativity in point-of-purchase advertising, first and foremost, is about building brands, sales, and *profits*. To reverse William Benton's famous quote, "If it isn't creative, it doesn't sell." Creativity in point-of-purchase advertising first requires a complete understanding of the exceedingly busy retail environment in which the product is being sold. Designers should go out and visit the store, as should product managers. The challenges for P-O-P advertising are immediately evident. Package facings and competitive displays vie for attention. Digital selling messages pulse overhead and laser beams trigger news of product specials as shoppers wheel their carts down the supermarket aisles. Commercials crackle over a public address system; television sets continue the pitch while consumers wait to check out.

"Cutting through the visual clutter" is an overused phrase in point-of-purchase, but it holds true; the job of a creative P-O-P is indeed to cut through that visual clutter and stand out.

The two key design principles of point-of-purchase advertising are especially challenging, but if followed, they help the creative process:

1. Keep the design simple, using symbols and not words wherever possible; and
2. Make the product the "star," not the display. David Ogilvy said it very well: "Make the product itself the hero of your advertising." Never lose sight of the fact that it is the *product* you are selling, not the display.

And, as in any creative endeavor, distance yourself from what you think you know to be true. One of the most common, creativity-stunting misconceptions is that point-of-purchase displays are a few steps short of a commodity. Nothing could be further from the truth. Creativity in point-of-purchase advertising first demands an understanding that effective P-O-P amid the cluttered retail environment requires *ownable* ideas. Generic, off-the-rack solutions are nearly always inadequate and are unnecessary given the wide choice of materials with which to work, as detailed in this chapter's section on "Types of P-O-P."

Following are four open-ended "rules" for opening the door to creativity in point-of-purchase advertising, including some examples of especially creative P-O-P programs.

1. **Be visual.** Anyone who walks into a supermarket and sees a floor display shaped like a giant Dixie Cup knows immediately what is being sold (see Exhibit 6.4). Putting freezer tape in a freezer makes the same statement, as does displaying champagne in an outsized champagne bottle replica.

   - Nikon wanted to show how sophisticated their least expensive camera was. The creative solution: laser cut the camera in half and enclose it in a case. The unit was placed on the counter where sales personnel could explain the product's benefits to customers. It was a very successful display — and one that did not feature a single word. Not even Nikon's name was on the box (see Exhibit 6.5).

   - Keds introduced a new line of children's washable sneakers with a tiny washer/dryer that churned and tumbled miniature images of the footwear (see Exhibit 6.6). This in-store advertisement sold product benefits with real soapsuds and water but without words.

2. **Involve the consumer.** As discussed, store help today is scarce to nonexistent. Every time you can involve the consumer, therefore, you are closer to closing a sale.

   - Teledyne actually helped customers understand what their new shower massage felt like, without taking a shower. The display featured a rubber membrane that the customer could touch. A pump created the sensation of the shower massage. It was an extremely effective merchandiser that won POPAI's "Display of the Year" (see Exhibit 6.7).

   - Revlon created an interactive display that was also a mechanical accomplishment because it used no electricity. The display used a combination of weights and levers to help customers learn their skin types so they could select the proper makeup (see Exhibit 6.8). An accompanying brochure brought the consumer closer to a sale.

3. **Provide information.** While big, bold images are great for capturing attention, the job of good P-O-P sometimes is simply to

EXHIBIT 6.4

EXHIBIT 6.5

merchandise information in a new and better way.
- Ford Motor Company wanted its service customers to hear about a new lifetime guarantee. Service center walls are typically packed with selling messages, so developing a poster or the like was not the best solution. Asking service managers to wear buttons reading "Ask me about the lifetime service guarantee" and embroidering the message on their uniforms were not practical options.

  But between the service adviser and the consumer was a clipboard on which the service manager wrote the customer's name and service requirements. The clipboard was redesigned so the customer could easily see the selling message (see Exhibit 6.9). In addition to accomplishing the merchandising objective, the clipboard proved to be better than the one previously used by dealers and has become a standard throughout the Ford Motor Company.
- Sony Corporation had 23 different television sets, and needed to place information about each model and its features at the point-of-sale. Because the sets are often sold in department stores and high-end retailers, however, signage was met with resistance. This situation spawned a merchandising device called Y.E.S., which stands for "Your Extra Salesperson."

  The Y.E.S. unit consists of a retractable panel printed

EXHIBIT 6.6

EXHIBIT 6.7

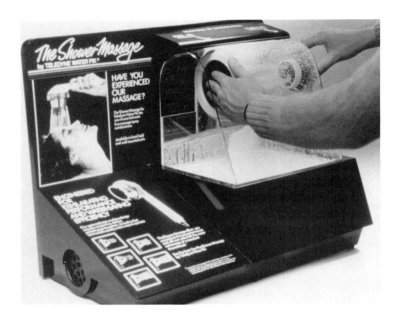

EXHIBIT 6.8

EXHIBIT 6.9

EXHIBIT 6.10

with product information that pulls out and scrolls back like a small window shade (see Exhibit 6.10). This breakthrough in-store advertising medium attached flat and discreetly — above, below, or beside the product — without disrupting store decor.

4. **Enhance the brand.** Building a brand's image does not necessarily mean translating its advertising campaign into an in-store setting. Displays that project moods, taste, prestige, glamour, and excitement are also ably communicated at the point-of-purchase.

  • Holly Farms, the chicken marketer, had a different problem: Raw chicken is probably the least attractive product in a supermarket. To overcome this, an illuminated billboard system featuring appetizing prepared chicken dishes was developed to fit over the poultry section in the meat department (see Exhibit 6.11). The graphics were changed monthly and free recipe cards were made available to the consumer.

  • Ray-Ban used a counter display that put the consumer in the mood for the glasses by using strong, lifestyle-reinforcing graphics (see Exhibit 6.12).

  • Sperry Top Sider combined various display components to create the ambiance of a yacht club. This boating environment set just the right tone for the brand's target audience (see Exhibit 6.13).

Creativity in point-of-purchase advertising takes many forms and can make a giant difference. A profit-driven creative approach can reduce the cost of producing or shipping P-O-P displays or programs. Creative construction can make it easier for a retailer to set up and, thereby, increase usage. Creative design can more effectively communicate to the consumer in the retail environment.

If it isn't creative, it doesn't sell. To bring out the best creative effort, both the buyer and creator of P-O-P must join together and get to know each other and each other's business. Then, within their respective organizations, others must be allowed to *dare* to approach point-of-purchase advertising in a fresh, new way. There is always a better way to do something, but we must be challenged to find it. And when that fresh, new approach is found, we must have the courage of our convictions to do what we believe will work.

Of course, all this is risky. You may strike out, but you will also hit some home runs rather than a few safe singles. So take risks. And above all, have fun. Without fun, creativity at point-of-purchase is only an academic exercise.

EXHIBIT 6.11

EXHIBIT 6.12

EXHIBIT 6.13

Larry Tucker has been prominent in the promotion and direct marketing fields for more than 20 years and is a recognized authority on target marketing, list analysis, promotion, and direct mail. For the past 16 years, his firm, Larry Tucker, Inc., has sponsored the nation's largest targeted co-op mailing program, "Jane Tucker's Supermarket of Savings" — now mailing almost 150 million co-op envelopes annually to growing families, older active adults (50+), and black and Hispanic or Latino families.

An active member of the Direct Marketing Association, the Promotion Marketing Association of America, and many other industry groups, he contributes frequently to industry publications and regularly addresses meetings of marketing executives.

CHAPTER 7

DIRECT RESPONSE

GENERATING COST-EFFECTIVE RESPONSE OR COUPON REDEMPTION WITH INSERTS, RIDE-ALONGS, AND CO-OP MAILINGS

Many marketers are responding to the escalating costs of "solo" mail by cutting down on new-customer acquisition programs. Not only are costs up substantially, they point out, but also the failure of these relatively expensive "outreach" mailing programs to break even on the bottom line has been very disappointing.

But cutting back on mail marketing is a shortsighted policy. Approximately 20 percent of your current customers move each year, and your third-class mail won't follow them. Other direct marketers and newly aggressive local retailers are constantly chipping away at your current customer base. It's now more important than ever before to keep a steady, reliable stream of new business flowing in.

Some companies have turned to television advertising, magazine ads, or catalog-request sections and other alternative media. But the most logical and potentially most profitable medium is *direct mail itself.*

Lots of Options. There are hundreds of alternatives to expensive "solo" mail. Co-op, statement-stuffer, ride-along, and package-insert programs are available at reasonable cost, ready to bring your selling proposition to millions of interested, qualified, ready-to-respond prospects at only a few pennies per insert. And there is now enough experience with these programs to be able to predict with confidence your probable success.

You can print your offers on insert sheets and place these in co-op mailing programs, which *share the costs* of postage, lists, envelopes, addressing, and inserting among a number of *noncompeting marketers.* Some programs will even design and print the insert for you. Or your insert can "ride along" in (or on) the packages of products being sent out to known recent buyers. There are also many "statement-stuffer" and invoice enclosure programs, from those reaching catalog buyers of specific products to magazine subscription billings, or even cable TV monthly mailings.

There are so many of these programs that the *Standard Rate & Data* directories have dedicated a separate section to listing them. Finding the ones that will work for you — and then utilizing these programs productively — can take quite a bit of research, testing, time, and money. But proper use of one or more of these wide-ranging programs can open up a significant and continuing source of profitable new customers.

During more than two decades in the direct-response field, I've seen hundreds of companies succeed in this area — and hundreds of others fail. Success hinges on the interplay of a number of factors: strategy, offer, pricing, timing, graphics, headline, copy, and even color, paper stock, and format.

Look to Your Past Successful Efforts. In starting up an insert campaign, one of the first things to bear in mind is that these programs can build naturally on your established strengths. Oftentimes, you can feature a proven product or offer that's been popular in your ads or in your solo or catalog mailings (or something similar). You'll want to start out with the time-tested price points, product features, offers, and promotional approaches that have drawn responses in the past.

Determining the Best Offer for Each Audience. Before you decide to *adapt* one of your standard or "control" offers or try to create a new offer out of the blue, you'll want to study the audience reached by the medium in which you'll be placing your inserts. Find out from the sponsor, manager, or broker as much as possible about these consumers: their ages, interests, income, lifestyles, and past purchasing habits. If the distribution is to catalog buyers, get a copy of a recent catalog. If lists of magazine subscribers are part of the distribution mix, get current copies of the publications, as well as advertising media kits and circulation statements, and examine them carefully (look particularly at the mail order ads, if any, in these publications). Data cards on lists are particularly useful, along with information on who rented the lists and for what offer.

Our company conducts continuing, extensive research on our own co-op recipients through surveys, focus groups, and other methods in order to help our participants and prospective clients learn more about our audience (including their purchase and usage of product or service categories). And we compare this data with information on response to other offers in the past for similar products or services.

Of course, you'll want to choose a medium that reaches *households with consumers who resemble your present profitable customer base.* A number of programs offer you a "profile" that's a good match to the majority or a distinct segment of your current buyers. Several programs have a strong skew toward families with young children, for example. Sports enthusiasts or outdoorsmen make up other distinct markets. Small-business owners are clearly identified in many programs. Working women are yet another identifiable group. Then there are pre-retirees over 50, the fast-aging "baby boomers" who represent the fastest-growing group in the nation. And the 65+ generation is also still expanding and is very responsive to its mail.

When you can reach many millions of potential customers with shared characteristics in one mailing (such as a targeted co-op), you have a real opportunity to improve the "pulling power" of your printed inserts very efficiently and with only a little cost and effort.

An Inexpensive Experiment. Almost any company can afford to prove for itself whether an insert program will work cost-effectively. Production charges can be held to a minimum — especially if you have photos or even color separations on hand. We regularly help our clients to position their offers and even to design attractive and eye-catching insert presentations.

You don't need very large quantities to start. To get a valid reading on response and to properly evaluate both the media and the insert itself, you can test as few as 10,000 pieces in the typical package-insert program. However, in a widely circulated program with several million recipients, it's wiser and more practical to schedule tests of 100,000+ pieces to get a reliable reading. Coupon testing generally requires a base of 100,000+, restricted to one or just a few markets.

Aiming for Long-Term Profitability. Although there are definitely marketers who consistently make money on the initial order, a number of the most successful users of insert programs don't aim to "break even" on their prospecting programs. They make their profit down the line with repeat orders, bounce-backs, subscriptions, or continuity programs. Their paramount concern is simply to bring in as many qualified responses as is reasonably possible.

Once you determine a format, price point, headline, copy, and graphics that bring in satisfactory (or better) response levels, you'll find that you can utilize insert programs year-round to keep new business flowing in. This can serve to "even out" the peaks and valleys from your established cycles of solo mail. And you may also be able to get the jump on your competition by using these regular, continuing programs to test new products, approaches, or strategies.

Customizing Your Graphics, Offers, and Copy. While many of the early ventures into this area utilized standardized inserts for inclusion in dozens of different programs, it has been proven over and over again that creating and designing inserts specifically for individual (or several similar) insert programs can bring much better results.

Smart marketers will "customize" *graphics, offers,* and *copy* on inserts going into targeted programs to attract the consumer's attention, using *language* that speaks to these identifiable prospects directly and forcefully. Our colleagues in general advertising follow a similar path as they practice "media mapping": a technique whereby packaged goods advertisers and others promote the same brands in a different manner to different audiences.

Not only are the models in the ads appropriate to the audience targeted by the publication or TV show, but also the *language* of the ad, the *style* of speaking or writing, the *offer,* and the *graphics* are fine-tuned to appeal directly to a "niche" audience, whether college students, young parents, senior citizens, Latinos, or blacks. For example, Dial soap is promoted as a "nose guard" in *Sports Illustrated,* as a "stress management tool" in *Fortune,* and as a "self-esteem boost" in

Parents. The copy and photos are designed to win the empathy of each group.

Your insert can feature self-identifying label words or buzzwords common to the specific group, such as "uh-huh" for Pepsi and "Mom" or "Grandma" or "Working Mothers" or "Fishermen" in headlines and body copy, along with appropriate photographs. You should speak directly and exclusively to the individual as part of this specific audience and keep generalities to a minimum. Be especially careful if you're addressing anything other than your own age group. This approach, if carried off well, will definitely make your offer seem more relevant and personally appealing to each person in your target audience.

Making Money at a Response Rate of 1 to 10 per 1,000. Typical response rates for an insert placed by mail marketers in a package or a co-op environment range from 1 to 10 per 1,000. But because the entire cost of participation (including printing) runs about 10 percent of the cost of solo mail, the cost-per-response figures balance out. The larger circulation programs let you reach millions of households in a very efficient manner, helping you to uncover new markets or to discover new "hot spots" quickly.

"Cents-off" coupons distributed to targeted audiences by mail, for packaged goods or health and beauty products, generate between 5 percent and 10 percent redemption (depending, of course, on factors such as the money value of the coupon, the product, and the applicability to the specific audience reached). That's two to three times the redemption generated by Sunday newspaper FSIs, and substantially more than is generated by "neighborhood/resident" mailings to every house on the block.

Any offer, copy, graphic, or format that can raise this response rate a fraction of a percentage point will pay off handsomely! At these low response levels, a very small improvement in response or redemption can make a big difference to the bottom line of a program — especially when you get up into the millions (or tens of millions) or total circulation spread out over a year or more.

The time, effort, and up-front expense involved in creating a "custom" insert will almost always pay off over the long run. You can sell the same thing to different people in dozens of ways — each most appropriate for the specific audience you're appealing to.

Look for Demographic and Lifestyle Indicators. We have found that millions of consumers in a given age group share a number of common interests, and they can often be motivated to respond by an approach that takes these interests into account. Older consumers, for example, are almost always interested in convenience, quality, or security; and they respond well to both endorsements and guarantees.

When you're advertising or promoting in a medium targeted largely to older consumers, you'll want your offer to appeal to their particular point of view. Remember that, by and large, these are experienced shoppers who are not easily swayed by exaggerated promises and definitely not willing to put up with shoddy products or poor fulfillment performance. Ply them with testimonials from authorities or from people their age who have a similar lifestyle. Let your graphics show vital and vigorous older people in the act of enjoying or using your product. Studies consistently show that older people envision themselves as five to 10 years younger than their actual chronological age, so bear that in mind as you select or create graphics and photos. Also include grandchildren, if appropriate.

Guarantees should be featured prominently and in no-nonsense language, with the signature of a company principal (or founder). Pictures of this individual in the office or in a buying location, and even of the factory or warehouse, can be placed within or near the guarantee box or "certificate" to give added credibility and assurance.

Remember to keep your type a bit larger to compensate for poorer eyesight. Conservative type styles, colors, and layout work best. Keep tones under type to a minimum. And, in general, avoid type reverses.

You'll want to *stress benefits* that show the older consumers exactly how your product or service can make their lives easier, more rewarding, or more enriching. Picture your product in actual use. Diagrams can be utilized to explain how something works or charts can be used to compare products or drive home a point. Older consumers are real readers; the more information you give them, the better.

Many senior consumers grew up in an era when the Sears and Montgomery Ward catalogs were staple sources of products they simply couldn't buy at the local stores. They're lifelong mail order shoppers. And now, with a bit more disposable income, credit cards, and a large extended family, shopping by mail can be a pleasurable and convenient experience for them. They may even become your very best continuing customers.

Shift Gears as the Audience Changes. Younger adults should be approached in a very different fashion, with emphasis on the new, the stylish, and quick gratification of their desires. Graphics should be brighter and more contemporary. These are impulsive, impatient, on-the-go people who are generally very active socially.

If you offer premiums to younger adults as an ordering incentive, you'll want to select items tuned in to their tastes. Audiotapes or videotapes, novelty telephones or radios, or stylish accessories seem to appeal strongly to this group.

Copy addressed to people under 25 should be brief and catchy. They won't sit still for long sentences or detailed explanations. Use photos or diagrams to explain a complex idea. Subscription terms should be kept short, and payment terms should be stretched out. Be sure to structure your offers and order form to avoid poor payout and bad credit as much as possible.

But there's definitely another shift once these young people settle down, get married, and have children. Responsibility (for the family unit, their credit rating, and the welfare of the children) become their paramount concerns. With the mini baby boom now going on, this is a vibrant and growing audience — one that is very profitable if it's approached properly. Offers aimed at young parents or working mothers can feature strong appeals to maternal concerns, stressing activities that can be shared with the children. Settings should be in a warm home environment or in shared family leisure activities. This is a terrific continuity audience, which can be developed to buy from you for years to come!

For busy parents, you'll want to emphasize time-saving or convenient features, product durability and safety, and good value. Information is a dominant need here, so reprints, booklets, manuals, or instructional videotapes are excellent premiums. Members of this audience will send away for product samples, and they are among the strongest requesters of catalogs, "soft" offers, "free" issues, and introductory deals. The overwhelming majority of these women work outside the home, and so convenience is something that they are willing and able to pay for.

Try to feature photos of a child of the approximate age of those in the majority of the households reached by the medium your insert will be carried in — babies, toddlers, preschoolers, school children, or teenagers. If two or more child age groups are involved, look for or create graphics that show a multichild family. You want the reader to identify as much as possible with your piece.

If a particular sport, recreational activity, or hobby is common to a significant number of the recipients of an insert-carrier program, by all means include a reference to this in your graphic and perhaps in your copy as well. Even a fishing hat on the table or a golf club casually propped by the door can help win over an audience of enthusiasts, without alienating or even alerting the others.

People representative of your target audience who are doing things that your audience does (or would like to be doing) can combine in a strong emotional appeal. Show grandparents with grandchildren and pet lovers with dogs, cats, birds, fish — whatever is most appropriate.

Although the creation and customization of these "individualized" inserts may cost from a few hundred to several thousand dollars initially, the additional "lift" they will bring should pay off your investment in a matter of months.

SELECTING AND FEATURING PRODUCTS FOR CO-OP OR PACKAGE-INSERT PROGRAMS

The range of products and services that can be profitably marketed in a co-op or package-insert environment is very broad, but effective use of this medium requires the application of *proven techniques* that can make the difference between success and disappointment.

Over the past 15 years of sponsoring widely circulated consumer co-op mailings, we've worked closely with major direct-response marketers in selecting, presenting, and promoting their products — consistently bringing them substantial new business from previously untapped sources, cost-effectively.

The product you offer doesn't need to be new or even novel. But it *does* have to be representative of your general line, and it should be perceived as an *outstanding value* by the type of person who will be asked to order it. Once your offer, headline, and graphics gain his or her attention and interest, the perception of a bargain price (or tempting terms) can convert prospect interest into customer action.

Remember that you've got to come up with a *combination* of an attractive (even novel) product and low price. That's what drives so many direct marketers to the novelty and premium shows and to frequent shopping trips to Europe and the Far East.

Creating a Unique Price/Feature Combination. You'll note the language: the "perception" of a bargain. That's a very important point, and one that's better reserved for the section on pricing. In general, successful offers to first-time buyers feature a one-time price under $20, including all charges. But price alone is rarely the most important key to a successful insert program. The audience you are trying to woo probably has never been properly introduced to you; they know very little about your company, so you'll have to make it easy and agreeable for them to do business with you for the first time by creating the assurances of a "risk-free" environment.

Many successful mail marketers create a special "loss leader" for a product offer — something that they have particular and sometimes unique success in manufacturing or importing. The product should be as universally appealing to the specific audience as possible (wallet, pocketbook, scarf, baby clothing, knife set, cookware, or collectibles, for example) and should carry a price that would seem to be less than that of a comparable item found in a retail store. If no comparable item is available in stores, so much the better!

Marketers of cosmetics, lotions, perfumes, and costume jewelry can offer terrific "bargains" up front because of the ratio of product cost to the perceived value. If you're also marketing a related product, you may want to offer one of these bargains as part of a "bargain package."

Try Adding the Personal Touch. The most ordinary belt or blouse or robe can be given additional value and attractiveness with personalization: the initialed belt buckle or the monogrammed initial have great appeal. Recipe books or family bibles with a family's name on the cover or binding may work very well. A family crest can easily be obtained for the 100 most common surnames. Even wine with personalized labels could be sold this way. Brainstorm how you can personalize your own products. Don't forget the continuing popularity of Zodiac signs as well.

Audience-Specific Products. If the co-op mailing your insert is included in (or the package or ride-along) is going to a *demographically definable* group of households, then your work may be made a bit easier. Special personalized mugs, plates, bibs, or spoons for babies are a perennial favorite among young mothers, along with anything that will increase household safety for the toddler or give the mother more free time by cutting her workload.

For new movers or newlyweds, other possibilities present themselves; stationery, embossed towels, or personalized doormats are just the tip of the iceberg. Change-of-address files from established catalog companies should be especially fertile ground.

For older consumers, items to make them more comfortable or safe in the home or car are long-established winners — everything from devices for safety and convenience in the bathtub to shoe inserts and foot massagers. Many retired people are frequent travelers (as are business executives), and you may want to offer them items as varied as magnifiers for map reading, auto compasses, or special security money carriers.

Coming in the Back Door. You may want to present your product with another approach. Instead of selling shoes or jewelry or cosmetics, you can recruit new "dealers" or sales representatives — all of whom get a special discount price, even on limited quantities. Or you can offer membership in a special "club" or "plan" to sell a wide variety of products. This requires a complex back-end, but you can reap benefits for years from your respondents.

Package Your Offer with Add-Ons. It's almost always a good idea to present your product along with a *built-in bonus,* especially if you're selling something intangible, such as life insurance. A detailed booklet on health-promoting diet habits and easy-to-do exercises may bring in many more inquiries, and it helps the insurance company in its long-term mission of cutting the mortality rate. A travel atlas will boost inquiries about an auto club, cruise line, travel agency, or moving service. A lawn-and-garden checklist can bring in leads for a lawn maintenance service. Printed materials are inexpensive to produce, yet they are perceived as being worth several dollars by the public.

If you're selling magazine subscriptions, it's been proven that reprints of published articles are excellent incentives. Or you may create a special annual or seasonal issue (or a directory or guide), and offer it free to all new paying subscribers, no matter when they begin.

With the decrease in cost for producing audiotapes and even videotapes, a number of magazine marketers are trying these as attractive incentives for the paid-up new subscriber. From sports highlights or training/instruction tapes for *Sports Illustrated* to home repair tapes for the fix-it publications and lure-tying tapes for the fishing books, your options are limited only by your imagination. And how about a model Ferrari or Lamborghini for the sports car magazine subscriber? Or a custom gearshift knob with the buyer's initial?

A few marketers are experimenting with offering two related items as their "product," with one being a promotional "loss leader." If two items go naturally together, and one of them is quickly perishable, you have a natural fit — for example, razor blades given away with a razor.

A general rule of thumb is that the closer the add-on is related to your basic product, the better quality of response you'll generate and the longer you'll keep the customer. When you combine relevance with "desirability," you've got a winner!

Making the Bargain Seem Even Better. You'll want your package to look like a terrific bargain. Adding a 10¢ carrying case to a $3 order for personalized pencils or a $3 cigar cutter or carrying case to a $30 order for a box of cigars is just good marketing strategy. Watch those TV ads: "But that's not all … ." One more incentive may tip the balance from interest to action.

Once you select a product or package of products, you should try to create a *unique positioning* for it. Your product may actually have one-of-a-kind features (a knife that never needs sharpening or pantyhose that never wear out). But more often, you'll want to create or point out singular benefits that your products offer — selling the "sizzle" instead of just the steak. The promise may be as important as the product, and the two should be sold as one dynamic marketing idea.

No Competition in Most Co-op Mailings. Most co-op mailings will guarantee you a competition-free environment — an "exclusive" on your own product or service category. Make sure that you spell these terms out carefully and completely as you look at different carrier programs. If you're selling women's clothing, for example, there may well be someone else in the mailing package who is selling men's clothing or women's handbags, shoes, or perfumes.

But what about scarves? Are you protected? Maybe you'll want to offer a free or reduced-price scarf with each order, or you'll want to use the back of your insert to showcase your own line of scarves. Try to corral as much as possible of the consumer's purchasing power in your own broad category. Discuss this frankly with the program sponsor, and get your parameters set down in a written and signed agreement.

Pricing Strategies to Increase Response. When you're planning to test various offers, pricing strategy is an important factor. Whether you're selling a $99 figurine or a $3.98 continuity item, your pricing must be perceived as a bargain by the audience perusing the insert.

If the normal perceived retail value of a category of products is relatively high (even though product cost may be relatively inexpensive), you have a lot of room to maneuver. With products such as perfume, beauty cream, jewelry, or decorative items, it's easy to give liberal partial-payment terms, extra bonuses, free samples, half-off prices, or "bill-me-later" options. We'll look at each of these approaches in just a moment.

However books, periodicals, and records/tapes/CDs represent a different challenge. Profit on the initial order may not be that great; as a matter of fact, the majority of companies in these fields expect to "buy" a new customer by *losing* money at the outset. Their overall, long-term profitability is dependent on generating multiple shipments to a paying customer (or a continuing paid subscription) extending over a number of months or years. With profitability spread out over time, a company with continuity programs can make compelling offers such as "6 Records for only 1¢" or "3 Books for 3 Bucks — No Commitment — No Kidding!"

In periodical publishing, where the need to maintain a substantial number of readers or a "rate base" for advertisers is a very important consideration, circulation directors may use a bag of tricks to bring in the initial orders. Requesting cash-with-order has become rare, and "Examine your first issue FREE at our risk" has become the benchmark offer. Even this liberal policy may not be tempting enough to draw the large number of responses that are needed, and premiums or special pricing and terms may be combined with this "no-risk" offer.

General auditing regulations require that your final price offered be no less than half the normal subscription-term rate. But since cover prices are generally higher, you can often offer $1 off a $1.50 cover-price magazine and stay within the guidelines.

Selling Merchandise with Minimum Risk. For items such as clothing, gifts, and knickknacks, the aim of companies prospecting for catalog buyers or long-term customers is often to break even on the first order, so that the cost of bringing in the new customer can be minimized. The other basic approach offers a free catalog or may ask for a nominal amount for the catalog (taking that or a larger sum off the first merchandise purchase).

Obviously, in programs dedicated to increasing catalog circulation, the total costs to the vendor of the entire operation (soliciting the order for the catalog, data entry, printing and mailing the catalog, and direct mail or telephone follow-up) must be factored into the final break-even figure. Some companies can manage to sell "loss leaders" at attractive prices to generate the first actual order. But all of them are "buying a new customer," banking on the projected "lifetime value" of the newly acquired customer. Catalog companies regularly rate their new customers after 18 or 24 months to determine "lifetime value." Future solicitation is then based on this evaluation.

Getting consumers to ask for a catalog and then getting them to buy from the catalog (or one of your subsequent solo mail offerings directed to them) becomes a more complex, "two-step" marketing task.

We'll deal with this in detail later on. In general, bringing in qualified leads can be a sound business practice when the ultimate sale is complicated or if it involves a big-ticket or long-term commitment.

For low-ticket or impulse items, insert programs can generate orders profitably if the right price point can be found. But this can change from one moment to another as other vendors rush to market with similar items. Sufficient response must obviously be generated to make these pay out, and this is one area where the combination of pricing and offer is critical.

Inserts can do a thorough, cost-effective job in each of these categories, bringing in hundreds of thousands of purchases (or millions of inquiries, sample requests, or catalog orders). Determining the right price point *and* pricing policy depends largely on your goal: to break even, make a profit, or "buy" a new customer at an acceptable price.

Higher Profit Margin Allows Higher Risk. Many items successfully marketed by mail are manufactured or obtained at a fraction of their normal selling price. Particularly for trendy, style-oriented products, cosmetics/scents, new high-tech items, or "collectibles," pricing may be "blind" — that is, the consumer has very little reference against which to judge it. Markups of 300 percent or more are not uncommon in these cases. And even in the field of books and audio or videotapes, the incremental manufacturing cost is only a small portion of the price asked.

In these cases, the marketer can take more risk up front in formulating tactics to bring in the initial order. "Send No Money Now: Examine in Your Own Home for 10 Days at Our Risk" is a financially sound offer for these products because it takes into account the substantial no-payments and the returned merchandise that will probably ensue. The added initial response gleaned from the majority who will pay (and stay), coupled with the substantial built-in profit margin, makes this type of offer profitable.

Spread Out the Payment Schedule. Of course, many marketers now allow consumers to make their credit card payments in several installments. "Only $9.95 a month for four months" may be a lot easier to swallow than a flat $39.80 as a price point. Some larger marketers even offer their own credit payment systems to holders of Visa, MasterCard, or Discover cards.

You can keep your pricing in the bargain range by breaking up the billed payments into two or three parts — a two-step program with billing for the first installment going out *after* the initial "send no money" order is received by the vendor and *before* shipment of the product. The first payment can completely cover the cost of the product and shipping. Those who pay the remaining one or two invoices amortize the media costs and provide the profit margin.

Satisfied customers will often respond to bounce-back advertising or subsequent solicitations as they pay the installments, and they provide a substantial profit bonus! And each billing cycle provides you with an opportunity to sell other items or add-ons.

Smaller Sizes, Samples, and Initial-Order Premiums. Another way to make your price more palatable is to offer a smaller size, the first piece in a series or set, or a reduced number of items in a grouping. This gives you a chance to add a premium (for example, a chess board with your first chess piece, a display cabinet with your first collectible figurine, a bookcase with your first classic book or encyclopedia volume).

Several food marketers offer "samples" of cheese or smoked meats or canned goods at greatly reduced prices. You can offer prospective long-term customers a choice between the "10-day supply" of vitamins or cosmetics at $3.98, while the "30-day supply" may be only $5.98. And don't be surprised if a number of $5.98 orders come streaming in!

Cash up front, "bill me," offering smaller quantities or starter sets — all of these are propositions that bear testing. You may well find that one approach works well in several related media but that other media produce better results with a totally different strategy. Only testing will reveal whether asking for a check (or credit card number) to accompany the order is better over the long run than offering another, more liberal option. My long-term experience has been that the easier you make it to place the order and get the initial commitment quickly, the more orders will flow in.

Connie Kennedy is a marketing consultant in Coppell, Texas, a suburb of Dallas. With more than 20 years experience on both the client and supplier sides, Kennedy has provided marketing consulting and full-service database marketing for clients such as Southwest Airlines, Frito-Lay, and Warner-Lambert.

Prior to consulting, Kennedy worked in product management at General Mills, was Director of Marketing at Mattel Electronics, Director of New Products at Taco Bell, and Vice President of Advertising at 800-Flowers. Her broad base of experience includes working with new products, sales promotion frequency and cross-sell programs, lead-generation programs, and extensive work in developing and testing database programs.

Kennedy is a member of the Direct Marketing Association (DMA) Council and the North Texas chapter of the DMA. She has a B.A. in Marketing from University of Arizona, an MBA from Arizona State University, and she is a graduate of the DMA Collegiate Institute.

CHAPTER 8

DATABASE MARKETING

DATABASE MARKETING DEFINED

Database marketing has become a buzzword. Many view it as a panacea for what ails marketing today. Some have already moved on to relationship marketing or integrated marketing. But database marketing is at the root of it all.

What is all the hype about? What is this new marketing technique called database marketing? Is it right for every business?

Database marketing has evolved from the recent dramatic changes in our world. Consumers face unprecedented choices. Table 8.1 shows the explosive growth in media vehicles and new products in the last 20 years.

TABLE 8.1
ACCELERATED CHOICE

	1970	1980	1990
Average no. TV channels	7	9	33
No. consumer magazines	1,075	1,490	2,265
No. products in average supermarket	12,400	14,145	25,855

The service economy rules where the manufacturing economy once prospered: 67 percent of the gross national product and seven out of 10 American workers are part of the service sector. Add to these changes the clutter and the decline in efficiency of the traditional mass media, and you have a very dynamic market, one that is not as easily forecasted as the one of old.

Contrary to popular opinion, loyalty is not dead. Businesses are simply not delivering what is required to foster loyalty. The differences between product A and product B are fewer and fewer. Customers are searching for companies that understand their needs and tailor their products and services to those needs. Only by building a strong relationship that recognizes those needs do you foster long-term loyalty.

These changes demand that marketing and sales promotion experts alike stay in tune with an ever-changing marketplace. To stay in tune, one must know who is shaping the change. Quite simply, the customer is. Essential to success today is understanding and meeting the needs of the customer. Because the needs that must be met are no longer needs shared by the masses, the new challenge is to market to the individual. A company must be driven by the characteristics, needs, desires, and preferences of the individual consumer. A relationship must be fostered customer by customer.

Database marketing is, in reality, a return to the very basics of marketing: know your customer and serve your customer through technology. The marketer of the 1990s can utilize the individual-based selling techniques of old. Once again, the proprietor knows his or her customers by name and the products they purchase. A new method of understanding and communicating with the customer is required. This new method is database marketing. The new medium is the database.

The advances of computer technology have made it possible to practice individualized marketing on a very large scale. The cost of storing vast quantities of information has dropped dramatically over the last 20 years, facilitating the development of marketing databases. Thus, keeping track of your customer's product preferences and purchase history is affordable. The database becomes the platform to market to individual customers based on their needs and desires.

One of our clients feels so strongly about the importance of customers and their relationship that the client capitalizes the first letter of customer wherever it appears. The capital C alerts all employees to who the real boss is. Our client is profitable in an industry in which the major players are losing money. You cannot underestimate the importance of the customer. And, you can no longer treat all customers the same.

Simply stated, database marketing is the promotion of products or services customer by customer, by means of an information source. The information source is the database. The database provides the information necessary to customize the communication to meet the needs and desires of the individual customer. Currently, the communication vehicles used in database marketing are the mail, interactive point-of-sale, and interactive telecommunication services.

DATABASE MARKETING APPLICATIONS

As with all business endeavors, the purpose of a marketing database is to positively impact the financial performance of a company. There are three fundamental strategies to achieve this. The first is the acquisition of new customers. The second is the retention of current customers. And the third is the maximization of the contribution of current customers. No matter what the business-building objective is, one of these three strategies would be employed in its pursuit.

Acquisition of New Customers. New customers come in two types. The first is a customer that is new to your product or category. Given the penetration of most products and services these days, this target may only be a marketing opportunity for truly new categories of products and services. The second group, the competitor's customers, is an opportunity for a much larger group of companies.

Both types of new customers can be part of a database. The decision about who to include on the database is made during the planning stage of the database, which will be discussed later in the chapter.

Highly targeted acquisition programs can be designed utilizing the individual level information that the database provides. Imagine, if you will, a database of your competitors' best customers and the ability to tailor your marketing programs to their needs, putting your company's best foot forward.

The automobile industry is a perfect example of this strategy. In any direct communication, success is predicated on addressing the right people at the right time with the right offer. Through the information derived from the licensing of motor vehicles, the automobile makers can populate a database with owners of competitors' automobiles. Through customer research, they have determined which competitive car owners are most likely to purchase next their make and model. For instance, a Thunderbird owner, when trading in the car, might consider a Cadillac, a Lincoln Town Car, or a Mercedes for the next purchase. Armed with this information, Cadillac knows which group of potential buyers to target.

The automobile industry, through an extensive analysis of car buying, has determined that the most likely time for people to trade in their car is four and a half years. The identification of these potential switching patterns is valuable, but what makes it powerful is the knowledge of approximately when someone will purchase a new car. By building a relationship just prior to the next purchase, the manufacturer ensures that his make and model will be included in the set of automobiles that will be considered. Thus, he has begun the sales process. The initial goal is to capture the next purchase occasion. The long-term goal is to create a relationship that lasts beyond one purchase and results in repeat purchases within his line of cars.

Retention of Current Customers. The airlines' frequent flier and hotels' frequent stayer programs are excellent examples of proactive retention programs. Using a database of all the flights and visits, the travel industry is able to fashion programs based on past behavior. For example, if a traveler normally takes a flight to Kansas City every month, an early warning system might alert the marketing and promotion team when two months go by without a trip. The airline or hotel has the ability to send a personalized message to the individuals offering a special perk on the next trip if she returns a satisfaction survey for previous trips. The program identifies if there is a problem and also provides an incentive to make sure the valued traveler is not flying on a competitive airline.

Another example of retention programs is reactive programs. The Tylenol product tampering scare of several years ago was dealt with very effectively by McNeil Consumer Products. The damage control plan would have been even stronger if a database of Tylenol users had been available. Imagine a letter sent within a matter of days to loyal Tylenol consumers explaining the extent of the product tampering, describing the steps the company was taking, and delivering a coupon to ensure the loyalty of this important group. A private, direct channel of communication to customers without a news media filter through a database would be invaluable.

All reactive programs do not involve product tampering or product liability. Many times marketers are faced with a direct assault on their most valued customers by a competitor. American Airlines recently was under attack in its home market of Dallas by Delta Airlines. Delta offered membership in its most-valued customer program, the Medallion level, to Dallas fliers. The offer did not require the Dallas-based fliers to comply with the normal Delta program requirements.

As a Platinum member of the American Advantage frequent flier program, I received a letter from Mr. Michael Gunn, Senior Vice President of Marketing, reinforcing how important my business was to American and contrasting my benefits as a member of the Platinum program against those of the Delta Medallion program (see Exhibit 8.1). The letter was received within days of Delta's announcing its offer in the mass media. This counterattack by American Airlines minimized the impact of the Delta offer.

Maximization of Customer Contribution. Imagine being able to tailor a promotion based on past behavior in your product or service category. A continuity program could be designed that would cause even the heaviest customer to make an incremental purchase. The information on the database can provide the foundation for programs to promote cross-selling of other products, trading up to a more expensive line, and increasing your share of purchases from a customer. An industry that employs a customer maximization strategy is financial services. These programs leverage the information available at an individual level to ensure your company receives the maximum purchases possible. The only way to truly maximize the volume and profits of a company is customer by customer, matching programs and incentives to individual customer behavior and potential.

An excellent example of a maximization program is the Weight Watchers' Winners! program. The program realizes an excellent cross-selling opportunity for both the weight-loss centers and the 250 portion-controlled food products that are sold through grocery stores. The Winners! program leverages the Weight Watchers' brand name across to different retail channels. The objectives are to foster continued membership in Weight Watchers and to generate incremental volume for the food products.

Membership solicitation utilizes both channels of distribution. New enrollees in the Weight Watchers weight-loss plan were automatically entered in the Winners! program. Shoppers were intercepted in the grocery store and given a chance to enroll. The enrollment kit included information on Weight Watchers meetings and the weight-loss program. The program consists of accumulating points for atten-

EXHIBIT 8.1

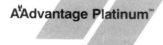

October 1, 1992

Ms. Connie Kennedy
614 Meadowview Ln   AAdvantage #B341786
Coppell, TX 75019-5746

Dear Ms. Kennedy,

Because you are one of our most frequent customers, we would like to take this
opportunity to thank you for your continued loyalty to American Airlines.
We hope that you are enjoying AAdvantage Platinum status, and we would like to
reinforce our commitment to providing you with the most innovative frequent
flyer program in the industry.

The AAdvantage Platinum program offers many benefits which some other
frequent flyer programs do not. For instance, on American you earn free
upgrades for *every* 10,000 miles you fly. As a Platinum member you *always*
earn bonus miles each and every time you fly on American or American Eagle. You
may upgrade from any fare--not just the full Coach fare. And AAdvantage Platinum
members may upgrade in advance of all other members of our frequent flyer program.

Finally, as an AAdvantage member, it's important to you that we provide the most
daily flights to more destinations than any other carrier at DFW including the
most international service and the most nonstop flights to Europe. The
frequency and the variety of our flight schedule give you far more choices to
fit your busy schedule and far greater opportunity to earn miles faster.

As you read in the September/October newsletter, we are making it even
easier to earn free trips this fall. When you fly either eight segments
or 12,000 miles on American Airlines or American Eagle with purchased
tickets, you'll earn a certificate for a free round-trip Main Cabin ticket
which may be used for travel within the contiguous 48 United States,
Canada, Mexico or the Caribbean. Two certificates are redeemable for one
free round-trip Main Cabin ticket to Hawaii, Europe, Latin America or
Japan. This offer is valid on flights September 8 through December 18, 1992,
so you may already be on the way to earning a free trip!

Your loyalty to American Airlines is very important to us, and we want to
continue to provide the best frequent flyer program in the Dallas/Fort Worth
area. We look forward to serving you again in the near future.

Sincerely,

Michael W. Gunn
Senior Vice President-Marketing
American Airlines

American Airlines® AAdvantage Platinum
MD 5200, P.O. Box 619281, Dallas/Fort Worth Airport, TX 75261-9281

dance at Weight Watchers meetings and the purchase of Weight Watchers food products. The points are redeemed for various gifts.

Additional mailings, coinciding with potential weight-loss plan dropout times, provided further encouragement to stay in the program through incentives and product information.

THE DATABASE MARKETING ALTERNATIVE

Database marketing is a viable alternative to other available sales methods for two key reasons — effectiveness and efficiency. The targeting ability of database marketing eliminates waste, thus increasing efficiency and effectiveness. Unlike mass media vehicles such as broadcast and print media, you only communicate with known customers of your products and services. A more relevant message is delivered because you know the individual characteristics, needs, desires, and preferences of each customer with whom you are communicating.

Table 8.2 outlines the cost per effective impression for various mass media vehicles and database marketing. An effective impression incorporates the cost to reach each customer and the impact of that impression (recall).

TABLE 8.2
COMPARISON OF DATABASE MARKETING TO MASS MEDIA

Media	Total Impressions (MM)	Category Incidence	Recall Rate	Effective Impressions* (MM)	Advertising Cost Effectiveness (CPI)
Mass (TV, Radio, Print)**	2,100	39%	24%	197	$0.15
FSI	50.7	39%	13%	2.6	$1.12
Database	15.0	95%	81%	11.5	$0.26

* Effective Impressions = Impressions x Category Incidence x Recall Rate.
** Budgets = Mass: $30.0MM, FSI: $3.0MM, Database: $3.0MM.

Should Everyone Have a Marketing Database? Eventually, everyone will. With continued improvements in data collection, computer processing, and data storage, the cost of building and maintaining a database will be affordable to all relevant companies. Today, not everyone who could benefit from a database can afford one.

To determine if you should develop a database, a cost/benefit analysis should be undertaken. On the cost side, you need to estimate how much it will cost to acquire and maintain the appropriate information on the database and deliver programs to the database. Exhibit 8.2 details itemized costs that should be considered.

EXHIBIT 8.2
COST CHECKLIST

Acquisition — Cost of the names, addresses, and pertinent information

Database design

Preparation of data for the database

- Merge/purge
- NCOA
- List clean
- Address standardization
- Normalization

Query system

Maintenance of database

- Updates
- NCOA
- Additions

Database marketing program costs

- Printing
- Postage
- Creative development
- Data entry
- List pull
- Incentive

As shown in this exhibit, there are two main categories of costs — database related and program related. The cost of building the base is directly related to the availability of the information. For instance, a video store has the name, address, and all transactions for each customer; whereas a consumer packaged goods company only knows the name, address, and sales associated with the intermediary — the retail outlet. The cost to develop a marketing database for the video store will be much less than for the consumer packaged goods company because the data are already available. The consumer packaged goods company will incur the additional cost of acquiring the data. If the database costs are fairly significant, you should consider whether to amortize that cost over a longer period of time than one year. The information has value beyond a year; therefore, a two- or three-year time frame should be considered.

The costs should be compared to the benefits that can be derived from a database. A simple way to do the comparison is to estimate the lifetime values (LTVs) of your customers and compare them to the database costs. To determine the LTV, one must first assume a time frame for a customer's "lifetime." Few products or services can assume a customer will buy from them during the entire time they are in the market for their product. Given the battle for share of market and customers' growing propensity for brand switching, a year may be the longest you can assume they would be in your franchise.

Your customer base does not have one lifetime value. There are as many lifetime values as there are customers. In the calculation of lifetime values, a value should be calculated for several pertinent groups. A database does not have to reflect your entire customer or prospect base. The database can be populated by subgroups such as heavy, medium, and light customers. The database could house only competitive or franchise customers. Any combination of the above subgroups is also possible.

When determining for which of the groups you should compute an LTV, you should consider that competitive customers represent 100 percent incremental volume. Heavy customers by definition will be worth more than medium or light customers, but you already have their purchases, right? Wrong, at least not in the majority of products and services today. Your heavy customers are not giving you 100 percent of their purchases in your category. Everyone knows that it is much easier to keep and increase share of purchases with current customers than to convert a competitive customer. The appropriate audience for the database could be *both* current and competitive customers.

Competitive conversion in these days means increasing the share of purchases customer by customer, not gaining 100 percent of their purchases. To obtain 50 percent of the purchases of a competitive heavy customer would be significant. The profit per purchase will aid in determining whether you include only heavy customers or consider including the next level of customers.

For the initial evaluation, an LTV should be calculated for all relevant customer groups. Exhibit 8.3 outlines the lifetime calculation for several audiences.

EXHIBIT 8.3
LIFETIME VALUE (LTV) CALCULATIONS

Formula:	LTV = Annual Purchases x Profit/Purchase
Average Customer:	LTV = 6 purchases/year x $6 profit/purchase
	LTV = $36
Heavy Customer:	LTV = 12 purchases/year x $6 profit/purchase
	LTV = $72

Now that you have the costs associated with database marketing and the LTV of your customer groups, you can determine the additional volume necessary to cover the cost. For example, if the cost of acquiring the pertinent information amortized over two years is $1 and the cost of the annual program is $9, the total annual costs would be $10. Based on the heavy customer example from Exhibit 8.3, only two incremental purchases per year are needed to cover the costs of the program and generate incremental profit.

To determine how likely the benefits of a database will outweigh the costs, you must consider how much of an impact the unique characteristics of this medium would have on your business. Table 8.2 showed how highly targeted, knowledge-based marketing can affect a business. In that example, the database was at a 3 to 1 cost disadvantage to the FSI but proved to be more effective and more efficient. You should search for case histories in relevant categories to determine what database marketing has been able to achieve. In this search, you will find response rates and incremental volume rates that will surprise you — as the cost per effective impression did.

BUILDING A MARKETING DATABASE

As with any successful endeavor, you plan before you build. The process of building a database is comprised of seven phases. The phases are detailed in Exhibit 8.4.

EXHIBIT 8.4
DATABASE BUILDING PROCESS

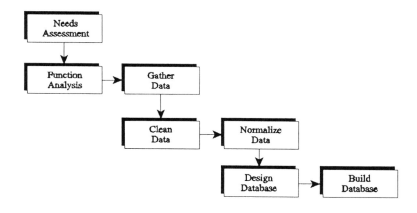

Needs Assessment. The first phase is the needs assessment. In this phase, you determine the objectives for the database. Thorough planning with an eye to the future is required when establishing the objectives for the database. Key areas that the objectives should cover are audience or target, expectations for the database (financial and marketing), who will be using the database, and the degree of interaction required. The objectives drive who will populate your database, what data structure you will use, how much it will cost, and who can access it.

For example, assume the objectives are (1) to convert competitive customers, (2) to deliver significant incremental volume in the first year, and (3) to provide an analytical tool for nontechnical staff. These objectives would result in a database that is made up of customers of your competition, is of a size sufficient to generate incremental volume in its first year, and has a user interface that a nontechnical person can master.

By identifying competitive customers as the target, you will not be populating your database with your own customers. If, in the future, you would like to begin communicating with your customers by means of the database, you will need to acquire the information and add it to the database. The database structure will need to be adapted, and a new data collection effort will have to be undertaken. Had the future need for current customer information been identified in the initial planning, the database would have been designed to carry the additional information, and the initial data collection could have included current customers, thus saving time and money.

The total cost of building a database is greatly affected by the size and the speed with which a database is built. Unless you have a captive audience and a system that traps all the information you need to market effectively (frequency of purchase, items purchased, brand, or source), it will probably take multiple screening efforts to build a database that has a high penetration in your target audience. To build a database of any size cost-effectively, one should balance speed and cost. The shorter the timeline, the more costly the data collection efforts are. Significant incremental volume in the first year may not be in the best interest of the long-term plan for that database. You may find that a lower incremental volume goal in the first year will lead to a higher cumulative profit from the database over several years.

If nontechnical personnel will be accessing the database, special design considerations come into play. What information will they access and what functions will they want to perform? For instance, will they want to print out mailing labels once they selected a group from the database? Or are they just interested in how many customers might qualify for a specific program? The first requires access to name and address and formatting for labels. The second requires access to purchase and demographic characteristics. These demands require very different access capabilities. Your plan will need to include a training component for those individuals utilizing the database.

Even though the cost of storing information has been drastically reduced, it is still very important to maintain only the characteristics of a customer that facilitate better targeting and improved communication. Maintaining extraneous information can negatively affect the performance of database processing, cause you to take your eye off the really important variables, and incur unnecessary costs to keep nonpertinent information current. Customer research can be very helpful in determining the key variables to place on the database. Segmentation studies and research that describes your customers, their attitudes, and their purchase behaviors will aid in identifying the information. Past research can be used or you may have to field a new research study. Validity and relevancy of the information are the key.

Therefore, as a part of the needs assessment, you must determine what information is required to meet the objectives you have set for the database. The checklist in Exhibit 8.5 lists the types of information that could be key for targeting and influencing purchase behavior through a database.

Function Analysis. This phase of the database building process focuses on what the database has to do from a technical standpoint to meet your objectives. The answers to the questions during this phase will aid in determining which software and hardware are required.

EXHIBIT 8.5
DATABASE CUSTOMER INFORMATION

Required:
   Name and address (business or home, depending on your industry)

Potential:
   Brand preferences

   Brand purchased most often

   Frequency of purchase

   Units purchased per occasion

   Demographics

   Lifestyle indicators

   Phone number

If you are able to track every transaction, you can add the following:

   Total lifetime sales

   Total annual sales

   Recency

   Sales by product purchased

   Combination of products purchased

EXHIBIT 8.6
FUNCTION ANALYSIS CHECKLIST

- ❏ Is 24-hour on-line access required?
- ❏ How many customers will be housed on the database?
- ❏ What type of response time is required for certain processes?
- ❏ How often will the information be updated?
- ❏ How much customer information will be stored?
- ❏ How many new customers are anticipated in the next one to three years?
- ❏ What provisions should be made for additional customer information?

Sample questions from this phase are listed in Exhibit 8.6, but a technical person well versed in marketing databases is an essential part of this process.

Internal vs. External. Once the needs assessment and function analysis are completed, the question of where and how to house the data must be answered. First, you must determine if the database can be built and maintained internally.

A marketing database is very different from a financial or inventory system. Typically, financial and inventory systems are not concerned with individual customer-level data, which are primary focuses of the marketing database. Financial and inventory systems are focused on current orders or weekly, monthly, quarterly, or annual sales. A marketing database must be able to relate data from a marketing perspective, not a financial or operational view. The architecture for the data is built around this perspective and will not resemble the structure of operational systems currently in use. The output of a marketing database includes customized promotional lists, opportunity identification, scoring, early warning systems, and reporting on past programs. Only some types of reporting will resemble functions that the current operations systems perform. There are off-the-shelf or licensed products that could meet part or all of your needs, and personnel could be trained in these systems. Your company's current in-house resources may or may not be able to adapt to the requirements of a marketing database.

When making the decision, it is important to consider both options. Housing the base internally will require additional head count, training, software, and potentially hardware. If the marketing department will have access to the database, you will also need a group to support these users. Any and all additional costs associated with housing the database internally should be compared to outsourcing the database.

Outsourcing the database provides several benefits. First, you will be able to access the knowledge of people who have years of experience in this area. Second, you will be a number-one priority even at month's close. Third, you will be able to choose a company that can provide one or all of the services required to implement database marketing. Building and maintaining the database is only one of the components of database marketing. A diagram of the components of database marketing is shown in Exhibit 8.7.

There are companies that provide all of these services, specialize in a few, or offer only one of the components. If an external source is the answer, you will be able to tap the service's experience in all the areas necessary. Finally, you own the data and, depending on your agreement, the software. The database could always be brought in-house at a future date, allowing you to develop the necessary resources over a period of time.

Database Architecture. The architecture or software in which your data are stored should be chosen based on functionality. Many people will tell you that you do not have a marketing database if you are utilizing a flat file format. The format is merely a record with the name and address and a string of information following it as shown in Exhibit 8.8.

EXHIBIT 8.7
DATABASE MARKETING COMPONENTS

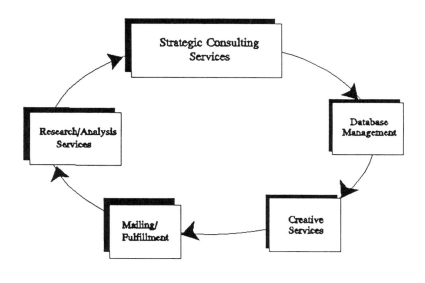

EXHIBIT 8.8
FLAT FILE DATABASE FORMAT

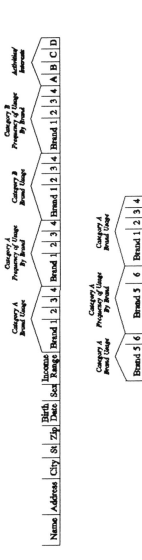

Many feel that you have to be in a table-driven or relational format to be a true database. The table-driven format links customer information by means of a set of tables. A diagram of a table-driven format is shown in Exhibit 8.9.

This format operates more efficiently than a flat file because you do not have to pass every record in the database each time you process. You search the tables to determine who should be included in the process, and then only access those that meet your specifications.

There are variations on these two formats. The flat file format can be linked by a series of indices to make it more efficient. A table-driven format can have direct on-line access. Both can reside on mainframe, mini, or personal computers.

The important criterion for deciding which software and hardware to employ is cost-effectiveness. Your objective is to be able to mine the gold from your database. To do that, you need to be able to direct the data from many different perspectives. Cost should not keep you from evaluating a potential opportunity.

Gather Data. Now that you have determined the information that should be included in the database, the source(s) of the data should be identified. Internal sources should be evaluated first due to their cost-effectiveness. The sources that are usually maintained internally are billing and inventory systems, customer service, panel or advisory boards, and mailing lists. The external sources are outlined in Exhibit 8.10.

EXHIBIT 8.9
TABLE-DRIVEN DATABASE FORMAT

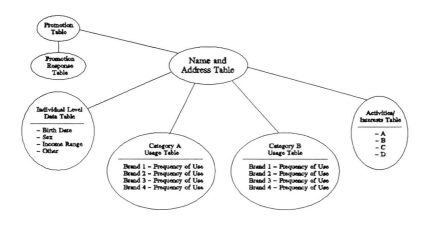

EXHIBIT 8.10
EXTERNAL SOURCES OF DATA

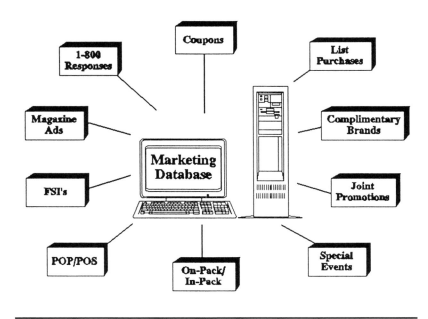

Information from promotions such as those listed above, is some-times saved. This past information should be evaluated before inclu-sion. The key is the time that has passed since the promotion. During that time, the respondents may have moved, changed brands, or entered a new stage of life.

The goal is to gather the information as cost-effectively as possi-ble. You will want to evaluate each source on the basis of cost per screened name, validity, and the time required to collect it. Some of the sources may not have all the information that you require. You may have to solicit the information from your customer or overlay the data from a syndicated source. It is very important to remember that you need individual customer-level information.

You can solicit the additional information from your customers at the time of their next purchase through a questionnaire in-pack, on-pack, or administered by a sales representative. A separate screening effort through the mail or by telephone could also be conducted at any time. The information that is gathered should be standardized across sources for ease of interpretation and implementation.

Demographics and some lifestyle information is available through syndicated sources. There are several large consumer and busi-ness databases that you can match to your database and then overlay the appropriate information on your customers' records. Some of the demographics are based on census information. In these instances, the information is carried down to the household level from either a zip code, census tract, or block group. The data assumes that the residents of a zip code, census tract, or block group are identical. Inferred data, such as census data, are not as powerful a targeting tool as actual behavior or respondent data.

Some of the most common sources of syndicated demographic or lifestyle consumer data are as follows:

- Acxiom Corporation
- Donnelley Marketing Services
- NDL
- R. L. Polk
- Database America
- Equifax

Business syndicated sources provide such information as Standard Industrial Classification (SIC) codes, total company sales, number and location of branches, and total sales. Dunn & Bradstreet has offered this type of information for many years.

Obviously, competitive customer information cannot be gathered in the same manner as information on your current customers. You will need to rely more on external sources — list purchase, mail or telephone screening, or promotions geared to bring in competitive customer information. Once again, the same information should be collected in the same format as it is with your current customers, and an overlay of syndicated data should be considered.

Clean Data. The information for your database will come most likely from multiple sources. Prior to loading the information into the database, several steps are required to "clean" the data. The first step is to place the data from the multiple sources in the same format. The name and address will be placed in the same fields, and the additional data will be given the same specific locations in each customer record.

Next, the customer names and addresses will be sent through a piece of software that standardizes the addresses according to U.S. Postal Service guidelines and corrects or adds zip codes and zip-plus-four. These changes increase the deliverability of any mailings from the database.

The next step is to eliminate duplicates. Duplicates can occur during data entry or are the result of a customer responding to more than one stimuli. When an exact duplicate has been identified, one of the records is deleted.

The final step in cleaning the data is the updating of the addresses. With more than 20 percent of all households moving every year, some of your customers will no longer be at the address contained in your information. By using the National Change of Address (NCOA), a service of the U.S. Postal Service, the addresses can be updated electronically. The source of NCOA is the change of address card you fill out to notify your mail carrier of your move.

Database Design. The first five phases provide the input for this phase. The architecture, hardware, functions, and information requirements shape the design of the database. In this phase, the actual detailed database design is completed. The design may encompass the writing of a customized database architecture or merely the customization of a licensed or off-the-shelf software package.

Tests of all functions occur during this phase. Modifications are made as necessary to meet the processing and marketing objectives.

Database Building. During this phase the information is loaded into the database. Final tests are conducted prior to the system's being released. Any further modifications are made during this time.

Care and Feeding of the Database. The value of a database is determined by two factors — the information contained on the database and the accessibility of the information. Information and accessibility are of equal importance. Imagine the right information but only a costly and tedious method of access. The converse, the wrong information but easy, affordable access, is equally as worthless. These areas were addressed in the needs assessment, function analysis, and design phases of the database building process, but they cannot be evaluated once and forgotten. Technology is in a state of constant change. Today's business environment is in an ever-increasing state of evolution. Your database will require changes over time to meet your processing and marketing objectives. Periodically, advances in pertinent technology should be reviewed. The marketing information contained on the database should be in constant review. After every program, the value of the information should be assessed. Market research should be employed on an ongoing basis to aid in this assessment. The types of market research and their purpose will be discussed in a later section.

For the information to be truly valuable, it must reflect the current environment. To maintain current information, the ongoing database marketing plan should include two methods for updating information. The first involves two of the processes described in the data cleaning phase of the database build. Addresses should be updated at a minimum on an annual basis. To supplement NCOA, you should consider requesting address corrections on all mailings. The cost of address corrections should be evaluated against the benefit. Addresses will need to be updated to meet changes in postal areas, such as zip codes and carrier routes.

The population of your database is not static. You will be adding and deleting members. Information will be updated through response to programs. The second area of maintenance accomplishes this through what are most commonly called adds and updates. An add is the process of adding new customers to the database. An update is the process of updating some part of an already existing customer record.

In an add, all steps of the cleaning process should be undertaken.

This process is similar to preparing the original names, addresses, and information for the database. You will need to make sure the "new" customer is not already on the database, a duplicate, and the data will need to be normalized to fit the database structure.

In an update, you are adding some information to an already existing customer record. The first step is to prepare the information for insertion in the database. If it is an address change, the address will need to be standardized to meet postal standards. If the information is sales, demographic, or lifestyle, the codes will need to be reviewed to determine if they match those already on the database. The second step is to locate the current record on the database and append or change the appropriate information.

Another type of update is aging. This update involves information based on time. For example, if age is a critical factor in your targeting, you would want to update a customer's age annually. Another example is recency, the time since a past purchase. To be able to update your customer information, you need a source for that information. The sales information can be captured through coupon response, rebates, refunds, or sales transactions. The competitive set, demographic, and lifestyle data may require what is called a rescreen. A rescreen involves a questionnaire or screener that is completed by the customer answering such questions as brands purchased on a regular basis, brands used most often, frequency of purchase, and demographics/pyschographics. The timing of the rescreens is dictated by how dynamic your business environment is and how critical these variables are to the performance of the database.

SHOULD TESTING BE PART OF THE PLAN?

Testing should always be part of the plan. The real question is which one of the two types of testing that should be considered. The first is the overall evaluation of the database marketing. Many times, your cost/benefit comparison will leave you in a gray area. The level of performance required from a database marketing program is the likes of which you have never seen before. At the same time, your intestinal judgment tells you there is something there. Remember that this is a new medium with pinpoint accuracy that can deliver sales results at unprecedented levels. A test can be constructed to confirm or deny your intestinal judgment. The key to constructing this test is to evaluate several alternatives for each of the key components of the program — namely target audience, list, creative, and offer. As with any effective media plan, frequency is part of the equation for success. You should test the effect of building a relationship and consider more than one mailing. A sample test matrix is shown in Table 8.3.

TABLE 8.3
TEST MATRIX

Target Audience	List Source	Creative	Offer
A	1	Newsletter	High
	2		Medium
	3	Brochure	Low
B	1	Newsletter	High
	2		Medium
	3	Brochure	Low

To determine the impact of the test, three measures should be included. Behavior is the most important variable to be measured. Response by test cell will provide the immediate reaction to the program. An estimate of incremental volume generated by the program measures the true effect of the initial reaction and can capture additional purchases tied to the program. The final measure is that of the attitudinal impact. Attitudes precede behavior. If in the attitudinal measure you find that your product or service is now favorably viewed by a group that was not predisposed to it prior to the mailing, you can anticipate that with continued communication they will try your products or service. All of these measures should be factored into the success of the program. Two questions need to be answered: Does database marketing make sense for your product or service? If so, what components were the most successful and should continue?

The second type of testing is ongoing. Direct mail organizations include a test cell in every mailing to see if they can improve on what they are currently doing. They will vary either the list, the offer, or the creative to see if they can surpass the response rate on their benchmark (most successful execution). If they do, the new execution becomes the benchmark, and the quest for an even more effective program continues. This constant testing is second nature in a medium that is as accountable as direct mail. Database marketing has this same accountability. With this medium, you can be continually fine-tuning your efforts. This does not mean that you are constantly in test mode. You are merely carving out a small portion of a large-scale program to evaluate an alternative.

HOW DO I EFFECTIVELY USE MY MARKETING DATABASE?

The first step is to develop a database marketing plan for each product or service that will utilize the database. You will want to consider long- and short-term objectives. Strategies to achieve those objectives should then be drafted. Many of the same types of strategies that are used in the mass media are appropriate for database marketing. You must keep in mind, however, the differences in the medium. These differences are not handicaps. They are opportunities.

For example, a marketing objective could be a 10 percent increase in customer loyalty. The strategy could be a continuity program covering a number of purchases. In a mass medium, you would deliver an offer in-pack, in print, or on broadcast media. For example, the offer could be to send in six proofs-of-purchase and receive a poster, seven and receive a baseball cap, and so on. All participants would receive the same offer. Typically, there would be no follow-up communication regarding the program.

In a continuity program delivered through database marketing, the alternatives are almost limitless. You can select any appropriate subgroup of your database for participation in the program. If you have been tracking loyalty, you could target a group that has been slipping or one that shows high potential for increasing its share of purchases with your company.

You are able to customize the offer based on the behavior of the target audience. You can target only customers who have recently reduced their number of purchases, as opposed to all customers who receive your mass communications. For example, one group may have purchased from you 10 times a quarter, but has now slipped to only eight purchases in a quarter. A second may have gone from eight to six purchases in a quarter. Through database marketing, you can customize a program for the first group to return to its prior purchase rate of 10 and then structure a stretch incentive to push it to 12. The second group would receive a program based on its past purchase rate of eight and a stretch objective of 10.

A series of follow-up communications can be used to support the program. In the beginning, they would elicit participation in the program. Then, the mailings could encourage meeting the various levels of the program. If, for example, the program is half over and a group of the participants is one purchase short of the first goal, the mailing could be tailored to encourage hitting the higher goal. The mailing could be personalized to include how many purchases have been made and how many more are needed to reach the higher level incentive.

The key to developing a database marketing plan is to take off the blinders of mass media. Think about your customers as individuals, not as "Women 18–34." Design plans that treat your customers the way you would if you knew them all by name.

Resources Required. If you had no prior experience, you would never develop a television commercial just because you have in-house creative capabilities. The same holds true for building a marketing database or designing and executing a database marketing program. You will need to develop the expertise in-house or form a relationship with an experienced database marketing supplier.

If the decision is to develop the expertise in-house, you must determine whether to hire experienced individuals, to train current employees, or to combine hiring and training. A combination of hiring and training is probably the best. As it was with direct marketing several years ago, there is no degree in database marketing. Colleges are not turning out trained professionals in this discipline. The training that has occurred has been in the trenches. Individuals have learned by experience — their own and those of their colleagues.

The Direct Marketing Association (DMA) and the National Center for Database Marketing do provide several single and multi-day seminars on the subject. Numerous books have been written on the discipline that can aid in training. Several of them are listed in the "Resources" section at the end of this chapter.

Even if the decision has been made to develop expertise in-house, you will probably need some outside help in executing your database marketing programs. There are two types of suppliers. The first is a full-service database marketing agency that supplies all the necessary components of database marketing, as outlined in Exhibit 8.11.

Similar to general advertising agencies, many full-service database marketing agencies will manage outside vendors to supply some of the components, such as printing and fulfillment. Generally, a full-service agency will maintain the database and provide the analytical services and the strategic consulting because the information is so important.

EXHIBIT 8.11
FULL-SERVICE DATABASE AGENCY

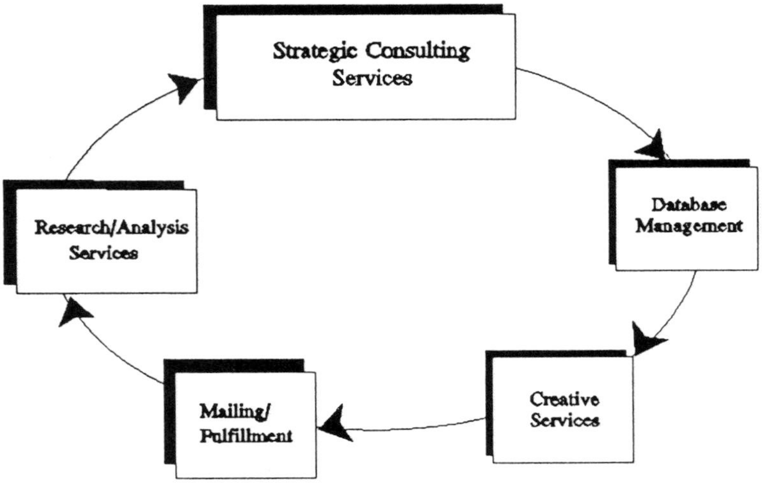

Information and the proper interpretation of that information are key to the success of a database marketing program. If correctly managed, the information will help drive your database activities. New volume opportunities will identify themselves through analysis of buying trends. Groups whose loyalty is eroding will raise their hands. In general, the database allows you to analyze your market and develop programs at the individual level. General advertising agencies that have branched into database marketing often employ a computer service bureau to maintain the database and utilize another source for analytical services.

The second type of supplier is one who specializes in one or two of the components. There are numerous consultants who specialize in database marketing. The consultants specialize in providing direction for the development of a database system and/or database marketing programs. Normally, they stop short of the execution of the plans; however, they can screen and recommend suppliers for the execution. Database marketing consultants can be very helpful in the early exploration of the medium.

Another type of specialist is a service bureau. A service bureau focuses on the systems and the data processing component. In working with these specialists, you should have a good working knowledge of your marketing and basic systems requirements.

There are numerous production suppliers that have experience in direct mail. Guided by a knowledgeable, on-staff database expert, you can use the services of a creative boutique to develop your creative product. Printers and fulfillment suppliers also provide some components of database marketing.

If multiple suppliers are your choice, a strong internal manager who has experience in database marketing will prove very valuable. Coordinating multiple suppliers will require someone who knows your company's database marketing vision and knows how to translate that vision across several entities. Database marketing is a process. Every program will provide learning that can be used to improve the next one. To maximize the value of your database marketing plan, continuity and involvement by someone from your organization at every level is key.

The checklist in Exhibit 8.12 can help you to determine which supplier is the best for you.

The Role of Research and Analysis. As stated above, the foundation of database marketing is information. For database marketing to be successful, research and analysis play a very important role. The database is rich with information that can guide you in marketing to the important group of customers that resides on it. The database tracks behavior. From time to time, it may need to be supplemented with customized research among specific groups. The customized research can help provide the reason behind the behavior. The reasons and the

---

EXHIBIT 8.12
SUPPLIER CHECKLIST

1. **Who will manage the database marketing effort?**

   What are their database marketing strengths?

   What are their database marketing weaknesses?

2. **What role do you want the supplier to play?**
   - ❏ Turnkey supplier
   - ❏ Systems supplier
   - ❏ Marketing consultant
   - ❏ Systems consultant
   - ❏ Consultant to select suppliers
   - ❏ Strategic consulting
   - ❏ Creative supplier
   - ❏ Fulfillment supplier
   - ❏ Research supplier
   - ❏ Analytical supplier

3. **What is the experience of the suppliers in your industry and in the role you would like them to play?**

4. **If the suppliers are turnkey suppliers that utilize outside resources for some of the components:**

   What are those components?

   What are the qualifications of those outside suppliers?

   How critical is an intimate understanding of those components to the success of your database marketing plan?

   Does the turnaround time for programs match your needs?

   Are the suppliers committed to database marketing or is it an add-on service?

---

associated attitudes help in the development of offers, creative, and program ideas. Custom research can help you understand if the purchases of your product were truly incremental or why an incentive did or did not work. Customer market research can even help you understand if an incentive is necessary. This information leads to more effective and efficient programs. As with any marketing program it is important to talk with your customers to better understand how to meet their needs.

Analysis of the database information plays a key role in two areas. The information on the database is the meat for a very actionable customer segmentation analysis. Traditionally, a segmentation analysis is conducted on a sample drawn from your total customers. At the conclusion of a traditional segmentation analysis, you know there are different subgroups among your entire customer base and how they differ.

You do not know where they live, and you do not have a direct line of communication with them. When the segmentation analysis is completed on your database, you do know where they live and can reach them through your database marketing communications. You can then track their reaction to your programs over time and continually refine the segments.

The second area in which analysis plays a key role is in the combining of customized research information and the information on the database. A sample of the database will be involved in a customized research study, but that information can be inferred from key characteristics and applied to a much larger population. Thus, you can enrich the database with attitudinal information to increase your understanding of all the members of your marketing database.

To be truly successful with database marketing, a strong research and analytical plot should be included in the overall plan. The research and analysis is not just a requirement during the first year. To understand your diverse and ever changing customer base, ongoing research and analysis will be required.

Common Mistakes. Probably the most common mistake is that of not capturing response to the programs at the individual level. Many times elaborate targeting up front will be negated because the response will be captured by a group code on the response vehicle. The group code is similar to the way your response vehicles now receive different codes based on the media vehicle. For example, if the database program included franchise and competitive customers, this method would result in an F1 code for the franchise group — *F* for "Franchise" and *1* for the program. This type of coding will only allow you to analyze the respondents by the predetermined groups. You will not be able to examine differences between nonrespondents and respondents. Nor will you be able to break the franchise group into subgroups, such as "bought in the last three months" or "haven't purchased in six months." Individual results are stressed because these lead to the most meaningful groups for future mailings. The individual-level results free you of the preconceived customer groups you are accustomed to and allow new customer groups to emerge.

Another common mistake when you begin using database marketing is to forget the back-end. The back-end is the pulling together of all the results of each program at the individual level. Even when the response information has been captured by individual, it can be hard to fight the old tendencies of analyzing preconceived groups and evaluating them at the individual level.

The tendency in the beginning is to view the marketing effort as a highly targeted program and evaluate response results in total to determine if the effort was a success. There will not be one response rate; there will be many different response rates. They are generated by the different target audiences and even subgroups of these different target audiences that were included in the program. In any program, there are winners and losers. For example, if your program included competitive and franchise customers, there is a response rate associated with competitive customers and another with franchise customers. Table 8.4 shows various subgroups that could be analyzed by their response rates.

TABLE 8.4
BACK-END ANALYSIS

Group	Subgroup
Franchise	Loyal franchise customers
	Franchise customers who use one other product or service (Dual)
	Franchise customers who use multiple products or services (3+)
	Competitive loyal competitive customers
	Dual competitive customers
	3+ competitive customers

Many times there is more than one way for a customer to respond. There may be multiple coupons, a coupon and a rebate offer, or a cumulative point program involving multiple purchases. A back-end analysis evaluates the breadth (total number of respondents) and depth (responding to multiple devices) of response for various groups and subgroups.

Because you have response at the individual customer level, you know who responded and who did not. Another level of analysis in the back-end work is this comparison of nonrespondents to respondents. The comparison helps you understand why a program was not appealing to the nonrespondents but was to the respondents. Differences between the two groups can be used in selection of future participants. The next program could exclude those who resemble the nonrespondents or a different, more appealing program could be offered to them.

New opportunities are discovered during the back-end analysis. The analysis of these individual results leads to revisions or discontinuance of programs. The costs of the program are compared to the value of the incremental volume generated by the program. This constant review with the ability to learn from previous efforts provides the ever-increasing efficiency of database marketing.

A final common mistake is satisfaction with the status quo. Early gains in database marketing may prove so rewarding that the hunger to market "smarter" diminishes. You overlook how fast your customers are changing.

The marketing database can keep pace with these changes, but it must constantly be evaluated and questioned. Does the database have the right information? Is the information as current as it should be? Are you letting the data talk to you? Do you have the right customers on the database? Is there another way to reduce costs? The list of questions is as endless as the quest for maximizing the value of database marketing. Truly knowing your customers provides the power to constantly improve on past performance.

THE FUTURE

Database marketing has been well served by recent advances in computer technology. Mini computers and microcomputers are handling the tasks that were once reserved for mainframes. Processing time has decreased. Many more of us marketing types are getting knee-deep in our data because of less technical interfaces, such as Apple and Microsoft Windows.

Technology will continue to shape the future of database marketing. Computer technology will continue to make strides in the data storage and processing area. These improvements will come in the form of multitask work stations, parallel processing, and wider usage of disk array. The move will continue to smaller platforms or machines. A key benefit of the movement to microcomputers (souped-up PCs) is the software that is already available and the number of companies that write software for these machines.

To move ahead, database marketing will require software that puts the marketers closer to their customers. The software will need to facilitate access and interpretation of the data by nontechnical people. The more marketers learn about their customers, the more they will want to know. The microcomputer environment has numerous packages to help the nontechnical person take advantage of the computer age. As more databases move to this platform, software will be developed to facilitate the two-way communication between marketers and customers by means of the marketing database.

Technology will affect database marketing in other arenas. The first is printing. Great strides have been made in developing truly personalized packages in cost-efficient, on-line systems. Addresses can trigger the imaging of a map showing the retail location closest to a customer. Coupon values can be varied from one customer to another based on purchase behavior. Copy can be adjusted to address the benefits that are key to one household against another.

Imaging technology will continue to improve. What if the logos, illustrations, and photos could be imaged package by package? A completely variable package might be achieved through four-color imaging. No longer would you need multiple press runs to customize a package for a certain audience. The marketing database would drive the development for a package customized to each customer's needs.

In the future, unlimited selective insertion will result in mass production of mail packages that have as many variations as your customer has needs. For example, if a large consumer packaged goods company wanted to do a mailing across its brands of pet food, diapers, and detergents, only a household that had a dog or a cat or a child in diapers would receive all three coupons. If there was a household with a dog and no child in the diaper-wearing ages, only a detergent and dog food promotional piece would be included.

This production capability will benefit more than just cooperative programs. Imagine a business-to-business, large-scale mailing that requires specification sheets and brochures for a number of products. On-line production of this piece could accommodate the information requirements of all your customers. To meet those requirements today, collation and insertion by hand or sending everyone every specification sheet and brochure is required. Mailings will be more effective and more affordable because they will contain only relevant information and will be produced in a mass production environment.

The final area of database marketing that will benefit from technology is that of communications. Currently, the message is primarily carried to the customer through the mail. Some database marketing applications use 800 numbers and interactive telecommunications to capture customer information to be added to the database. In the future, new communications channels will be available to database marketers. One of these is interactive television.

A company by the name of TV Answer is developing a two-way communications tool that works through your television. The technology is similar to a cellular telephone network. Radio waves transmit signals between users' home units and central cell sites. The information can then be transmitted via satellites to TV Answer's headquarters and other designated destinations.

A customer will be able to request product information, check bank balances, and transfer funds. TV Answer will even have a direct link for ordering different products, such as catalog items, delivered food, flowers, and distilled spirits. The service will introduce interactive programming. The viewers will play along with sporting events and voice their opinions on news and talk-show programs.

In the beginning, direct communication by marketers to only certain customers will not be available. Marketers will be able to gather more information for their databases through the customers' requests through TV Answer. Imagine a prime-time network television commercial for Jeep Cherokee. Every household can view the commercial, but only TV Answer households can react to it instantaneously. Their screen will have a menu of actions from which to choose. Viewers could request that a salesperson give them a call or that a brochure be sent out. This information is communicated to Chrysler, and a sales lead for a new Jeep Cherokee has been generated.

Another use of the service is the capturing of new members for your marketing database. Questions regarding brand and service preferences can be answered, and the information can be added to the database. As the technology progresses, marketers may be able to communicate selectively with households in the interactive program.

Privacy issues can have a positive or negative effect on the future of database marketing. If direct and database marketers continue to respect the customer's right to privacy and only use information to better serve, the impact will be positive. The Direct Marketing Association (DMA) and its members are active in self-regulation regarding the use of sensitive information. The DMA has a service called Mail Preference Service. You can request that your name be taken off all mailing lists. Members of the DMA then use this list to delete individuals who are not interested in receiving direct mail.

Database marketing will continue to evolve as changes in technology bring marketers closer to their customers. Information will become easier to obtain, and the methods of interpreting it will become even more sophisticated. Developments in communication will facilitate the direct communication and relationship-building of old.

RESOURCES

Organizations:
Direct Marketing Association (DMA)
11 West 42nd Street
New York, NY 10036-8096
(212) 768-7277

National Center for Database Marketing
109 58th Avenue
St. Petersburg Beach, FL 33706
(813) 367-5629

Books:
Maximarketing
Stan Rapp and Tom Collins
McGraw-Hill Book Company, New York, 1987

The Great Marketing Revolution
Stan Rapp and Tom Collins
McGraw-Hill Book Company, New York, 1990

Relationship Marketing
Regis McKenna
Addison-Wesley Publishing Co., Inc.; Reading, MA; 1991

Integrated Direct Marketing
Ernan Roman
McGraw-Hill Book Company, New York, 1988

Publications:
Target Marketing
North American Publishing Co.
401 N. Broad St.
Philadelphia, PA 19108

Direct
Cowles Business Media, Inc.
911 Hope Street
Six River Bend Center
Box 4949
Stamford, CT 06907-0949

DM News
Mill Hollow Corp.
19 W. 21st St.
New York, NY 10010

Neil L. Fraser's experience with co-op advertising goes back over 30 years to his work with a distributor of General Electric and Sunbeam appliances. While with the distributor, Fraser helped develop pioneering distributor/dealer co-op advertising programs. Fraser left that post to join an Atlanta advertising agency as an account executive. He became the firm's Vice President before organizing Fraser Advertising, Inc., in 1963.

As an advertising agency executive, Fraser has worked on many different types of co-op advertising. He developed and administered distributor/dealer programs on local and national levels for brand name products such as Carrier Air Conditioning, RCA Television, Whirlpool Appliances, Westinghouse Appliances, and Magnavox Television. His industrial co-op experience includes programs for distributors of Caterpillar Tractors and International Construction Equipment. He developed and is current administrator of the Network Services Authorized Sales Representative co-op programs for Southern Bell and South Central Bell. In addition to conventional vertical co-op programs, Fraser has set up horizontal co-op advertising campaigns for several clients.

Fraser has written on the subject of co-op advertising for many different trade publications. A Glossary of Cooperative Advertising was developed by Fraser and published in 1984 by Commerce Communications. He has been a speaker on co-op at meetings around the country and abroad. His educational work in this specialized area was recognized in 1988 when he was named one of the six original members of the Co-op Hall of Fame.

CHAPTER 9

CO-OP ADVERTISING

COOPERATIVE ADVERTISING'S PLACE IN MARKETING

Cooperative or co-op advertising is the sharing of advertising costs between mutually interested businesses, usually retailers and their suppliers. The basis for co-op goes back to 1903, when the Warner Brothers Company, makers of Warners Rust Proof Corsets, issued the first known co-op plan. Today's marketers will find Warner's words to be familiar:

> One of our chief helps in promoting the sale of our corsets is to assist you locally in bringing the particular styles you carry to the eye of your customer through local means.

In an advertising brochure dated 1907, Warner told its retailers that cooperation is:

> … a word that has become inseparably associated with our selling plans. It means that we work with you and for you in enlarging your corset business if you work with us and for us. This cooperative advertising that you and we do together naturally advertises our corsets as well as your shop.

As Warner so accurately stated at the beginning of the century, cooperative advertising serves the mutual needs of manufacturers and retailers for local advertising. Why is this local advertising needed? Because it is a valuable force in moving merchandise and meeting competition. Without the advertising that co-op helps to provide, most merchants are at a disadvantage in the retail arena, with resulting lost sales and lost profits.

Since the turn of the century, co-op has earned a secure place in the marketing of goods and services. Today, the use of this advertising and promotional technique is increasing, and its role in marketing is becoming more important.

While there are no reliable statistics on the amount of money spent each year on co-op advertising, estimates suggest that in retailing, co-op funding supports more than 20 percent of all advertising expenditures. Co-op also is used to advertise and promote the sale of industrial products and in the marketing of services. Across a wide range of industries, shared advertising cost is vital to the success of both large and small businesses in almost every segment of our economy.

To understand co-op's role in advertising and its importance in the sale of goods and services, you must examine those elements that make up a co-op advertising program and the motivation behind them, beginning with the manufacturer-retailer relationship. Most co-op dollars are spent within this vertical chain of production, distribution, and sales. The vertical co-op chain starts when a manufacturer establishes a program, either at the retail or wholesale level, to support local advertising and sales promotion by offering to pay part, or even all, of the cost. As part of this support, the manufacturer also may provide material for use in the retailer's advertising or sales promotion programs. The co-op support is not unconditional. There are usually extensive rules with the co-op offer to be sure that the retailer or wholesaler actually advertises or promotes the manufacturer's products.

A manufacturer's conventional advertising is a responsibility of its advertising department. Media used, timing, and content are under complete control. The manufacturer's co-op advertising is under the control of a customer, the retailer, who usually decides on timing, media used, and advertising content, within the restrictions of the manufacturer's co-op policy. In addition, the retailer's advertising will usually have a feature lacking in the manufacturer's advertising: price and where to buy.

Manufacturers who run conventional advertising campaigns in the mass media (television, radio, newspapers, magazines) are pre-selling to create demand. Their intent is to make customers go to retail stores to look for the advertised products. Such advertising does not identify specific places where the products are sold and gives pricing only in the familiar "suggested retail" form. Manufacturers' advertising may also be intended to create consumer demand so retailers will want to sell the advertised products.

Since co-op advertising runs at the level where products are being sold, its intent is to attract customers into specific stores by identifying products with prices and a retail location. Those products have already been purchased by the retail store, and may or may not have been "presold" by the manufacturers' advertising.

Co-op and the Law. When a manufacturer offers co-op funds or assistance to a retailer, our unique antitrust laws become involved. Those laws started with the Sherman Act of 1890, a move to break up the cartels and trusts that controlled the economy of that period. There were loopholes in the Sherman Act that were closed by the Clayton Act of 1914. But the Clayton Act overlooked one very large loophole: advertising and promotional allowances. During the 1920s big retailers used that loophole to gain price advantages from their suppliers and stifle competition from smaller stores. The worst offenders in this area were the grocery chains, with the A&P being the most aggressive and visible offender. In 1936 the Robinson-Patman Act passed, specifically prohibiting discriminatory practices when using promotional allowances in the sale of commodities in interstate commerce. The laws do not apply to intrastate commerce or to the sale of anything but commodities. Those three pieces of legislation are known as our "antitrust laws." They are intended to prevent discriminatory pricing and price fixing and to maintain open and competitive free trade. Since the provision of co-op money for advertising and promotion reduces advertising and promotion expense, it affects the price at which a product sells at retail. That is why the antitrust laws regulate co-op advertising and all promotional allowances.

In 1969, a landmark ruling by the U.S. Supreme Court ordered the Federal Trade Commission to lay down guidelines for the use of advertising and promotional allowances. Those guidelines, known as the "Meyer Guides," define the rules of co-op advertising. Anyone involved in the use of co-op and promotional allowances should have a copy of these guides, which can be obtained from the Federal Trade Commission.

As a result of the antitrust laws and the court decision, co-op advertising and promotional allowances are almost universal in our marketing system. The laws have helped in assuring that co-op funds are available to all retail outlets that sell products whose manufacturers offer co-op and in making that co-op proportionally equal to the co-op given to other competing retail customers. In other free market economies, where there are no such laws, co-op is still offered on an arbitrary and unfair basis.

Co-op's Basic Conflict. A basic conflict of interest in the co-op system is revealed on examination of the motives behind manufacturer and retailer advertising programs. Manufacturers want advertising to boost sales of the products they make, regardless of where those products are sold. Retailers run advertising to bring people into their stores to buy whatever they sell, not necessarily the items shown in advertising.

When manufacturers fund retail advertising through co-op programs, bringing traffic into a store, the retailer may sell another manufacturer's products. Taking that chance is part of the co-op picture. The two conflicting sales goals have successfully coexisted for many years, even if they have been a source of friction between the co-op parties.

Internal Co-op Conflict. Budgeting advertising funds for co-op can produce internal conflict at the manufacturer's level, with a tug-of-war over allocation of dollars between national and local advertising programs. While co-op sometimes wins the money, national advertising has all the glamor and usually gets all the creative efforts. Co-op, on the other hand, is frequently produced by in-house advertising departments working with sales personnel and receiving little management attention. Co-op is, nevertheless, a real marketing workhorse, and its importance cannot be overemphasized.

Co-op's Influence on the Sale of Various Products. The types of products or services sold influence the value of co-op and determine its application. The sale of basic products — basic products available everywhere, such as razor blades, soap, and toothpaste — are less likely to depend on co-op funds for promotion or advertising. The sale of these products, where prices are too low for sustained local advertising by individual retailers, usually depends on manufacturer advertising in mass media, packaging, or point-of-purchase displays. Retailers of higher-cost merchandise, such as appliances, clothes, or home furnishings, are more likely to use co-op.

Selling higher-priced products also is more dependent on the ability of retail outlets to identify with brand names through local advertising and to feature the prices and locations at which those are sold. The importance of co-op in the marketing mix can be roughly divided between product categories as shown in Table 9.1.

There are, of course, exceptions to these examples. Co-op is used in the marketing of many low unit-cost products sold in groceries and drugstores, where it is frequently provided in the form of point-of-purchase material instead of advertising dollars. Co-op also is an important element in the local advertising of hardware stores, automotive parts stores, and in the retail advertising of brand name food products run by grocery chains. Co-op advertising for low unit-cost items usually appears in so-called "omnibus" ads containing a variety of products. Newspapers are filled with such advertising by chains. Much of that advertising is by their suppliers.

How Co-op Is Provided. Most co-op programs assign funds for local advertising based on the amount of their customers' purchases. The most commonly used system is that of the percentage accrual, in which a percentage factor assigned to retailer purchases accrues in a co-op account and is available for use in co-op advertising.

TABLE 9.1

Co-op Is Less Important	Co-op Plays a Significant Role
Convenience goods	Items shopped for, such as clothing
Mass-merchandised packaged goods	Infrequent purchases
Impulse purchase items	Appliances and home entertainment
Self-selling products	Furniture and durable goods
Utilitarian products	High brand-loyalty products
Easily understood products	Technical products
Low-cost items	Specialty products or services
Everyday items	Hobby or recreational products
High-cost items	Ego-enhancing goods

Another form of co-op funding is the promotion or unit allowance, extensively used in the marketing of packaged goods, groceries, pharmaceuticals, and products for the automotive aftermarket. This type of co-op funding automatically allocates promotional money on cases, dozens, pounds, or any other unit factor, at the time of the product's purchase.

The promotional or unit allowance and accrual co-op are parallel marketing tools, but the marketing motivation behind each one's use may be quite different. Accrual co-op, tied directly to the dollar value of a retailer's past or most recent purchases, is an after-sale device intended to help the retailer move the supplier's products out of the store. A specific co-op advertising commitment by the retailer is part of the accrual plan. Unit allowances are generally presale marketing tools intended to get merchandise into a retail establishment. Making an advertising commitment on the retailer's part is not always required to get the allowance, which is available as soon as the purchase is completed.

The least complicated of all co-op funding is the "open-ended" system. Here the supplier matches the retailer's expenditures without limits as long as the advertising or promotion helps the sale of its products. Most co-op suppliers fear the lack of control that an open-ended policy implies. Yet a carefully structured policy of this kind can be the most effective way of applying co-op.

Manufacturers' Use of Co-op. A general insight into exactly why manufacturers use co-op is demonstrated by the following list of the reasons they give when asked about the purpose of their co-op programs:

- Building sales for the most profitable product line
- Supporting the most profitable product line
- Building sales for a weaker product line
- Introducing a new product
- Meeting competitors' efforts
- Leveling out peaks and valleys of demand by timing of program
- Acceding to requests of retailers, wholesalers, distributors, and others
- Building sales in a particular region
- Heightening brand awareness
- Controlling local ad content
- Stretching advertising budgets

Most suppliers offering co-op do so for one or more of these specific reasons. On the average, however, fewer than half have systems in place with which to measure the effectiveness of their co-op programs in accomplishing their stated goals.

MANUFACTURERS' GOALS IN CO-OP ADVERTISING

By taking the responses given by manufacturers as their reasons for having co-op programs, each area of co-op motivation can be analyzed.

Building Sales. Increasing sales is an easily recognized basis for any advertising or promotion program. The statement is modified to include "our most profitable product line." Co-op is not so limiting, and may be offered to support a manufacturer's complete line of products, sometimes with the intention of making an unprofitable line into a profitable one.

Exactly how does co-op act to build sales? The movement of products at the retail level is influenced by the support of co-op programs that supply both advertising money and promotional assistance. A manufacturer may advertise and promote products at the national level, but unless customers know where and at what price they can buy those products, the national advertising will have little effect. To bridge that gap, manufacturers offer co-op to their retailers.

Co-op also has extended effects that increase its selling potential. Co-op advertising at the local level serves to identify a retailer with a product line and a brand name. That retailer becomes recognized as a source of a manufacturer's products, and this recognition has a durability that goes beyond individual ads. In addition, many co-op programs seek to further solidify local ties. They do so through sharing in the cost of signs, Yellow Pages listings, uniforms, truck painting, in-store displays, and other ways of linking retailers to manufacturers and brand names. A retailer's investment in brand identification makes it more difficult to buy competing brands and builds repeat orders for the co-op supplier.

Another way in which co-op builds sales is through its influence over other retailers in the same market area. Stores check the advertising of their competitors very closely. A strong co-op advertising program, visible to competing stores, can open the door to a manufacturer's rep and help in securing new sales outlets. Co-op advertising run by strong retailers also can serve as an "umbrella" for smaller retailers. Customers seeing ads run by large stores may look for the same products at retailers in their neighborhoods. A co-op campaign run by major department stores featuring a brand name product will frequently produce traffic for smaller stores selling the same product.

Supporting Most Profitable Products. The qualification of "most profitable product line" is another important aspect of co-op. Many suppliers give this factor as a sole justification for offering co-op support. Many manufacturers feel that most of their profits come from specific segments of their product line and that all advertising and marketing efforts should promote these products. The remaining products may be less profitable but still necessary as part of the mixture required by the marketplace. An example of such a situation would be a manufacturer who produces four different models of an appliance simply to meet the overall need of the market and be recognized as a full-line supplier, knowing that 75 percent of sales and profits is going to come from only two of those models. The manufacturer might well limit a co-op program to the two models accounting for 75 percent of sales because the other two models, with perhaps specialized applications, do not warrant co-op support.

Boosting a Weak Product Line. Co-op can be very useful in strengthening a weak product line. When research or field reports indicate a line should have a greater market share based on product features and consumer demand, special co-op programs help improve the picture. Channeling funds into advertising and promotional support for the weak line can produce the extra local exposure needed to increase sales and make the product line more appealing to retailers. Such co-op support might take various forms, including increased cost sharing, reduction of restrictions on local ads, or even paying all the retailers' advertising costs. Because of its flexibility as a marketing tool, co-op is a problem solver in this and many other marketing situations.

Introducing New Products. Co-op is used to launch new products in much the same way it is used to boost weak product lines. The promotion of new products is a far more common application of the co-op concept than is the practice of strengthening weak products. An enhanced co-op program is almost a necessity when placing new items on the retail market. In some cases product introduction turns out to be a manufacturer's first venture into co-op after finding that wholesalers and retailers will not accept the new line without a supporting promotional program.

Meeting the Competition. Having a co-op program that equals or surpasses one that is offered by the competition should be an important part of any sales strategy. A strong and well-organized scheme of advertising support can be as important as the features of the product line itself when retailer buyers are deciding which lines to carry and promote. On the other hand, the inadequacy of a co-op program can turn retailers toward competing suppliers who are willing to provide the kind of help needed in the marketplace.

Unfortunately, many co-op programs rest entirely on the "we do it because the competition does" principle. Simply having a co-op program because it is an industry practice is like wearing a suit because everyone else wears one, without considering fashion, color, cut, and all the other ways clothing can improve appearance and make a good impression on others.

Leveling Sales by Timing. One of co-op's tangible advantages is the supplier's ability to time advertising emphasis to take advantage of seasonal demands or to compensate for off-season slumps. Examples of seasonal advertising efforts can be seen in the traditional emphasis placed by the toy industry on pre-Christmas promotions. As a result, this industry has suffered from off-season inventory costs and cash flow problems. Toy manufacturers now try to increase promotional activity at other times of the year to level out sales. The home comfort industry places co-op emphasis on the preseason advertising of air conditioning and heating equipment. Co-op also is used for seasonal emphasis in the marketing of sporting goods and recreational products. Whenever timing is a factor in selling, co-op programs can be adjusted to meet marketing requirements.

Meeting the Requests of Retailers and Wholesalers. Since co-op has become an integral part of our marketing system, wholesalers and retailers ask for and sometimes demand co-op from their suppliers. Buyers habitually pressure sales representatives for co-op before purchasing their goods. When those salespeople represent companies that do not offer co-op and find that they are losing sales, they apply pressure on management to provide the needed assistance. It is at this point that many co-op programs are born.

Building Sales by Region. Co-op has the additional advantage of being the type of advertising that can be used selectively by region as a market-strengthening device.

Co-op plans may vary to meet the demands of different markets. If a supplier has a low level of sales in a particular area, extra co-op funds can be channeled into that area as a way to increase sales promotion activity. The same co-op program enhancements used to launch new products or to strengthen weak product lines can apply when trying to improve regional sales. In these cases, many co-op programs go beyond "sweetening the co-op pot" by tailoring campaigns and advertising messages to offset specific weaknesses in given areas and by supplementing advertising with displays, sales incentive programs, or signs. In addition, market-building programs often employ extra advertising run entirely by the manufacturer or distributor that is tied directly to an increased level of retailer advertising — that is, if retailers agree to run a certain amount of advertising based on normal co-op, the supplier agrees to run additional advertising at no cost to the retailers. Co-op policies can be adjusted to allow for factors such as the higher rates paid for advertising in metropolitan markets by underwriting some of the additional costs.

Heightening Brand Awareness. While few manufacturers give brand awareness as a reason for offering co-op, this may be because the idea is completely accepted and is no longer a prime consideration.

When looking only at numbers, national and mass media advertising can give a manufacturer both product and brand name exposure at very low cost. Yet seeing the manufacturer's products and brand name in a local newspaper or hearing them advertised on a local radio or TV station in direct connection with a local merchant is important to the overall impression made on the consuming public. Local ads not only tell the customer where to buy and at what price, but they give the significant extra impact of bringing a selling message close to home, increasing consumer confidence in both the manufacturer and the product. Even when no substantial sales result directly from the local advertising, consistent efforts will leave a lasting impression on the market area.

Control of Advertising. Co-op has always produced a struggle between the parties involved over control of the advertising funded under the terms of the co-op agreement. When supporting local advertising, suppliers want to exercise some degree of control over spending and over the content of the advertising. The majority of manufacturers offering co-op place limitations on the media used, and many carefully watch the content of retail level ads as well. Industry trends currently show that suppliers are continually increasing their control over co-op usage.

Considering the large sums of money involved, co-op controls are justified. But restrictions in a co-op policy can be carried too far, making a co-op plan so inflexible that it becomes useless in practical application. Providing market flexibility while retaining necessary control is a primary goal in good co-op planning.

The struggle over who controls co-op, manufacturers or retailers, will always be an underlying element of discord in all co-op advertising, whether or not the policies are flexible. Retailers feel that they know their markets and should be able to decide which advertising is best for their stores. Manufacturers feel that they should direct their co-op so that local advertising conforms to the goals of overall marketing strategies. The conflict is a basic one: retailers trying to use co-op to promote a place of business and suppliers using co-op to sell a brand name or product line. Which party comes out ahead in the power struggle usually depends on who can exert the most financial leverage. Large retailers and chains usually get their way unless dealing with suppliers who are strong enough to resist, while smaller retailers have to live within the limits imposed by co-op policies.

The small retailer, in fact, sometimes stands to benefit from controlled co-op. Many advertising programs pool dealer funds for greater impact on a market. Some wholesalers, for instance, manage entire programs by establishing a fund from available retailer co-op to be used for advertising throughout that wholesaler's territory, benefitting all sales outlets in that territory.

Many manufacturer- and wholesaler-controlled programs bill participating retailers only for their share of the cost, thus avoiding paperwork and the traditional co-op paradox of having customers send bills to suppliers. There are other controlled co-op systems in which advertising itself, in the form of packages of radio or television spots, newspaper space, or billboards, is offered to retailers instead of co-op funding. Such programs are directed by suppliers with minimum input from the retailers involved.

The development of so-called "vendor support" advertising gives co-op a new twist. This type of co-op program is produced by retail chains putting together entire promotional packages, then enlisting (or demanding) the support of their suppliers.

Co-op interests large retailing organizations primarily for the money it provides to pay for their advertising, and they resist any sort of co-op policy restrictions. It is not unusual to see products in department store ads identified with their manufacturers only in the body copy. This occurs even when those manufacturers' co-op policies say that brand names and logos must be prominent for the advertising to qualify for co-op.

Another method now used by large retailers and chains to gain control of co-op money is that of turning their catalogs into advertising media in which space is "sold" to vendors. In this fashion, stores can often get around a co-op policy's funding requirements based on allowances or accruals on purchases. Partially because catalogs supply extra money from the manufacturers, the use of this advertising medium currently ranks second only to the use of newspapers.

Two more parties are active participants in the struggle for co-op funds at the retail level: the media and advertising agencies. Newspapers, the traditional co-op media, are losing ground to catalogs and flyers and to broadcast media. Advertising agencies, which once stayed away from retail advertising, are becoming increasingly involved in co-op and in both regional and national co-op programs for their clients. In addition, strong retailing chains, frequently aided by advertising agencies, are pushing hard to get more "vendor support" to supplement their advertising programs. Broadcast sales management is also aware of the extra advertising dollars co-op can bring in. Many TV and radio stations have co-op coordinators on their staffs to work on developing retail advertising and helping local merchants to get extra co-op funds.

Finally, there is the growth of cable television together with the changes it brings to retail marketing through specialized programming and the ability to localize coverage. As technology changes and laws against cable monopolies take effect, new ways to advertise and sell at retail are around the corner. These will include interactive systems for in-home shopping and electronic "Yellow Pages." Vendor co-op support will be a part of this new advertising field.

Stretching Advertising Budgets. The importance of cost-efficiency is far down the line in any survey of manufacturer motivation for using co-op. Yet co-op is an advertising bargain. When advertising in newspapers, for example, manufacturers have only to look at the difference in the rates they pay, the so-called national rates, and the local rates paid by retailers, to realize that space bought under co-op agreements can increase advertising levels. Local broadcast time, too, is often a more economical buy at the local level than at the national level. When retailer participation becomes part of the program, advertising dollars are stretched even farther.

There are exceptions to this principle. Some manufacturers will pay their retailers 100 percent of a national newspaper rate just to get local advertising, preferring to have the advertising run over a retailer's name even with no cost advantage. In the packaged goods industry, advertising allowances are provided merely for having products featured in an ad, with the allowance bearing no relation to the cost of the ad space. Since there are sound marketing considerations in each case, co-op still serves its basic purpose.

Co-op programs can also be "tuned" for cost-efficiency. With the computer data now available on advertising rates, co-op can change market by market, with sharing based on actual advertising costs in each location. Manufacturers and service bureaus are becoming increasingly sophisticated in the techniques of cost-efficient co-op administration.

Summary. To be successful in the marketplace, co-op advertising has to meet the goals of both manufacturers and retailers by creating demand for a product and bringing buyers into the stores where it is being sold. Manufacturers want to sell their products; retailers want traffic coming into their store to buy any product sold there.

From the manufacturers' standpoint, co-op can perform all the many marketing tasks mentioned: boosting weak products, launching new products, strengthening weak markets, timing promotional emphasis, meeting the advertising demands of wholesalers and retailers, establishing control over local advertising, and extending advertising budgets. In accomplishing these goals, co-op can go far beyond the funding of local advertising programs for retailers. Co-op can share the cost of many other promotional expenses such as in-store demonstrations, audiovisual aids, displays, packaging, coupons, contests and prizes, premiums, bonuses, and sales incentives. The range of co-op application is almost unlimited, extending to such exotic retail promotion devices as inflatables, laser skywriting, rolling billboards, or any other conceivable method of tying a product name and a retail source together.

Co-op is now used in more ways than ever before and is increasingly important to both manufacturers and retailers. The amount of money spent for local retail advertising, much of it funded by co-op, continues to grow each year. However, with the rising cost of advertising, the amount of additional exposure gained is not proportionate to the increase in expenditures. This fast-rising cost factor makes it necessary that co-op programs be even more effective and efficient, placing future emphasis on co-op's value in the marketing of both consumer and industrial products.

RETAILER GOALS IN CO-OP ADVERTISING

Here are some statements often made by retailers when asked how they feel about co-op advertising:

Co-op is too much trouble. I wouldn't use it if it weren't for the money.

I love it!

Co-op is a curse; stores are too dependent on the money, advertising only the merchandise that comes with the largest number of co-op dollars.

Viewpoints as divergent as these are not uncommon when talking about co-op to anyone in retailing. The first opinion, however, reflects the essence of co-op at the retailer level — money to fund advertising. The use of that money may be as variable as the world of retailing itself, but it forms part of the two basic reasons why most retailers want co-op: getting money to fund advertising and to extend store promotion budgets and getting help with the creation and expansion of store advertising programs. Within those two frameworks — funding and promotional assistance — co-op must fit the basic needs of retail advertising. These common goals include the following:

1. Creative and timely advertising programs that will enhance the image of the stores involved and bring customer traffic into those stores.
2. Advertising of products that are needed and wanted in the store's market area at prices that are competitive and attractive to consumers.
3. Linking of stores to brand name products, frequently through advertising and promotional programs that coincide with national or regional promotions on the part of the vendors.

Except to exclusive dealerships, brand recognition is least important to the retailer. Good retail advertising is structured on offering merchandise that people want to buy, not on co-op dollars. Retailers who carry a variety of merchandise may find it impossible to use all the co-op available from their many suppliers, choosing to advertise only products they feel will produce traffic in their stores.

Co-op as a Money Source. Estimates on how much of the co-op money made available by manufacturers, distributors, and other vendors is spent are varied and unreliable. Media organizations like to talk about the huge sums of co-op dollars that are left "on the table," with concurrent scrambling to get at those elusive dollars.

Current estimates of co-op funding place the amount available in the broad range of $12 to $20 billion annually, which gives an idea of the vast importance co-op holds as a source of advertising funds.

Unquestionably, poor communication between suppliers and customers, combined with ignorance about co-op application, means that fewer co-op dollars are spent than are technically available. But co-op is not a handout nor an open bank account; it is a practical marketing device that is valuable under certain conditions.

As the parties to co-op arrangements (vendors, retailers, and wholesalers) work out better and more effective methods of co-op application, the amount of co-op money spent will increase in relation to the amount that is technically available but never used.

Who spends most of the available co-op funds is a better documented area of marketing information. The large retailing organizations spend most of the co-op money available from their suppliers. Approximately 200 retailers account for some 65 percent of all retail advertising dollars and a correspondingly high percentage of available co-op money.

Co-op and the Big Retailers. To the large organizations who dominate retailing, co-op is primarily a money source. These stores seldom buy merchandise solely on the basis of co-op, but among vendors competing for the business of these large retailers, those having the best or the most flexible co-op programs will be favored.

It is not unusual for a major retailing organization to have an advertising budget that runs into hundreds of millions of dollars annually. Nor is it unlikely that 25 percent of that budget will come from co-op suppliers.

Manufacturers dealing with such retailing giants as Woolworth's, JC Penney, Kmart, Wal Mart, and others must set up co-op programs that fit in with the planning and logistics involved in major promotional efforts. Woolworth's, for instance, includes co-op in the planning and preparation of more than 50 tabloids each year, each with a circulation of more than 15 million, produced in 26 different printing plants across the country.

Handling the major production tasks of programs such as Woolworth's tabloids requires making advertising plans far in advance of actual ad dates. To do their planning, retailers such as Woolworth's expect to have the financial and material commitment of their suppliers from six to eight months ahead of time. Co-op programs unable to make this kind of commitment run the risk of having the products they sell omitted from the advertising programs of large retailing firms.

Collecting co-op money becomes another major task when it assumes the scale found in large organizations. Large retailers can carry millions of dollars in co-op receivables on their books, with many of them 90 to 120 days old. The failure of manufacturers to promptly process retailer claims for co-op can lead to the failure of their co-op programs and negate much of the efforts made by their sales forces. It also can lead to the very common problem of off-invoice deductions for co-op funds without proper claims and documentation, an administrative nightmare.

Large retailers look to their vendors for the same co-op terms: policies that allow products to be featured within the stores' advertising formats, commitments for funding and support far in advance of actual advertising dates, and prompt payment of co-op claims with a minimum of paperwork.

Co-op's Benefits for Smaller Retailers. A good example of what a small retailer can do with co-op money from suppliers can be found in the example of a small clothing store in Cape Cod, Massachusetts. In 1974, the store had an advertising budget of $15,000. Co-op was a minor part of that budget, with only about $2,000 coming from suppliers. The decision was made to adopt a more aggressive advertising program and to seek out co-op funds that might be available by querying all the store's suppliers. The result was the expansion of a $15,000 ad budget to $28,000 using funds from more than 100 different co-op plans.

Another example is an air-conditioning contractor in Augusta, Georgia, who launched his business with advertising that made him, within five years, the largest contractor in the area just by aggressive use of co-op funding from his primary brand name supplier. The contractor, realizing that his competitors were not advertising, even though they had available co-op money, mounted a concentrated television, newspaper, and billboard program that quickly established the name of his business and linked it firmly with the well-known name of the manufacturer he represented, producing a rush of business. Without the strong co-op support this contractor received, his company could not have grown so quickly in so short a time.

Extra Market Effects from Co-op. The air-conditioning contractor's success story has a secondary twist that illustrates the influence co-op can have on an entire market. The contractor's highly visible advertising program spurred his formerly dormant competitors into mounting vigorous advertising efforts using co-op from their suppliers. The result was a tremendous increase in the sale of air-conditioning equipment in the Augusta area. Consumers benefitted from more competitive pricing, and the media were the beneficiaries of many extra advertising dollars.

This air-conditioning contractor's initial co-op advertising efforts and later joint advertising programs involving a group of dealers selling the same brand of equipment did not come about just from co-op funding. The planning and coordination of the advertising were largely the work of the manufacturer's distributor sales force. The sales staff made the dealers aware of what could be done with co-op and worked with them every step of the way. This brings up another important element in good co-op programs: the partnership that develops between the supplier and the retailer in achieving their common goals of increased sales. Like any good business partnership, the successful co-op arrangement takes effort by all concerned.

Co-op Limitations on Retailers. Success stories, such as those of the clothing store and the air-conditioning contractor, abound in the examination of co-op's application in marketing. Co-op is, however, sometimes as capable of limiting a retailer's advertising as it is of expanding it. The majority of co-op programs in use today run contrary to a basic rule of marketing — namely, that advertising and sales promotion should generate sales. Instead, with the accrual system, the programs use the level of a retailer's purchases to determine co-op funding. It is a convenient accounting device used in some form by more than 70 percent of all the U.S. manufacturers who offer co-op to their customers. It is also a device that retailers do not like for the very reason stated: advertising plans are tied to current or past purchases and not to potential sales. The accrual system not only inhibits retail advertising planning, but also frequently puts co-op money where it is not required and starves developing market areas of needed promotional funds. Building flexibility into the co-op accrual system can help avoid these problems. Money can be assigned before purchases are made based on previous purchasing levels. In new markets, or for new dealers, initial funding can be introduced based on anticipated sales, with accruals allowed to catch up as the retailer's business develops.

Co-op and Grocery Retailing. Even in this introductory examination of co-op, it is worth separating grocery retailing from other types of retailing. Once again those unreliable but ubiquitous estimates say that the grocery trade spends 60 percent of all co-op money. Grocery retailing has undergone significant changes, with today's supermarkets carrying a tremendous variety of nongrocery items. This product mix brings more co-op plans into their marketing pictures. At the same time, the grocery industry is faced with intense competition and marginal profits. The industry has tried to increase the cost-effectiveness of advertising and promotion as a partial answer to its problems; consequently, there is more extensive use of co-op.

Grocery retailers are now employing co-op in new and different ways and are aggressively seeking additional funds from their suppliers. Many suppliers have, in turn, altered co-op plans to make those plans more useful to the grocery trade and have developed special co-op programs just for grocery marketing. Packaged goods manufacturers have, for instance, reduced a customary dependence on national advertising for demand effect and have turned toward providing their grocery customers with co-op programs that will provide more localized advertising. Part of this shift has involved the increasing use of television in grocery store advertising. Sales messages similar to those in nationally run television ads can be used at the local level. On the other hand, the traditional grocery store newspaper ad contained little more than product name and price. A "donut" is a prerecorded commercial with a "hole" in the middle to insert current information. For example, a supermarket that advertises frequently will produce a donut spot to highlight its products on sale each week. The commercial is standard except for the inserted message. Donut commercials save money by eliminating the need to produce a new commercial for each new product offering or sale announcement. More extensive use of donut commercials also lends itself to co-op advertising; these commercials carry standard opening and closing messages identifying the store but may feature several different products and prices in the center section. Grocery stores also rely on point-of-purchase sales tools, including videos and in-store "broadcasting" over their public address systems. Some chains are experimenting with the sale of spot advertising on their in-store audio systems to community merchants, so manufacturers are now having to adjust their co-op policies to include this new "medium."

Intense competition among suppliers to the grocery industry has brought about a phenomenon directly affecting promotional budgets. Because product movement in grocery stores is dependent on visibility, shelf space has become the measure of sales success. This has produced the "slotting allowance," which is a charge paid by a manufacturer to get products onto the shelves of a grocery chain, with no related advertising or promotion activity.

Extra Retailer Benefits. When using the air-conditioning contractor as an example of a small retailer's successful use of co-op funds, it was noted that the vendor's sales representative in the territory was due much of the credit. Perhaps the real drama of the co-op marketing technique is seen in a situation such as this one and not in the allocation of megadollar budgets. Co-op works hardest when it is a retailer's basic source of advertising assistance, as well as financial support. To many small retailers, who often know very little about advertising, the co-op arrangement plays a vital part in the survival and growth of their businesses. Help received from knowledgeable manufacturer or media sales representatives in planning promotions, advertising copy, and materials supplied by vendors, and opportunities to participate in joint advertising programs using pooled co-op money, are all tremendously important to retailers who lack the ability and the staff needed to handle their own advertising and promotion programs.

In addition to assistance in the use of conventional advertising media such as newspapers, radio, and television, small retailers also benefit from all the extras included in most well-planned co-op programs, such as signs, point-of-purchase material, Yellow Pages listings, product catalogs and literature, and even uniforms for service personnel.

Summary. The function of co-op is more limited at the retailers' level than it is at the manufacturers' level because retailers' goals are more immediate in nature. Retailers want to run advertising that will bring traffic into their stores and only secondarily to link their establishments with national brand name products. Most retailers, particularly large ones, can be very selective about which products to advertise, and they will not use co-op simply because it is available to them. Smaller retailers are far more dependent on co-op to enhance their advertising budgets and for the additional advertising help and material that comes with many manufacturer co-op programs.

Retailers and manufacturers share the common advertising and promotional goal of selling merchandise to the public, but retailers are also selling their places of business. In pursuing this latter aim, retailers use co-op and try to exercise as much control as possible over its application. The struggle for control of funds produces one of the basic conflicts of the co-op system. Co-op itself, however, provides sound benefits to both parties. The manufacturers who offer co-op encourage promotion and sales of their products by retailers, get local exposure, and reduce advertising costs. The retailers benefit from the co-op funding by the availability of more professionally prepared advertising material and by being linked to a nationally recognized brand name. These joint benefits have given co-op a secure place in our marketing system.

THE WHOLESALER'S PLACE IN THE CO-OP CHAIN

In the vertical chain of co-op advertising that links the manufacturer to the retailer, there is quite frequently a middleman: the wholesaler or distributor. The presence of the wholesaler can have varying degrees of influence on the co-op arrangement, depending on the way in which a manufacturer establishes a co-op program.

Wholesalers and distributors, when handling a particular product line, may have exclusive sales territories. Some manufacturers may also sell their products directly to larger retailers within their distributors' sales territories. In other cases, the types of products sold may not lend themselves to exclusive distributorships and are available to the market through several wholesalers with overlapping sales territories. These different methods of distribution influence how co-op advertising reaches the retailer by way of a wholesaler.

Types of Wholesaler Co-op Plans. Manufacturers who sell through exclusive distributorships set up co-op plans in which the distributor is the customer. Under these plans no direct payments are made to retailers; all co-op funds go to the distributor. The manufacturer's policy is, however, tied to retail-level advertising with the requirement that proof of such advertising be available for audit. The distributor is expected to have a co-op policy with rules that conform to the manufacturer's co-op specifications. The distributor may also share advertising costs with the manufacturer, becoming a co-op provider in the process. The manufacturer is expected to be sure that distributors provide co-op to competing retailers on a proportionately equal basis. This can be a source of problems, because it is difficult for a manufacturer to determine how much product each retailer has purchased from the distributor. Distributors and wholesalers may be required, when using manufacturer co-op money, to furnish records of retailer purchases to verify their eligibility.

In other types of policies, wholesalers may be no more than conduits for co-op information and materials. Retailers make their claims for reimbursement directly to the manufacturer or service organization, providing wholesaler invoices as proofs of their purchases.

Combination Retailer and Wholesaler Plans. When a manufacturer sells directly to some retailers in one market and through wholesalers to others, co-op policies may differ for each category of customer. While the policies may vary, each must result in providing competing retailers with proportionately equal benefits. Combination programs have to base co-op funding on two different price structures — the one paid by the direct purchasing retailer and the one paid by the wholesaler. To provide comparable benefits for those retailers buying from the wholesaler sometimes requires the addition of the wholesaler's money to the co-op funding. It is still the manufacturer's responsibility to be sure that the proportionately equal doctrine is adhered to at the retailer level.

Wholesaler Co-op Objectives. When using co-op, wholesalers share the goals of both the manufacturers they represent and the retailers who are their customers. Most wholesaler advertising and promotional programs contain the following two basic objectives:

1. **Building market share.** Increasing market penetration for product lines handled is a distributor or wholesaler's main promotional aim. To expand sales, distributors usually try to involve as many retail customers as possible in organized advertising efforts built on specific products and brand names. Such wholesaler organized and directed advertising may pool available dealer co-op money to mount joint advertising that covers an entire sales territory. When conducting this type of promotional program, the wholesaler's goals closely parallel those of the manufacturer, with emphasis given to product, brand name, and features. The difference is in the ability of the wholesaler to adapt to small markets with advertising that includes both pricing and localized promotional offers and is centered on individual retailers. This is something that manufacturers can seldom do except when selling directly through large retailers and chains.

2. **Building the wholesale organization.** Wholesalers can use co-op as a device to build up their businesses by increasing sales to retail customers and helping to get new customers. Most wholesalers are keenly aware of how important retail advertising is to their success, and they aim at keeping continuous promotional activity going in which their retailers can par-

ticipate, which makes them better sources than competing wholesalers. To fund various promotion programs, wholesalers will use whatever co-op money is available.

Multiproduct wholesalers are interested in obtaining co-op help and money from a number of suppliers, pooling the money to fund various advertising programs. Examples of this type of wholesaler advertising are the circulars and newspaper inserts of hardware stores and automotive parts stores, which are usually produced by their wholesalers using co-op funds. The advertising is intended to generate sales by increasing store traffic, which is the motive for the retailer's use of co-op.

How Manufacturers Gain from Wholesaler Co-op Efforts. Because many national co-op programs are too broad in scope to fit individual market needs, there are real advantages in channeling those programs through wholesalers. Being one step closer to the retail firing line, wholesalers can adapt co-op to regional or local market needs and are very often innovative in doing this. Many manufacturers have taken successful distributor programs and built them into national co-op programs. Other manufacturers make it a point to share information on successful advertising among their distributors.

From a practical standpoint, using or adapting good wholesaler co-op programs is a way to get field-tested advertising into a national co-op offering. This also makes a good case for closer coordination between national and distributor sales promotion personnel and the structuring of such organizations as distributor advertising councils to discuss common marketing goals.

Wholesaler Contribution to Co-op. When manufacturers distribute their products through wholesalers, the intermediary firm plays an important role in the application of co-op, a role often overlooked or minimized in outside studies of co-op marketing techniques. The salesperson in the field, usually the wholesaler's representative, is charged with persuading retailers to advertise and to use their co-op funding. The local sales representative must also work with groups of retailers in his or her territory, showing them how to use co-op material and helping them to set up joint co-op advertising. In addition to selling products to these retailers, the wholesaler's representative has to function as a sales promotion adviser.

Wholesaler management also must be familiar with the use of co-op and structure co-op advertising programs that cover entire sales territories, handling all the administrative problems that go with those programs. Necessity has made wholesalers particularly adept at using co-op, and manufacturers can normally count on them to take all available co-op money. These organizations deserve more credit and recognition than they are given when co-op is written about or discussed.

INGREDIENT PRODUCER CO-OP PLANS

In addition to manufacturers, retailers, and wholesalers, another party sometimes enters the co-op picture — a producer of the ingredients contained in a finished product. The makers of synthetic fibers, for example, are interested in the sale of carpets; cotton growers, in the sale of clothing; orange growers, in the sale of orange juices; and coffee growers, in the sale of coffee. Fabrics have been leaders in this field, but many other basic ingredient manufacturers promote end products at retail through ingredient co-op plans.

Ingredient producer co-op plans differ from conventional co-op because there is no direct buyer-seller relationship, so the offer of co-op is not a pricing factor. Ingredient producers can choose where and how they feel their money can be best used.

Most ingredient producer co-op money is connected with promotions of higher-priced merchandise. The programs are set up through powerful retailers who can influence a market. Ingredient co-op policies want the ingredient to be prominently identified either by brand name or through a logo or promotional name used by a trade association in its own advertising. The aim of these programs is to sell the consumer on the desirability of the ingredient, to help establish the ingredient as a selling advantage to the retailer, and to encourage use of the ingredient by manufacturers.

Because the retailer may be several steps removed from the supplier of ingredient co-op, there is no practical way of relating money to sales. Ingredient plans usually designate advertising dollars by market, by retailer, and by medium; then they tie these limits to specific types of products advertised within given time periods. The lack of a buyer-seller relationship has been held to exclude ingredient co-op plans from the Robinson-Patman Act's restrictions that require proportionately equal co-op offerings to competing retailers.

The use of ingredient co-op funds produces the problem of a retailer taking money from two sources and making claims against both. Manufacturer co-op plans must be written to require that extra funding be deducted from a claim before the manufacturer's share is calculated.

INDUSTRIAL CO-OP ADVERTISING

Shared advertising cost in the form of programs similar to those offered for consumer products is also a part of marketing for a number of industrial products. This is an area where the use of co-op is rapidly increasing.

The basic concepts of industrial co-op are the same as those found in consumer goods co-op, but the style is different because the industrial co-op advertiser is speaking to other businesses. The industrial advertiser who uses co-op is rarely trying to attract floor traffic but instead is trying to establish a business as a source for sales and service on a particular product line and to open doors for salespeople. Industrial co-op plans are usually smaller and more limited than their consumer co-op equivalents, so they are likely to be less formal and restricted. Many business-to-business co-op programs do not have written policies, making funds available on demand or through arrangements set up by supplier sales reps.

Many consumer goods manufacturers also make industrial products and so offer co-op in both areas. There is also an overlap of consumer and industrial markets for any number of products such as automobiles, appliances, and electronics.

In business-to-business advertising, manufacturers find many of the co-op advantages known to their counterparts in retail advertising, for example, closer association with sales outlets, lower regional advertising costs, or better adaptation of advertising to market needs. Unlike retail outlets, however, most industrial product sales outlets are tied closely to their suppliers, so their local co-op–funded advertising can be a more accurate reflection of the manufacturers' national programs.

CO-OP IN SERVICE INDUSTRIES

The U.S. economy has become one that derives most of its income from the sale of services instead of manufactured products. As it has in the marketing of manufactured products, co-op has found a place in the marketing of services.

Co-op is usually applied in the promotion of services only where there is a vertical relationship similar to the one found in the manufacturer-retailer chain. In the sale of services, there is no product and only an after-the-fact income based on charges to the consumer. Expenses do not involve inventories or large capital investments in manufacturing plants and materials, only direct overhead plus labor costs. Because there is no product or "commodity" involved in the sale of services, the restrictions of the Robinson-Patman Act and the FTC guidelines do not apply to co-op programs in this field of marketing.

The techniques of mass marketing are as applicable to services as they are to consumer products. Individual real estate firms, quick copy shops, personnel agencies, wedding photographers, income tax preparers, karate studios, auto rental agencies, and many of the thousands of service organizations that now serve the consuming public can more effectively promote under a recognizable brand name backed up with national advertising. The marketing device used for cohesive promotion of services is often the license-to-sell authorization or the franchise agreement, which can give even the smallest shops a national identity and framework for advertising — a vertical relationship selling a name instead of a product.

Advertising and promotion plans are part of most franchising and licensing agreements, but co-op is not always present. Without merchandise to sell and with income derived from franchise fees or service charges, it is difficult to set a basis for co-op funding.

In franchise organizations, there is a reluctance on the part of franchise management to become involved in sharing advertising costs with franchise holders, who are independent businesses operating under a common framework. But franchise service businesses are encouraged to advertise by the franchiser through the offer of limited co-op — with participation based on factors such as the number of franchises in a trade area — by making fixed amounts of co-op money available each year or by establishing co-op as a percentage of the franchise's sales. In addition, the franchiser will supply various types of local advertising and promotion material and lay out promotional plans for the franchise holder.

Co-op for services is part of the promotion planning of many different types of manufacturers when the services are vital to the sale of their products. In the automobile industry, co-op advertising is provided for service because the sale of cars is dependent on service availability. In areas such as heating and air conditioning or home appliances, co-op for service advertising is important because a large volume of new product sales comes from replacement of the old or defective equipment found during service calls. Appliance manufacturers have also discovered and are promoting a new source of revenue: the extended service contract. In the aircraft industry, manufacturers provide co-op to flight schools that use their aircraft, with the knowledge that training pilots is necessary to the continued sale of airplanes. Regional telephone companies, so long restricted by regulations, now market a variety of business and consumer services through independent sales organizations and retailers. Co-op is playing an important role in the expansion of these services. A good example can be found in the cellular telephone market, where co-op and sales incentive funds provided by the service suppliers support advertising, sales commissions, and even the cost of the telephone equipment itself.

HORIZONTAL CO-OP ADVERTISING

Advertising among franchise shops, while sometimes backed with co-op from the franchiser, is more often a joint agreement among all the franchises in a trade area to pool resources for advertising. This is an example of how co-op becomes horizontal instead of vertical, because the cost sharing is all at the same marketing level.

Horizontal co-op also figures in many vertical co-op programs, because the pooling of retailer funds is a common method used to increase advertising levels in various markets. In such cases, vertical co-op from a manufacturer or wholesaler and horizontal co-op from groups of retailers are pooled to fund a regional or area-wide advertising campaign. Since this type of joint effort may include competing retailers, the advertising and the co-op arrangement has to stay clear of preferential treatment or specific pricing.

Even where there is no vertical participation, horizontal co-op is a common marketing device. Groups of automobile dealers pool funds to increase brand awareness without factory participation, as do retailer groups selling many other consumer products.

There are hundreds of other examples of common business interests producing jointly funded advertising. Industrial advertising also sees a great deal of this type of promotional effort, sometimes under the auspices of trade associations, sometimes as a result of promotion-minded groups within an industry that band together to achieve more advertising impact.

MUTUAL-INTEREST HORIZONTAL CO-OP

Horizontal co-op can be found in advertising done by different businesses that get customers from each other's services. Airlines may offer co-op to travel agencies. Credit card companies may offer co-op advertising to businesses such as hotels, car rental outlets, and major department stores that honor their cards.

Wherever one form of business can scratch another's back, there is the potential for mutual-interest horizontal co-op advertising. A substantial amount of co-op falls into this category, and it is sometimes part of a vertical co-op arrangement in the same way as ingredient co-op. In the days of cheap energy, for instance, power companies would augment co-op funds available from manufacturers of electric appliances as a way of increasing the demand for electricity. Today they offer similar advertising incentives to retailers for selling energy-efficient appliances. That funding goes to retailers who also may receive manufacturer co-op, thus substantially expanding their advertising budgets.

WHEN SHARING IS A POSITIVE FORCE

Wherever co-op appears in our marketing-oriented economy, it is a positive force that aids in the efficient movement of all types of products and in the sale of many different services. Approximately half of the retail advertising in newspapers is co-op funded. A large amount of broadcast advertising revenue is derived from co-op, and an increasing amount of magazine advertising is now coming from this marketing device. It would be fair to say that not just advertising, but co-op advertising, is the financial underpinning of our society's major communications systems and of our free press.

Co-op is often misunderstood, frequently cumbersome, and has many drawbacks and disadvantages; but it has withstood the test of time in our marketing system and continues to gain in importance and become more widespread in application each year. Knowing how to use co-op and what it involves is important to anyone in the field of retail marketing.

COMPONENTS OF A CO-OP POLICY

All co-op policies should be written documents that clearly spell out the terms under which co-op funds are offered by a vendor to a retailer. Those terms involve the following:

1. Funding. Above all, co-op is a financial arrangement, money paid out for services rendered. The amount of funding is very basic to any co-op policy. The vendor must decide how to accrue or assign money to customers in the form of co-op or other promotional allowances. That financial decision rests on the various aims of the co-op program — for example, product line profitability, market needs, or competitive conditions. Once the method of funding is decided, then a system must be set up to make the assignments and to track the funding as it accrues to retailers. In writing the co-op policy, the conditions for funding must be made very clear to the retailer or wholesaler. Because funding is so very basic to co-op, it is also a major source of problems. Retailers consider accrued co-op money as if it were in a reserve for their use. Co-op, however, is neither a handout nor a bank account. To get the co-op money, a retailer must fulfill the requirements of the co-op policy for advertising or promoting a product.

Manufacturers do not accrue the amount of money based on customer purchases that is stated in their co-op policies. Instead, they use their own or their industry's experience on co-op usage and accrue only the amount they think will be used.

2. Advertising conditions. The co-op policy must define exactly what the retailer must do in the form of advertising or promotion to get co-op reimbursement. These conditions fall into five general categories:

Amount of reimbursement. The policy must show how much of the advertising cost the supplier will pay. In most co-op policies the cost sharing is equal, or 50-50. But there are many variations, with some that pay 100 percent or more of the retailer's advertising cost. Market and industry factors enter in to how much a supplier pays in co-op.

Approved media. Here is where a supplier can direct the use of co-op funds to the areas most helpful to the sale of its products. Certain media, for example, can be emphasized by setting co-op at a level higher than the amount paid for other media.

Advertising content. These rules tell the retailer how the supplier's products must appear and be described in local advertising, how logos must be used, what trademark and tradename restrictions apply, and where pre-approval is required.

Timing of advertising. This condition specifies the period in which the co-op policy is in effect, usually a calendar or fiscal year, and whether there are any seasonal limitations on advertised products and funding.

Reimbursement procedures. This rule spells out what the retailer must do to get co-op reimbursement from the supplier. This includes how and when to file a co-op claim and what proof of advertising is required in the form of media invoices, tearsheets, or scripts.

Making these co-op specifications and requirements should be done in simple, readable terms. The conditions themselves should not be difficult to fulfill, and they should fit in with both the supplier's and the retailer's capabilities and objectives. Many co-op policies are too complicated, with resulting loss in advertising and promotion effort at the retail level — exactly the opposite of what co-op is intended to accomplish for the supplier.

Karen Raugust has been Editor of The Licensing Letter, *a month-ly newsletter published by EPM Communications, Inc., since 1991. In addition to writing and editing* TLL, *Raugust writes EPM's other licensing-related publications, including the* Licensing Business Profit and Opportunity Outlook *and the* Licensing Business Databook. *She also serves as Editor of the* EPM Licensing Business Sourcebook *and contributes to EPM's* Entertainment Marketing Letter. *Raugust acts as a consultant to the licensing community through EPM's 60-Minutes Consultant service, and she is frequently quoted in the business and consumer press.*

Raugust has a B.A. from Carleton College and an MBA from Columbia University.

CHAPTER 10

PRODUCT LICENSING AND TIE-INS

Both retail licensing (the purchase of the rights to a legally protected name, logo, design, or likeness for use on an item to be sold for profit) and promotional tie-ins (licensing agreements for an advertising or promotional use) have grown exponentially over the last decade. Retail sales of licensed products in North America, for example, have tripled from a total of $20.6 billion in 1982 to $62.2 billion in 1992, according to figures compiled by *The Licensing Letter*. Since 1990, growth has leveled off; the market for licensed products has matured after close to 15 years of enormous growth. In addition, a recession adversely affected retailing in the early 1990s.

Still, a $60 billion-plus business is significant, and product licensing has become recognized as an effective way for an owner of a legally protected name, graphic, or likeness (a property) to earn significant revenue. A manufacturer who associates with a particular property (the licensee) stands to increase awareness of its products without having to build a brand from scratch. Simply being linked with a licensed property is not in itself enough to guarantee increased sales, of course. But licensing, as part of a total marketing strategy, can be a successful sales tool if the fit between product and property is a logical one.

The potential of a licensed property to drive product sales has been proven by such examples as the Teenage Mutant Ninja Turtles and *Star Wars*. According to the companies that handle these licensing programs, merchandise based on the Turtles surpassed $5 billion at retail in six years beginning in 1987, while products based on the *Star Wars* movie trilogy rang up more than $2.5 billion over six years starting in 1977. In the sports area, retail sales of both Major League Baseball and National Football League merchandise surpass $2 billion annually.

While these examples illustrate the *potential* of a large licensing program, it is not accurate to say that such blockbusters are the only way to make money through licensing. Smaller, more targeted programs also can be lucrative for the property owner (the licensor) and effective marketing tools for the manufacturers permitted to make property-based merchandise. For example, the television show *Northern Exposure* spawned a licensing program focusing on cold-weather wear and a limited number of collectible items, marketed to its core audience primarily through direct response.

It is also important to realize when thinking about licensing that there are two types of programs: those based on classic, evergreen properties (Mickey Mouse, Looney Tunes, or Peanuts, for example), and those based on short-term, "hot" properties (such as 1989's

Batman movie, which tallied worldwide retail sales of $1.3 billion, or 1990's *The Simpsons*, which sold over $2.1 billion worth of products worldwide, mostly in the space of a year and a half). A short-term property, if well managed, allows the licensor and licensees to garner significant revenues over a short period by selling merchandise in several — even hundreds — of product categories. The classic property, on the other hand, brings in less revenue in a given year than a "hot" property might at its peak, but it will be a steady business for its licensor and associated manufacturers over many years. This scenario assumes that the program is managed so that it does not oversaturate the market with products, thus causing the property's demise. Licensors and licensees who use licensing as a primary focus of their business strategy generally prefer to combine a selection of short-term properties with some steady, evergreen ones.

As in product licensing, promotional tie-ins can also utilize both evergreen and short-term properties. A tie-in is a form of licensing agreement whereby a company pays a fee for the right to use a property in conjunction with an advertising or promotional campaign (that is, for nonretail product uses). It is difficult to come up with a figure for the value of tie-ins, in part because much of the "payment" comes in the form of trade-outs (that is, the donation of something of value to the promotion in return for something else of value without cash changing hands). *Entertainment Marketing Letter,* an industry publication, estimated the value of tie-ins involving video releases alone at $110 million in 1991; that figure was higher in 1992. (The $110 million incorporates the total value of measurable media time and space, trade-out exposure, premiums, cash payments, and the value of on-cassette advertising by all promotional partners for all of the video promotions done that year.)

On the high end of the spectrum, a single multipartner tie-in can be valued as high as $50 to $60 million. Examples include a tie-in surrounding the video release of Walt Disney's *Beauty & the Beast* in 1992, or the CBS television network's promotion supporting its fall 1992 schedule, which involved Nabisco and Kmart as primary promotional partners.

While tie-ins can have a high monetary value attached to them in terms of what is brought to the table by the various partners, they can also be lucrative sales tools. As in the case of product licensing, however, the fit between the partners, the property, and the promotional elements must be sound.

While huge corporations with deep pockets, such as Coca-Cola and Pepsi, McDonald's and Burger King, and Nabisco, play a major role in tie-ins, there is also room for smaller companies to engage in creative promotions. A small marketer can participate as one of many partners (which spreads the costs over several players). Or, it can develop a targeted tie-in, such as with a special-interest videocassette.

For example, in 1992 Nutrasweet tied in successfully with an exercise video starring the actress Cher. It can also link itself with past hits, such as classic films, or with less-than-hit characters that are popular with its target audience.

PRODUCT LICENSING

The main players of any licensing agreement are the *licensor* (the property owner) and the *licensee* (the purchaser of the rights to the property). The *property* is the trademarked or copyrighted entity, be it a character, design, name, logo, sports league or team, event, or likeness. In some cases, a *licensing agent* will also be involved. The agent acts on behalf of the licensor in seeking appropriate licensees, negotiating contracts, and overseeing the licensing program. *Manufacturers' representatives* sometimes act on behalf of licensees in seeking appropriate licensed properties for their products.

The types of properties licensed out for other products fall into 10 major categories:
- **Art**, which includes copyrighted designs and fine art for use on a wide range of products;
- **Celebrities and estates**, which include the likenesses and names of famous people such as James Dean, Marilyn Monroe, Laurel & Hardy, and many others;
- **Designer names**, particularly in fashion and home furnishings, such as Gloria Vanderbilt, Ralph Lauren, Donna Karan, and Bob Timberlake;
- **Entertainment and character properties**, which comprise films, television, classic cartoon characters, and comic book superheroes;
- **Music and musical artists**, including Elvis Presley, New Kids On The Block, and the Grateful Dead;
- **Nonprofit organizations**, such as the World Wildlife Fund and other environmental groups, relief organizations including CARE, medical research and money-raising organizations;
- **Publishing**, which includes book characters such as Waldo from the *Where's Waldo?* series, or Babar the elephant*,* as well as magazines (*Playboy, Cosmopolitan*) and book titles (*The Baby-Sitter's Club*);
- **Sports**, incorporating all four major leagues and colleges, as well as other sports entities such as the Olympics, NASCAR auto racing, soccer, wrestling, and so forth;
- **Trademarks and corporate brands**, from all areas, especially apparel brands (J.G. Hook), footwear (Converse), automotive trademarks (Jeep, Harley-Davidson), and food and beverage brands (Betty Crocker, Coca-Cola, Budweiser); and
- **Toys and games**, that license out into other products, such as

Barbie, LEGO, G.I. Joe, Transformers, Hot Wheels, and videogame characters such as Super Mario Brothers and Sonic the Hedgehog.

Table 10.1 shows the relative importance of each of these segments in terms of the amount of retail sales attributable to them in 1992. Trademark licensing ranks as the largest segment, followed by characters/entertainment and sports licensing.

Each of these types of properties is licensed out for innumerable product categories. In fact, almost every type of product you can imagine has been associated at one time or another with some kind of license — hot dogs, milk caps, condoms, you name it. The major categories, however, are listed in Table 10.2, along with their relative retail sales for 1992.

Many manufacturing companies find that both licensing in (that is, purchasing rights to a property for one of their products) and licensing out (selling the rights to their own properties) fit into their strategy; thus, they act as licensors and licensees. For example, the toy manufacturer Mattel oversees licensing programs based on its own properties, Barbie and Hot Wheels, extending to apparel, accessories, and many other products. Meanwhile, they also manufacture toys under license from other companies, such as plush toys based on Walt Disney animated films, fashion dolls based on the television show *Beverly Hills 90210,* and Nickelodeon brand games and activity toys.

The Licensor's Role. From the licensor's point of view, licensing is lucrative monetarily. In fact, for some films, the advances from licensing agreements help pay for the production of the film itself; the film's existence is predicated upon expected future licensing income. In addition, licensing increases awareness of a new property. For example, consumers will be exposed to their local sports teams not only through print and broadcast advertising and sportscasts, but also by the logoed products in nearly every department of the stores where they shop.

Property owners also use licensing to extend a franchise into new product categories in which the company does not have expertise, and new distribution channels where the brand does not currently exist. For example, Marvel Entertainment manufactures comic books. But in order to extend its "X-Men" and "Superheroes" brands into new product categories (such as toys), it opts to license its brands to other manufacturers because its own expertise is in publishing. Licensing also minimizes the financial risk of developing new products from the licensor's point of view, because the research and development costs generally lie with the licensee.

On the other hand, the licensor does face some challenges. These include the possibility of diluting the property's value if licensees produce poor-quality products, and the probability of shortening a property's life span if the market becomes oversaturated with products. The

TABLE 10.1

1992 Shares of Licensed Product Retail Sales by Property Type
(Dollar Figures in Billions)

Property Type	1992 Retail Sales	Pct. All Sales
Art	$4.4	7.1%
Celebrity/Estate	$2.4	3.9%
Designer Names	$5.0	8.0%
Entertainment/Character	$14.1	22.7%
Music	$0.9	1.4%
Non-Profit	$0.6	1.0%
Publishing	$1.4	2.3%
Sports	$12.1	19.5%
Trademarks/Brands	$18.6	29.9%
Toys/Games	$2.5	4.0%
Other	$0.2	0.3%
TOTAL	$62.2	100.0%

Source: The Licensing Letter

© Copyright 1993 EPM Communications

TABLE 10.2

1992 Shares of Licensed Product Retail Sales by Product Category
(Dollar Figures in Billions)

Product Category	1992 Retail Sales	Pct. All Sales
Accessories	$5.9	9.5%
Apparel	$10.7	17.2%
Domestics	$4.0	6.4%
Electronics	$1.0	1.6%
Food/Beverage	$5.0	8.0%
Footwear	$1.9	3.1%
Furniture/Home Furnishings	$0.7	1.1%
Gifts/Novelties	$5.5	8.8%
Health/Beauty	$3.5	5.6%
Housewares	$2.0	3.2%
Infant Products	$2.0	3.2%
Music/Video	$1.1	1.8%
Publishing	$4.1	6.6%
Sporting Goods	$2.1	3.4%
Stationery/Paper	$2.9	4.7%
Toys/Games	$6.6	10.6%
Videogames/Software	$3.0	4.8%
Other	$0.2	0.3%
TOTAL	$62.2	100.0%

Source: The Licensing Letter

© Copyright 1993 EPM Communications

property's brand image can also be hurt if branded products end up in the wrong distribution channel — that is, if a product based on an upscale brand, perceived by consumers to be of high quality, ends up in a mass market chain, the brand itself and all associated licensed products will risk being hurt.

To minimize the effect of these challenges and to help ensure the success of the program, the licensor's responsibilities include the following:

- Adequately protecting the copyrights and trademarks involved for all properties in all geographic areas where licensing will be undertaken and for all appropriate product categories;
- Maintaining the quality and value inherent in the property itself through specifying appropriate art and logos for licensees' use and instituting a rigorous product approval process;
- Selecting quality licensees, keeping a rein on the number of manufacturers and product categories to avoid market oversaturation;
- Supporting licensees and retailers by creating and maintaining the property's awareness through point-of-sale materials and other in-store signage, by arranging tie-ins and publicity, by encouraging licensees to work together in cross-promotions, and by convincing retailers of the benefit of displaying all licensed products together in one area of the store; and
- Extending the franchise and keeping it fresh through line extensions (for example, focusing on the Baby Bart and Maggie characters of *The Simpsons* appeals to new mothers), sub-brands (Walt Disney's Princess Collection as a sub-brand for girls, incorporating princesses from various Disney films), sequels (the Ninja Turtles' three films over six years), and new media (such as *Batman: The Animated Series* to extend the *Batman* film property).

A licensing program offering all of these elements would be an ideal scenario; however, many licensors do not provide the whole package. This situation is slowly beginning to change as the market for licensed properties matures. Licensors are beginning to realize that the long-term success of their programs requires them to take responsibility for more than just trademarking and copyrighting their properties and arranging for licensees. And manufacturers and retailers are starting to demand all of the elements listed above before signing on to a property.

The Licensee's Contribution. For the manufacturer that pays for the right to use a property in association with its products, licensing provides the immediate awareness that is attached to a known entity, thus providing brand awareness without having to build a brand from scratch. The property itself generates awareness in the minds of consumers, with little need for additional advertising by the manufacturer to create that awareness. The various licensed products based on the same property also serve to advertise each other throughout the store and across various distribution channels.

An association with a licensed property can also create an entry into a new distribution channel to which a manufacturer does not currently sell. For example, a particular apparel manufacturer may not be selling to Wal Mart. But an exclusive association with a hot character license may be a significant incentive for Wal Mart to try the firm as a new resource; if the relationship is successful, the retailer may continue to work with the vendor on some of its other, nonlicensed brands.

In addition, a license can give a product an immediate image of quality with its consumers, who may not be familiar with the manufacturer's own name or brands. The food brand Betty Crocker, for example, is perceived by consumers as a high-quality, valued food brand. Consumers translate that same perception of quality to Betty Crocker-licensed housewares products. This image automatically provides a distinct competitive advantage to the bakeware or appliance manufacturer who holds such a license (see Exhibit 10.1).

Licensing can also exhibit a down side for the manufacturer. Any new, unproven property — especially films or television shows — may flop, in which case consumers might hold unfavorable opinions

EXHIBIT 10.1

about merchandise associated with it; perhaps they may not even have heard of the property at all. Second, for all types of properties, a portion of the payment — sometimes a large amount of money — is usually paid up front as an advance and is nonrefundable. Thus, if the property fails or if the fit between property and product is not right, the manufacturer loses the advance money, as well as any development and manufacturing costs.

Timing is another important issue. A short window of opportunity exists for peak sales on entertainment-based merchandise (about six weeks for the average stand-alone film), which means that any delay in production or delivery can cause a significant chunk of potential sales to be lost.

Licensees are responsible for product development and manufacturing of the product (subject to the specifications of and product approvals by the licensor), as well as selling to their own distribution channels. (Manufacturers that bring a large range of distribution channels to the party often have the advantage over other companies in terms of being selected as a licensee.) Potential licensees are sometimes expected to provide advertising to trade and consumer channels, as well.

Evaluation of Potential Partners. Negotiations can be initiated by either the licensor or the potential licensee. Both sides need to carefully evaluate each other as potential partners — the personal relationship between licensee and licensor is among the most important elements of the agreement. While licensing agreements can be terminated at the end of the contract period if either side fails to perform up to expectations, both partners would prefer to select a company that they can trust to keep up its end of the bargain.

A licensor looks for the following information from potential licensees in order to evaluate their requests for a license:
- Product quality (in the form of samples, current catalogs, promotional materials, or price lists);
- Distribution channels, including largest retail accounts and contact names of buyers at those outlets (The fit of distribution channels — upscale or mass market — with the property's image is as important as the number of outlets);
- Annual gross sales and volume for recent years;
- Annual advertising and promotion budgets for several prior years;
- Credit information;
- Proposed merchandise that the licensee plans to manufacture under license and samples of those products;
- Proposed timing — that is, when the various products will be introduced at retail; and
- Projected sales for the potential licensed merchandise.

In turn, prospective licensees must also evaluate the licensors —

simply owning a popular property is not enough to provide the basis for an agreement. Licensees need to evaluate whether the property is short-term or evergreen and which type better fits their strategic goals. Is the target customer for the property the same as the licensee's target audience? Does the property itself — animated series, film, live-action series, sports event, personality, design, trademarked brand — provide excitement or value and promise to maintain its current image? What types of support does the licensor provide to licensees and retailers in terms of promotion and advertising? How does the licensor plan to maintain the longevity of the property and keep it fresh? What other licensees are involved in the program? Manufacturers should feel free to ask for a licensee list and contact references.

Agents and Manufacturers' Representatives. Some licensors assign their properties to licensing agents, who represent that property — often exclusively — in various geographic territories or for selected product categories. Agents have contacts throughout the industry and are able to help with the licensee selection process, oversee royalty payments, expedite product approvals, and assist in identifying appropriate product categories for a licensor to fill. With their expertise, agents can be beneficial to new licensors because they will significantly shorten the learning curve. Many agents focus on one segment of licensing, be it trademarks, entertainment licenses, designers, or sports properties. Agencies range from one-person operations representing only one or a few properties to relatively large entities representing a long list of clients. In return for their expertise, agents are paid a percentage — usually between 25 percent and 50 percent — of royalty income.

Licensees, on the other hand, occasionally retain manufacturers' representatives or consultants to help them identify appropriate licensed properties for their products. They, too, have extensive contacts within the industry and are able to help manufacturers launch and maintain their licensing efforts.

Trademark and Copyright. Since licensing centers around the use of various rights to a protected trademark, logo, design, or likeness, adequately protecting the copyrights and/or trademarks in question is an essential part of the licensor's role. The following brief definitions do not even begin to skim the surface of the legal intricacies involved in trademark and copyright protection; they are meant as a simple launching point.

Copyright is legal protection for intellectual works including artistic and literary endeavors, among others, whether published or unpublished. Art and graphics to be licensed must be copyrighted. Titles, short phrases, names, and type cannot be copyrighted. In general, copyrights last until 50 years after the author's or artist's death (for works created after January 1, 1978).

Words, names, symbols, and combinations of these must be

trademarked. Logos and short phrases associated with brands ("Diet Pepsi, Uh-Huh") are also trademarked. Company names (trade names) cannot be trademarked, but brands must be, in order to be legally protected.

For information on copyright definitions, procedures, duration, and costs, contact the Copyright Office of the Library of Congress, in Washington, D.C. Trademarks are under the jurisdiction of the U.S. Patent and Trademark Office, also in Washington, D.C.

Because the licensing business really hinges on the existence of a legally protected entity — all of the information in this chapter is moot if the property is not adequately protected in every area where licensing will be undertaken — the lawyer you select should preferably specialize in the licensing business. Several such attorneys exist, now that licensing has become such a widespread activity among many diverse types of companies.

Payment. The royalty is the main component of payment for the right to use a property in conjunction with a retail product. Royalties are paid as a percentage of the wholesale price of all products sold. They are negotiable on a case-by-case basis — there is no business-wide standard royalty — and they vary greatly, from a low of 2–3 percent for some agreements to as high as 18–20 percent for others. Royalties average just over 7 percent across all property types and product categories.

A number of factors play a role in determining the specific royalty rate. The popularity of the property affects the rate; the more people who want a particular property, the higher its price will be. Short-term entertainment properties that are unique in some way, for example, generally command a higher rate than a corporate trademark or art property where hundreds of fairly similar properties compete. A film that is expected to be the star performer of the year in terms of sales of licensed merchandise can command 10 percent to 12 percent (even as high as 16 percent on occasion), while an artist's design may result in a range of 3 percent to 6 percent.

The product category affects royalty rates as well. Products with lower profit margins end up with lower royalty rates; low margins only allow for a certain royalty percentage before licensing becomes non-cost-effective. Food product manufacturers, for instance, generally pay low royalties of 2 percent to 3 percent, while a fine-art poster producer may pay 10 percent for the rights to the same property. Children's apparel firms fall in the middle, at 4–8 percent (see Table 10.3).

Some manufacturer expenses are subtracted from the royalty payment (although this, too, is negotiable). Cash discounts, freight charges, and returns are often deductible, while advertising costs are not. A cap of 2 percent to 5 percent of royalty income is usually placed on the allowable deductions.

TABLE 10.3

Average Royalty by Product Category, 1992

Product Category	Average Royalty	Range
Accessories	7.5%	3-15%
Apparel	7.5%	4-12%
Domestics	6.0%	3-10%
Electronics (non-game)	7.5%	5-10%
Food & Beverage	3.0%	1-5%
Footwear	6.0%	4-11%
Furniture/Home Furnishings	6.0%	2-10%
Gifts/Novelties	8.5%	3-12%
Health/Beauty	7.0%	3-10%
Housewares	6.0%	3-10%
Infant Products	6.5%	5-10%
Music/Video	8.5%	5-20%
Premiums	7.0%	4-10%
Publishing	7.5%	4-12%
Sporting Goods	6.0%	3-10%
Stationery/Paper Goods	8.5%	4-12%
Toys/Games	8.0%	4-12%
Videogames/Software	8.5%	5-20%
OVERALL AVERAGE	7.1%	

Source: The Licensing Letter

© Copyright 1993 EPM Communications

After a royalty rate is negotiated, the partners agree on an annual guarantee. The guarantee is typically a percentage of the royalties expected to be generated each year by the licensed products. It is non-refundable and is paid, usually quarterly, whether or not the product line generates sales high enough to warrant that amount of royalties for that period. The purpose of the guarantee is to protect the licensor in case sales of the product line do not meet expectations due to a lack of effort by the licensee.

Guarantees are paid "against royalties." That is, royalties are accrued — but not paid — up to the level of the guarantee. After sales generate royalties equal to the guarantee amount, additional royalties are paid to the licensor as further sales warrant.

Like royalties, guarantee amounts vary widely; for example, they can be as small as $3,000 for low-priced stationery items or as much as $750,000 or higher for some items. Separate guarantees may be required for different products manufactured by a single licensee or for different geographic areas for which a single licensee has rights, to make sure that an equitable level of attention is paid to each product and each region.

Part of the guarantee (typically from 25 percent to 50 percent, but this varies) is usually paid up front as an advance at the time of contract signing. The periodic guarantee payments are then adjusted accordingly to reflect the amount paid up front. If a guarantee is particularly small, the entire guarantee may be paid as an advance.

Contracts. Contracts vary depending on the individual agreement and, as mentioned in the section on trademarks and copyrights, it is advisable to retain an attorney who is specifically versed in the licensing business. While each agreement is different, the following elements are among those that will be included in virtually all contracts:

- The contract should identify the parties entering into the agreement.
- It should specify the length of the agreement. The average duration of most contracts is two or three years with an option to renew, but this may vary. A first agreement with a firm may be only a year in duration, while a contract with a known, successful licensee may be long term, even up to 10 years.
- The contract should list the specific merchandise being produced under license, including a description of the products and any traits that distinguish them from other similar merchandise (for example, a particular design or the specific materials used in manufacturing).
- The agreement should outline the specific geographic territory or territories covered by the agreement.
- It should summarize the specific distribution outlets covered by the contract (for example, department and specialty stores, mass market outlets, specific locations, or direct mail outlets).
- The agreement should clarify who owns what rights, such as rights to new entities created by the licensee based on the property.
- The contract should outline conditions for the agreement's termination and put in writing the sell-off procedures that will occur after termination.
- It should specify what happens in case of infringement by a third party — who can bring suit, who pays legal costs, and who keeps the monetary results of the suit, if any.

PROMOTIONAL TIE-INS

A promotional tie-in is typically a licensing agreement for the use of a property that is promotional in nature (as opposed to permitting the creation of a product for sale). Consequently, since there is no sales figure upon which to base a royalty, the core element of payment is a flat fee, with other additional costs added on as applicable. The cost structures of certain tie-ins can become quite complicated, depending on the nature of the promotion, and in many cases the amount of the flat fee itself is hidden among all the other elements of payment.

A tie-in can be as simple as the use of a character in a print ad. On the other hand, it can be as complicated as a multi-tier, multi-partner promotion involving premiums, advertising in various channels, rebates, packaged goods promotions, sweepstakes and contests involving mail-ins, and interactive phone technology — all targeting both consumers and the trade (retailers or distributors) Tie-ins can involve sports personalities and events, nonprofit entities, or entertainment properties. Timing is variable as well; a film tie-in, for example, can coincide with theatrical release, video release, or subsequent broadcast and cable airings.

Tie-in Participants. For licensors, tie-ins serve the purpose of generating awareness for their properties, thus advertising the event or entity itself (as well as related products made by licensees, if any). Tie-ins also enable the property to become known in channels where it would normally not be advertised. Filmgoers traditionally become aware of new films through print or broadcast advertising or through in-theater trailers, for example, but a tie-in allows the message to get to the consumer in other outlets, such as grocery stores and fast food restaurants. Last, but certainly not least, tie-ins are lucrative for licensors. The income earned through tie-ins can be as important a factor for them as the marketing benefits, depending on the property.

Entertainment companies (besides the licensor, if the property is in the entertainment area) also can be involved in tie-ins. Theater chains, home video distributors, music companies, film studios, and cable and broadcast networks are all frequent tie-in partners. Product licensees can also be involved in tie-ins, either through the provision of premiums or through participation in cross-promotions as part of the tie-in. Comic books, trading cards, plastic cups, squeeze bottles, plush figures, plastic figurines, and small toys are particularly popular for premiums, as well as to cross-package with other licensed merchandise. The provision of premiums can be a relatively risk-free way for authorized manufacturers to sell large quantities of licensed products.

Retailers are often involved in tie-ins, too. They benefit from their participation by attracting increased store traffic during the time period of the tie-in and by generating additional sales for licensed products based on the entity being promoted. (Other products may also see greater sales during the tie-in period due to the increased store traffic.) Retailer partners can also raise awareness of their company name by associating with a high-profile property. Tie-ins can be expensive for the retailer, however, and can be risky, especially for short-term entertainment properties. If a film flops, most of the potential benefits of the tie-in will not occur, but the money paid up front cannot be recouped. Among the types of retail outlets frequently involved in tie-ins are fast food restaurants, mass market chains, department and independent stores, grocery stores, video retailers, and toy stores, among others.

Tie-ins often include other product manufacturers, in addition to licensees. Their involvement usually incorporates changes in their product packaging to promote the tie-in; it can also include other elements, such as cents-off coupons or cross-promotions with licensed products or with other manufacturers involved in the same tie-in. The manufacturers hope their participation will lead to increased sales because of the excitement of their association with the property. They usually receive increased advertising exposure through being mentioned in ads by other partners, above and beyond their own promotional efforts. Much of their contribution to the promotion is in the form of packaging, hangtags, and other promotional exposure, rather than cash payments. Food and beverage companies; apparel, accessory, and footwear manufacturers; and health and beauty firms are among the most frequent participants, but many others are involved as well.

Finally, various media partners are also involved in tie-ins. They can include radio stations in local markets, local television stations and national networks, and print media — magazines nationally and newspapers locally. Their participation allows the other partners further opportunity to promote the tie-in at less cost, since the media partners usually donate space or time, thus saving significantly on advertising costs. In return, the media partner benefits from the cachet of being associated with a highly visible property.

Most tie-in promotions in the 1990s involve multiple partners, with the exception of straightforward advertising uses or some long-term associations with classic characters. Bringing in several companies spreads the cost of the tie-in over more players, thus making it more cost-effective for each partner. In addition, the participation of more partners maximizes consumers' exposure to the tie-in in as many outlets as possible. On the other hand, the more partners there are, the more problems are likely to arise. Coordination among partners becomes more difficult, as does the timing of the tie-in, with lead times (required time periods between signing the contract and implementing the promotion) varying from partner to partner. Flexibility, trust, and communication among the players are all essential ingredients in order for a multi-partner promotion to work.

Techniques. Virtually any sales promotion technique can be used in a tie-in with a nonprofit, sports, or entertainment entity. The main element of the tie-in is the licensed property, so the promotion will focus on that. A major use for the property itself is using its likeness or logo in advertising — for example, television, print, newspaper inserts — or on packaging. In addition, personal appearances by a film or sports star or a costumed character at retail outlets, local promotional events, press functions, and so forth, are also often included as tie-in components. And contest prizes can involve meeting key personalities associated with the property, seeing behind-the-scenes action such as a locker room or film set, or attending an event such as a film opening, a concert, or a sports event.

The other elements of a tie-in — components that support the use of the property itself — are common to any cross-promotion. Since most are discussed in depth elsewhere in this book, the following is a brief rundown of possibilities that are commonly considered for entertainment, sports, or nonprofit tie-ins:

- **Use of premiums.** These can be give-aways or self-liquidators, offered on-site or via direct response. In general, the premiums will be directly related to the property. They are either purchased from the retail licensee, or licensed separately as unique products for the tie-in only. Sometimes premiums are purchased specifically for the tie-in from a contracted manufacturer rather than as a licensing arrangement. The main concern regarding use of premiums, from the manufacturer's point of view, is that the premium items do not cut into sales of similar products made by retail licensees.

- **Rebates and cents-off coupons,** including bounce-back arrangements in which several promotional partners become involved. Rebates and coupons can be included on-pack, in free-standing inserts, and in newspaper or other print advertising.

- **Contests and sweepstakes,** fulfilled through mail-in mechanisms or interactive phone technology. These techniques can be targeted toward the trade or to consumers, or both in many cases.

- **Advertising on videocassettes.** Advertisers are unconvinced of the effectiveness of this technique, due to concerns that viewers fast-forward through the commercials and start viewing at the beginning of the film, or at the trailers. In addition, it is difficult to measure the effectiveness of such ads, and an accurate cost per thousand, upon which advertising agents base pricing, does not exist. Still, some tie-ins — especially those involving nonprofit groups and theatrical-film or special-interest videocasette releases — do include ads on cassette, sometimes simply to promote the nonprofit group's activities and sometimes with an 800 or 900 number that encourages donations or allows viewers to participate in a contest or sweepstakes.

- **Media support.** Media support usually includes a tag for the promotion in print and on-air advertising (often part of existing media schedules) by the various partners. It can also include involvement by magazines or networks that are themselves partners in the promotion and that donate advertising space or editorial coverage in return for being associated with the tie-in. This is often the case when one of the partners is a nonprofit entity, since the media partners feel that the association with a cause is a good public relations effort in the eyes of their constituents.

Incidentally, the use of nonprofit overlays to sports or entertainment promotions is on the rise. Bringing in a nonprofit partner along with the retailers, packaged goods companies, and property owners adds an additional element to the promotion in terms of goodwill for the partners. Conversely, the added excitement of the sports or entertainment tie-in can benefit the nonprofit group by increasing awareness and donations.

Case Studies. As noted, tie-ins can be simple, or they can be complex, multipartner arrangements. The following examples demonstrate the wide breadth of techniques and combinations of elements that can occur. Tie-ins arose out of the need for marketers to distinguish themselves from their competitors (to help them break out of the clutter with a "unique" promotion). But as the number of tie-ins increases, the promotion alone is not enough to provide that distinction. Increasingly more creativity is needed to make a tie-in truly unique.

An example of a straightforward use of a classic character for broadcast advertising occurred in early 1993, when Taco Bell licensed the characters Rocky and Bullwinkle for a series of animated ads. The fast food restaurant wanted to distinguish its menu from what it termed "boring burgers" offered by other chains, and it used original animation featuring the offbeat characters to get its message across. The selection of classic characters meant that the company would appeal both to older consumers, who were familiar with Rocky and Bullwinkle from their youth, as well as to younger consumers, who have been introduced to the characters since 1991. The campaign was supplemented by in-restaurant posters, tray liners, and carry-out bags and cups; Taco Bell employees wore Rocky and Bullwinkle T-shirts as well.

An early 1993 Tropicana tie-in with Hemdale Home Video illustrates single-partner promotion of a videocassette release. Tropicana chose to tie in with the video release of *Little Nemo*, an animated children's theatrical film, to promote its Tropicana Triplets boxed juices. Tropicana offered a $5.00 rebate on each videocassette of the film purchased, and it promoted the rebate on packages of Tropicana Triplets in 25,000 stores and in its national advertising. Tropicana also offered a free premium — a *Little Nemo* activity set produced by licensee Colorforms. Hemdale cross-promoted Tropicana in its advertising and promotional displays, as well as placing a Tropicana message on the videocassette.

In the sports area, the National Basketball Association tied in with McDonald's in March of 1993 with a national promotion called McDonald's NBA Fantasy Packs (see Exhibit 10.2). The tie-in involved prizes from several NBA sponsors, including Norwegian Cruise Lines, Bausch & Lomb, American Airlines, ITT Sheraton, and Dollar Rent A Car. Items from several NBA licensees were also offered as prizes, such as fantasy salaries from Sports Fantasy Contracts, uniforms from Champion, jackets from Starter, and apparel and basketballs from Spalding. Licensee Upper Deck created a set of trading cards especially for the promotion. In addition, NBA players

EXHIBIT 10.2

were involved (a one-on-one game with Michael Jordan), and some winners earned the opportunity to participate in NBA events or win tickets to games.

Nickelodeon launched a new block of programming in late summer of 1992 with a $20 million multi-partner promotion. It included an on-air sweepstakes sponsored by Sega, Kraft Handi-Snacks, and Pizza Hut; trading card premiums packaged with Capri-Sun Fruit Drinks; tune-in messages on packages of Kraft Handi-Snacks, which also advertised Nickelodeon merchandise available with proofs-of-purchase of Handi-Snacks; tune-in messages on Sega videogame cassettes; a Nickelodeon spread in *Sega Visions* magazine; sponsorship of Sega's mall tour by Nickelodeon; and tune-in messages on grocery bags in Kroger and Shop-Rite stores.

Payment. "Payment" is difficult to quantify when discussing tie-ins. Much of the payment comes in the form of trade-outs, so no cash actually changes hands. In fact, the licensing fee itself is often not even quantified; rather, the elements that each partner has to offer are negotiated through give-and-take until all partners are satisfied that what they will get out of the promotion — in terms of increased sales, increased awareness, goodwill, or whatever their goals may be — exceeds what they are putting into it, whether it be cash, added impressions for the other partners, or other components of value to the tie-in. While the licensor may sometimes receive cash for the right to use its property —

especially for a relatively simple tie-in such as the use of a character in an ad — in other cases, no cash at all may change hands.

In lieu of cash, the promotional partners may contribute other added value. For example, one partner may be responsible for providing premiums. Another partner may offer some type of advertising, perhaps in the form of a tag on existing print advertising. A partner's contribution may involve promoting the tie-in on-air during time already reserved for its ongoing ad campaign. This incremental media is considered part of the value of the promotion, even though the advertiser is not paying anything more than what it normally would pay — it is just putting it toward the tie-in instead of toward other uses.

In the case of a media partner, the contribution may involve the provision of free airtime or print space devoted to the tie-in. Similarly, a video marketer could offer free space for advertising on a cassette, or a manufacturer may provide space to promote the tie-in on its packaging or on hangtags. Again, this cost is an incremental one because the company would need to print packaging or hangtags for the products anyway; the additional costs are mainly in the form of creative input, as well as slightly higher printing costs that may arise as a result of shorter print runs.

There are other ways partners can contribute to a tie-in. A retailer or the licensor, for example, may offer in-store support such as signage or point-of-sale materials, countertop cards, or in-store flyers devoted to the tie-in. Another partner may contribute the operational costs of overseeing contests and sweepstakes, including fulfillment of premiums and prizes.

Measurement of Results. It is difficult to quantify many of the benefits of a tie-in, such as increased awareness, much less to trace which results are attributable to which part of the promotion. In addition, one of the major difficulties in terms of measuring the success of a tie-in is to try to ascertain which results, if any, are traceable to the use of the property itself, rather than being attributable to other elements of the promotion.

Some of the measurable elements include, of course, the number of coupon redemptions, the number of contest entries, the number of calls generated by interactive phone lines, and the number of premiums sold or given away. The elements that are measurable but not necessarily traceable include the following: increased attendance at films over previous comparable films, which may have been affected as much as or more by the quality of the film as by the tie-ins surrounding it; increased sales over nonpromotional periods or over other similar tie-ins with different properties; increased traffic at retail outlets over other time periods; and awareness of the property and of the tie-in partners' brands, as measured through recall studies at periodic intervals during and after the tie-in.

Of course, some elements of the tie-in cannot be measured at all, including goodwill generated by a tie-in toward a product, brand, or company, or the "excitement" associated with a product due to its connection with an entertainment or sports property. These attributes, while not measurable, are ironically among the major reasons for involvement in a licensed tie-in.

Issues and Challenges. Entertainment, sports, and nonprofit tie-ins — while they can be wildly successful — are not without their challenges. For example, lead times may vary between property owners and other tie-in partners. A film studio may be working on a lead time of as long as 24 months for a particularly hot film, while a packaged goods company may prefer a lead time of nine to 12 months. Both may be able to work with as narrow a lead time as four months, however, if the deal is important enough to them and the cost is right. Flexibility by both partners is required to minimize lead-time differences.

Another timing problem can occur, particularly with film tie-ins, due to the fact that release dates are changeable. A film's theatrical or video release may be moved up a week, for example, forcing tie-in partners to have all promotional elements in place a week earlier, with little advance notice. Or, a film may be delayed by six months if production is not running smoothly or if preview audiences pan the film, thus forcing last-minute changes. A packaged goods or retail company, whose promotional schedule is set a year or more in advance, will suffer; the promotion will most likely be canceled, and the sunk costs associated with it forfeited.

In the case of licensed or property-specific premiums being used in a tie-in, care must be taken that the premiums do not hurt retail sales of similar products. This risk can be minimized by making all affected parties aware of the premium use from the beginning — while there is still time to make changes.

Another timing issue is that of potential repeatability — or lack thereof — associated with various properties. A sports tie-in may be optimal if a company wants the opportunity to repeat a successful promotion year after year during the same selling period, thus facilitating planning and coordination with sales forces, wholesalers, and retailers. A successful Super Bowl promotion, with slight annual variations and improvements, may occur year after year. On the other hand, there is no guarantee that a successful film promotion may be repeated. The chance that a sequel of a hit film will be made is good, and getting better, but there is no telling when that sequel will occur — in what selling season or in what year.

If the tie-in partner's goal is to have an ongoing, long-term promotional arrangement with a property, then a classic character or a well-known nonprofit may serve the purpose best. Sports tie-ins can also work to some extent but, even if the tie-in doesn't involve an annual event like the World Series or Super Bowl, there is still an inherent seasonality to sports properties because their respective seasons do not last year-round. A long-term tie-in does not bring with it the "excitement" and high profile of a tie-in with a (what is hoped to be) hot film or a major sports event, but it does provide a point of difference between the tie-in partner and its competitors, and is usually less risky.

Aside from the challenges involving timing, tie-ins also carry with them certain risks inherent to the properties themselves. Entertainment properties may not be a hit, for example. People won't be attracted to a tie-in if its central element is unknown or if potential customers actively dislike it. One way to guard against this risk is to maximize the impact of the tie-in by scheduling it in the months or weeks *before* a film opens or a television series premieres. That way, although the tie-in partners do not receive the same benefit they would have if the property had been popular, at least they received enough value ahead of time, while excitement was building, to rationalize the costs involved.

In the case of films, more and more tie-in partners are choosing to associate their brands with videocassette rather than theatrical releases. That way, the property has a track record and is thus perceived as less risky. In addition, videos — particularly those for children, which are more often sold than rented — offer the added benefit of repeat viewing. Children like to see the film over and over, thus maximizing the awareness of the property itself and products associated with it through licensing or tie-ins.

Both entertainment and sports properties carry with them the risk of controversy. Athletes can be injured or be indicted for drug use or gambling or some other activity with which a tie-in partner does not want to be associated and over which it has no control. Entertainment personalities can be controversial as well, and films rated PG-13 or older can contain themes that unexpectedly offend a tie-in partner's target audience. These occurrences not only negate any benefits of the tie-in but also can actually hurt sales (or attract negative perceptions by consumers toward the partners). Tie-ins with cartoon characters, G-rated films, sports leagues rather than individual athletes, and estates of deceased celebrities are common ways to avoid this risk.

Finally, another challenge inherent in entertainment promotions in particular is the risk that key personalities will not want to participate in a commercial venture such as a tie-in. If the use of the star or the star's likeness is crucial to the structure of a partner's tie-in, it is essential that likeness approvals are acquired up front. Promises by the studios that likeness approvals are no problem should be double-checked by talking directly to the talent or the talent's agency representatives. On the other hand, successful promotions can be built around films or television programs without the use of the stars. If the promotion does focus on the star, however, the partner should be sure that the star is agreeable before it's too late and the tie-in has to be redone at the last minute, at the sacrifice of dollars and perhaps quality.

CONCLUSIONS

Simply associating with a popular property is not enough to effectively differentiate a product or brand from its competitors; thought and creativity need to go into tie-ins and product licensing relationships in order to make them successful. Rather than an automatic way to sell merchandise, licensing and tie-ins are now recognized as effective marketing tools, used in conjunction with the rest of a company's marketing strategy.

As a result, not only "hit" properties are used for tie-ins and licensing. The fit between the property and its licensees and tie-in partners is more important than the overall popularity of the property. There are times when companies will successfully tie in with the high-profile "hits" — they still generate excitement and widespread, short-term awareness. But different companies have different marketing needs, and there are many properties out there that can fit the bill, depending on a marketer's specific goals.

Licensing and tie-ins should be part of a company's overall marketing strategy, not the only facet of that strategy. Risks should be minimized as much as possible (although marketers should be aware that most licensing and tie-in deals are inherently risky). And all properties should be considered — not just the obvious hot entertainment properties, but smaller properties, long-term classics, trademarks, nonprofits, sports outside of the major sports leagues, and so forth.

Flexibility and trust among the partners are key to a successful relationship. Those two elements — as well as open communication among all players — will help allow the creation of a unique tie-in, will minimize risks, and will enable the partners to adapt to unforeseen contingencies.

Paul Stanley is President and Creative Director of PS Productions, Inc., Chicago, which he established in 1974. PS is the largest entertainment event marketing agency in the country. Previously, Stanley was President/Creative Director of the SR&B Advertising Agency in Detroit, Michigan, for 12 years. He also managed a record company, founded the Royal Oak Music Theater and Castle Farms outdoor venue in Charlevoix, Michigan, and was a concert promoter throughout Michigan for 14 years, promoting more than 2,000 concerts and events. Stanley produced, wrote, and hosted his own television show out of Detroit called Takin It to the Street.*

Stanley designed the first corporate sponsorship of a rock/music tour and created and trademarked the entertainment event concepts of Sponsownership™, Multiple Tiered/Modular Programs™, and Trade Learning Customization™. His PS Productions agency creates and executes corporate sponsorships for clients that include Procter & Gamble, Philip Morris, Kraft, Frito Lay, Borden, the Dial Corporation, Chrysler, Alberto-Culver, and many more. He is also founding judge of Adweek Magazine*'s Annual Event of the Year Awards.*

Stanley will soon complete a master's degree in advertising from Michigan State University with an eye to teaching event marketing at the college level.

CHAPTER 11

EVENT MARKETING — IT'S NOT THE EVENT THAT MATTERS

Event marketing is one of the most powerful marketing tools in existence today. The results, measured against the initial objectives of the sponsor, continually exceed marketer's expectations. In fact, marketer's reactions to the event medium have gone from caution, skepticism, and downright aversion to "We haven't seen this type of retail support and record sales in years." The sophistication of the event marketing medium has continued to increase to the point where the industry is projected to top $5 billion in 1993!

The first real event marketing music sponsorship program, "Ford Motor Company Presents The Rockets" (a rock and roll band big in the Midwest in the late 1970s), was created to reach college students and "talk" to them "on their own turf." A four-college market tour was scheduled with the primary objective of gaining "a warm feeling" from the college target and moving the attitude needle toward Ford in a positive manner. Ford implemented consumer research to evaluate this program, and the results baffled Ford's own research people. The needle didn't just move, it soared off the page! From "do you think Ford makes a good product" to "would you buy a Ford," the response was extremely positive.

One year later, "Jovan Cologne Presents the Rolling Stones" came to life, and an industry was on its way. Event marketing got everyone's attention.

When dealing with event marketing, it's not the event that matters most. Without grasping that basic premise, the power and essence of this very innovative marketing tool cannot be understood. The measure of an event marketing program's success is in how you *leverage* the event, not the event itself. By looking at the individual players and figuring out what the objectives of each are and then working to satisfy those individual objectives, the whole event program returns results that are much more than the sum of its parts.

Most of what is done in event marketing is common sense. Still, when properly used, event marketing is the most powerful results-oriented and "fail-safe" means of achieving marketing objectives today.

WHAT IS AN EVENT?

The fundamental notion behind an event sponsorship is that a sponsor/marketer associates with an event property — entertainers, sports, Olympics, Superbowl, etc. — and "trades off" on the popularity of that event to fulfill its marketing objectives. Sponsownership™, a concept trademarked in the early 1980s, is a sponsorship that is owned by the sponsor. This ownership not only allows sponsors/marketers to utilize and leverage the event to achieve their marketing objectives, it also allows them to take in revenues generated by the event itself (ticket sales, merchandise sales). It allows marketers to build and control their own events for years to come, thus building equity and longevity into their own marketing programs. Because of their effectiveness and profitability, sponsownerships are sure to become the marketing avenue of choice for sponsors over the next few years.

To understand better what event marketing is, several examples of successful event sponsorships and sponsownerships are briefly described in this section. While most of these concentrate particularly on entertainment events for packaged goods marketers, the basic principles remain the same for all events. An event can be created and utilized to support, sell, or market any product or service, from the automotive industry to electronics. The event can focus on entertainment, sports, or some other theme created especially for a brand's image. The same principles also apply whether your need is of a national scope or a one-market execution. Despite the fact that each event is ultimately quite different from the others in its theme, scope, and audience, keep in mind: "It's not the event, it's how you leverage the event."

- **"AT&T College Comedy Tour."** A sponsownership program designed for AT&T featuring leading comedians on 20 college campuses. The tour was also taped for an MTV special. It required securing all talent, booking college campuses, and producing the tour and TV special. The program was tied to AT&T service sign-up and image enhancement.
- **"Sparkle Crest Presents The ABC Family Fun Fair."** A multicharacter mall tour (20 weeks) for ABC Television, sponsored by Procter & Gamble. It became the number one mall tour in audience attraction (40,000+ per market) and mall satisfaction. The Sparkle Crest objective was to launch a new product, to gain retail support, and to enhance image. Retailers could not keep the product in stock. ABC's objective was to promote its Saturday morning lineup, and it went from third to first in ratings.
- **"Procter & Gamble Presents Barry Manilow."** A test program developed to meet the exact marketing objectives (displays, incremental cases) of P&G's Era and Ivory Liquid brands. The promotion it achieved was so successful, it was expanded to 20 markets. Another similar event followed, consisting of a 20-city, multiple-brand extension of the test program, leveraging Manilow's Broadway show with media and trade support to obtain incremental case sales and to enhance trade relations.
- **"The Wrangler Country Showdown."** The world's largest talent contest: tie-ins with 400 radio stations, 2,000+ Dodge

dealers, local tie-ins with 500+ Wrangler retailers, talent competitions at 52 state fairs, and a national talent contest showdown finish at The Grand Ole Opry in Nashville. The event leveraged $13.5 million in free media coverage.

- **"Chivas Regal Presents Frank Sinatra's Diamond Jubilee."** Chivas and Sinatra, two legends, teamed up to produce one of the most outstanding music marketing tours ever staged. The national tour tied in with consumer sweepstakes, trade hospitality, POP displays, a CD/cassette offer, and a 900 line. It was designed to produce high visibility and an awareness for the brand, retail support, display, and consumer sales.

- **"Borden Snacks Presents The Beach Boys."** The concert tour promoted 16 brands in 75 markets. The event was designed to increase display and feature support incentives and span three generations of consumers. Strong consumer takeaway/sell-through was built into the promotional program. Unique venues (baseball parks and a charity tie-in to the Better Homes Foundation) added even more power to the promotion. It was the biggest and most successful promotion in Borden Snacks' history (see Exhibit 11.1).

- **"Alberto VO5 Presents The Moody Blues."** This was an industry first in the health and beauty aids category. It was designed to gain increased display and feature support, incremental consumer takeaway, and expanded distribution within the top 50 ADIs. Results surpassed even the most optimistic of the company's projections (see Exhibit 11.2).

- **"Swift-Eckrich Presents Meet The Greats of Baseball."** This event was a 27-market mall tour, featuring Major League Baseball alumni. It was designed to increase trade support, stimulate incremental takeaway, and raise awareness of all deli products during the key summer season. Events included a one-of-a-kind photo exhibit, baseball clinics, and photo sessions and autograph signing by former baseball stars. Tie-ins with local deli counters included free photos and autographs and chances to win tickets to 1993 spring training exhibition games with proofs-of-purchase. The promotion achieved more than 90 percent total trade participation on initial sell-in.

A HISTORICAL PERSPECTIVE

Event marketing is not really a new idea. Rather, it is the updated use of very sound marketing and promotional disciplines that have been molded to fit today's marketplace. To really understand why events have become such a successful promotional tool, consider what they offer:

- An exciting, memorable, often entertaining environment, exclusively available to the sponsor and free from competitive

EXHIBIT 11.1

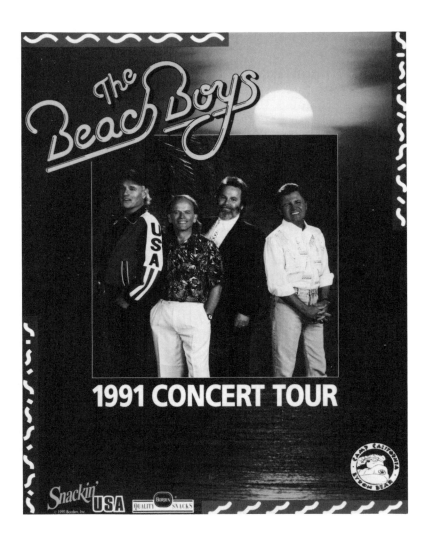

EXHIBIT 11.2

clutter and distractions;

- A completely captive and receptive audience, who is often quite demographically homogeneous and thus desirable from a targeting point of view;
- An opportunity to satisfy all the key players in the marketing arena, including the consumer, the trade, and the media, simply by capitalizing on and leveraging the event's popularity; and
- A tool that can enhance a brand's image and shift some marketing clout and power back into the hands of the manufacturer once again.

Events offer what no other medium today can, and in many respects, events offer the best of what radio, television, and advertising used to offer, only in today's marketplace. Consider history.

In the early days of brand advertising, marketers set out to create a brand image. With the invention of radio, advertisers found that by creating programming they, in fact, created an "event" that consumers tuned in to hear religiously every week. This captive audience was in a relaxed and receptive mode — a perfect disposition for creating and selling a brand image. By building this brand image, marketers could realize trial and sales objectives, putting *power in the brand*, a brand that Ms./Mr. Consumer would actually ask for. This brand power allowed manufacturers to dictate the retailers and receive more shelf space, line extensions, display support, and, later, feature pricing and trade advertising. They could also use that brand power to generate support for their new and lesser known brands.

As consumers bought into brand imaging primarily through radio events, a new, more powerful medium came upon the scene. The power of television would become unsurpassed in its reach and effectiveness for decades. With television came the need for new and different programming that would attract the desired demographics, hold the consumers' attention, and open their minds to advertisers' messages. Television was new, entertaining, exciting, innovative, and *live*. The shows themselves were events. Milton Berle, Jack Parr, Steve Allen, and Ed Sullivan became events that flowed into America's living rooms. Procter & Gamble created the soap opera, hooking millions of consumers who were a captive audience to their messages. Commercials were live, often starring the celebrities themselves as endorsers, adding a new dimension of credibility. Even the commercials were entertaining and captivating. Television brought even more power to the manufacturer/advertiser over the trade.

Fast-forward to the 1990s. Today, there is a whole new ball game, and brand power is almost gone, at least in terms of the retail trade. The number of competitive brands is at an all-time high. Couponing and discounting are a way of life. Retail deals and dollars have never before been spent at such a pace. Marketers have come to learn that the best way to sell products is through retail trade support, off-shelf displays, feature ads, and feature pricing. Manufacturers created their own monster by initially paying for this support, and now they cannot find a way out. Kraft General Foods, as an example, spent over $1.5 billion on "trade deals" in 1992. What is worse, the company is not really sure where all the money went!

The trade has never been more powerful than it is today. A majority of retailers don't even make their money selling products anymore; they make it on trade deals, case allowances, slotting allowances, diverting, forward-buying, co-oping, and many other ways that marketers, not long ago, had never even heard of. If one manufacturer isn't willing to pay, there are plenty of other manufacturers in line that will. Further, price seems to be playing a continued major role in consumer purchases, which results in a continuing decline in brand profits and equity. If that weren't enough to make it downright tough to sell products, look what has happened to the advertising world.

Never before have there been more media vying for consumer attention than there are today. Gone are the days of a few television networks, radio stations, and print vehicles. Cable television alone provides more than 100 channels. With the coming of skylink (a very affordable home satellite dish), the choices will be staggering. Couple that with a very mobile society, more women in the workplace, and an overall squeeze on consumer time, you now have a consumer who is almost impossible to reach through traditional marketing vehicles.

Marketers have at last realized that a national marketing strategy can no longer work, and they need local market strategies. Local promotions allow a marketer to adapt to a market from consumer, trade, and media perspectives. However, the question remains, "How do we implement that strategy?"

Unfortunately, to date, the primary strategy has basically been to "pay off the trade" while dumping millions of coupons on the consumer. That strategy, however, is no longer as effective because everybody's doing it, and manufacturers have created a merry-go-round they cannot seem to stop.

Enter event marketing. Event marketing can deliver everyone's objectives simultaneously. Events create a "win-win-win" scenario. No other medium can make that claim. For instance, if you're going to take money away from the trade, then you'd better have something else to offer in its place. And to do this, you must think about the objectives and needs of the trade. Understanding and unlocking those goals and needs are the key.

Event marketing is not about the numbers of people who show up at a concert or tennis match. It's also not about hanging a banner at the event. Promotional success shouldn't be about ticket sales, either. It is all about leveraging the event to meet everyone's objectives in that market. Unfortunately, early on, too many people based their whole promotion on the success of the event itself, and to some extent, they still do. In reality, the main focus should be on the three to four weeks prior to and following the event. This period is the key to successful event marketing.

MAKING EVENTS WORK FOR YOU

The following information on event marketing will deal with the nuts and bolts of creating, executing, and measuring the success of an event marketing promotion. Please remember that the basics are the same, whether you utilize sports or entertainment or you create your own event (Sponsownerships™). It is also wise to have an experienced event marketing firm with a proven track record to handle most of the event execution workload and to provide daily assistance if necessary.

It all starts with the marketer's/sponsor's objectives. Because event marketing is multidimensional, it can simultaneously deliver multiple objectives. Therefore, all objectives must be identified. For example, what objectives might event marketing accomplish for a laundry detergent?
- Trial and incremental sales
- Trade support, displays, features, promotional pricing, incremental case orders
- Reaching women ages 25 to 49
- Key selling or competitive timing
- Brand image and awareness

- Publicity
- Easy sell-in for the sales force
- Sales force enthusiasm
- Trade relations building
- Cost-effectiveness
- Easy/turnkey execution

Once marketers/sponsors have carefully identified all the objectives they wish to achieve, the criteria by which the success of the program are measured must be determined. While some may question whether event marketing results are, in fact, measurable, the reality is that events provide more measurable results than most other advertising media and promotion techniques.

The key and "soul" to successful event marketing is to remember the following: *Marketers achieve their objectives through event marketing by achieving the objectives of others. Marketers' success depends on influencing the trade, the consumer, their sales force, and the media to do their bidding.* No other medium has the direct ability to allow all who are important to a marketer's goals to achieve those goals simultaneously. Therefore, after identifying the objectives (manufacturer/sponsor), you must look at the objectives of the other players who will be affected by the event promotion.

This diagram may also be expanded to include other "players" (depending on the manufacturer/sponsor) such as franchisees, bottlers, promoters, and brokers.

These players' objectives, and how those objectives can be met through an event program, will be discussed in the following sections.

THE TRADE

Traffic and sales are primary objectives of the trade. Today, when manufacturers run an advertising campaign, theoretically, they are creating demand for their product, which should create traffic to retail and, of course, sales for both retailers and manufacturers. Why, then, are manufacturers spending billions of dollars a year "paying off the trade" if trade objectives are being met through manufacturers' advertising?

What if manufacturers could, in fact, meet the trade's objectives while meeting their own? To do this through an event marketing program, the trade's objectives must first be identified and built into the program. Obviously, the trade wants traffic and sales as stated earlier. But what else do retailers desire?

Retailers want to be a part of something big in their community or, at the very least, to not be left out of something big! They like to be a part of localized media. They need to turn sales quickly. They like to reward their own employees in special ways. They like new profit centers that earn a healthy markup, especially when those profit centers require no cash outlay against those profits. They want to reward their customers for their shopping loyalty. They like to be a part of something that is not the everyday "ho-hum" that has become the way of doing business. And one last thing that members of the trade enjoy is something that can include their own families — a work, yet family, experience.

Accomplishing all of this may seem like a big challenge, but the reality is that an event marketing program can, in fact, be designed to deliver *all* of these objectives and desires to the trade in exchange for the trade's achieving a marketer's/sponsor's objectives. Competition among retail trades is fierce. That fact can be used to a manufacturer's advantage.

Here is a summary of retailers' objectives: traffic, sales and quick turns, new profit centers, local media, staying competitive, rewarding their customers and employees, something new and innovative, community involvement potential, and something that is family-oriented for themselves.

Members of the trade are, of course, key to any manufacturer, but they are only part of the equation in achieving sponsor/marketing objectives today. Other players will also help achieve the trade's objectives.

THE FIELD/SALES FORCE

The field, of course, is the sales force of a manufacturer and the direct link between the retailer and the manufacturer. The field may be directly employed by the manufacturer or may include independent brokers or direct delivery systems (for example, truck or route drivers). The field is, of course, critical to any manufacturer, and an event program can be designed to achieve the objectives of the field as well.

Whether they are direct salespeople or brokers, today's field pretty much faces the same obstacles, problems, and frustrations. With all of the megamergers of the 1980s, the field is overloaded and inundated with brands, demands, and quotas. Personnel in the field have sales quotas to meet on multiple brands; they have to introduce new products and line extensions. They usually deal from a position of weakness with the trade and, of course, the competition has never been greater or more fierce. In addition, they are usually responsible for putting up point-of-sale and special displays, and their duties do not end there.

What this means is the field does not want or need any extra workload — period.

And it is wise to recognize that the field personnel can make or break any event promotion or, at the very least, hinder it. One key benefit of event marketing for the sponsor brand is in focusing the full attention of the sales force on the sponsoring brand.

What else can event marketing do for the field and its objectives? Let's look at some of these objectives. The field needs to increase sales. Salespeoples' bonuses are most likely tied to sales performance.

To do this, they know they must:

- Gain as many retail displays, extended displays, and end aisles as possible;
- Gain trade features and support pricing;
- Have promotional overlays to drive consumer takeaway; and
- Beat their competition.

Event marketing can achieve all of these objectives and more. How? An untold benefit of event marketing is its ability to boost field morale. This is a major plus. When people are happier and more excited, they sell better.

Event marketing gives the field something to bring to the "Lion's Den" (aka "the trade buyer") — something new, exciting, and most important, built for the trade's own objectives and with no competitive equal.

Event marketing allows field personnel to be big shots in their own markets because they are "hosting" the event and, therefore, are in control of prime tickets, special merchandise, special media, and most often, powerful backstage or private party passes. These items can be highly leveraged.

Think about this. If the field from brand A offers the trade this comprehensive, integrated event program with all of its perks, what does the field from competitive brand B counter with? Another case deal? More coupons? The fact remains, event marketing has no apples-to-apples comparison. This noncomparison factor packs one big cannon for the field. Therefore, the sponsoring brand can *finally* regain some much-needed and long-lost power.

It is important to teach field personnel that with all they are bringing to the trade — the event, the media, the customization, the traffic and sales builders, to name a few — they owe their customers *nothing* more. Consequently, for once, they can get up and walk away from an uncooperative retailer. That retailer is only hurting itself; nine times out of 10, the other retailers will not only "pick up the slack" but also will actually support the promotion beyond normal levels. Event marketing works, and smart retailers will not want to be left out.

The concept of the field walking away from the table or not throwing cash at the retailers is a refreshing change for the field. The only problem is that some field personnel are so "shell-shocked" or trade brainwashed that they actually need to be retrained. It is vital to train and communicate with the field exactly what the event program is about, how it works, and how it works for the other players. Field personnel are the direct link to the market and the trade. Supply them with field training films and other helpful collateral materials. More important, explain how the trade can use that power to achieve its own objectives.

Furthermore, it is important to equip the field with trade sell-in videos which can explain to retailers the event promotion and its power overall. These tools can even be customized for each individual trade and/or buyer. These selling tools can be created with a little touch of fun, as well, because it's all right to have some fun for a change.

The field is key. Yet, the field is also very busy. So remember those two points when executing an event promotion, and design the promotion for easy field execution. Make sure the program is initially very well communicated to field personnel with a chance for them to ask questions. Weekly sell-in success stories can be exchanged between different field personnel in different markets, as can funny stories, tips, and experiences. Encourage the field to "get creative with the promotion" if it chooses and to have some fun, or, as the field force for the "Borden Snacks Presents The Beach Boys" event promotion would come to say, "Have some fun, fun, fun!"

Today, field personnel utilizing an event in this way are gaining *multiple* display periods and multiple feature ads from the trade, in addition to the mandatory displays directly tied to the event marketing promotion time frame. First-quarter event promotions can and have been leveraged by the field for not only first-quarter support but also for Labor Day displays as well! New product distributions and line extensions have also been successfully leveraged with the trade against the event promotion.

THE MEDIA

The media, on both national and local levels, are just as competitive as any other business today. They are also a powerful partner in an event promotion. They can be utilized to create consumer awareness, call the consumers to action, provide further leverage with the trade, and contribute a host of additional benefits to the brand, sponsor, or event.

Start with the media at the same starting place as with all "players" in an event promotion — with their own objectives. Whether dealing with a television network or a local affiliate, a radio network or a local station, a cable network or a local cable system, a local newspaper, *USA Today*, or a magazine, they *all* want increased viewers or listeners or readers. They want to be able to offer exclusives/rewards to their audiences, and they also want to make money.

Can an event promotion offer a media partner or partners the ability to achieve those objectives? You bet!

By offering a station a multifaceted package, it is possible to meet and surpass not only the station's objectives but also those of the sponsors as well. A typical package would include the following:

- Exclusive tangibles (front row tickets, backstage passes, new artist releases);
- Exclusive intangibles (presenting station, exclusive on-stage welcomes);
- Value-added sales opportunities (ancillary media tie-ins that

media partner can sell off);
- Special programming (also a media sales opportunity); and
- Cash spot buys.

The biggest surprise to most sponsors is that the event promotion can actually allow the media partner(s) to sell parts of the program to noncompeting companies/brands without detracting from the promotion or the sponsors' presence/objectives. On the contrary, the more the media partner(s) sell, the more the promotion, brand image, and special offers are promoted! These are "value-added" sales opportunities for the station and an extended promotion for the sponsor. The media can even approach the sponsoring trades and put together other ancillary media tie-ins that further benefit the sponsor and the trade.

The key with the media is the word *leveraging*. Typically, an event will generate, on purchased media, ratios that range from $4.00 in promotion for every dollar spent to $30.00 in promotion for every dollar spent. That's a lot of media in every local market that is not only promoting the event, brand, and special consumer offers, but which is also choking out competitors. What is the competition going to do? Buy more straight brand-image advertising? The event sponsor should only hope so, since it will be purely wasted cash that the competition cannot use elsewhere.

One hundred thousand dollars was spent overall in event media buys across 75 markets on the "Borden Snacks Presents The Beach Boys" event promotion. More than $2 million in *measured* media was received in return, in support of the brands, the promotion, and the consumer offers. The majority of this media power was focused on trade and sponsoring brand displays. This created a lot of trade traffic and sales, which fulfilled two big trade objectives. This kind of synergy among the "players" can be leveraged by the sponsoring brand for its own objectives. How do you beat that? You don't.

How can a high level of media support be achieved? Look for ways to build exclusive benefits into a program based on the media's objectives. That can include, as stated, ways that the media can sell promotional parts of an event to noncompetitors, ways the media can attract listeners or viewers while tying to the sponsoring brand's displays and products, exclusive perks such as live remotes from the event site, exclusive access to interviews with entertainment or sports celebrities who are sponsored, and exclusive event merchandise.

Creating special programming for radio and/or television that can be bartered with the local stations is an effective ancillary to an event program. Media hypes customize the programming locally with their stations or news personalities and sell off time in the program. The program is, of course, tied to the sponsored event, artist, or sports celebrity, and the time reserved for the sponsor or special broadcast program provider may be utilized by the sponsor to further promote its brands, events, or consumer offers, and as leverage with the trade.

These are but a few ideas. Depending on the event, be creative and remember to keep the media's objectives in mind. Believe me, they will hear you loud and clear.

PUBLICITY

This is a good time to mention the endless publicity opportunities that exist with event promotions. Publicity is not paid media; it's news stories, articles, and interviews that primarily promote sponsor or brand image and awareness on both a national and local market-by-market basis.

If an event includes an entertainer, sports celebrity, movie star, politician, or other high-profile personality, there is a walking spokesperson who can interact with every medium in every market and on a national level, as well. After all, that's what shows such as *Good Morning America, David Letterman, The Tonight Show, Donahue, Oprah*, and others are all about and need! Take advantage of the publicity they can give! Local radio disc jockeys love guests or phone-in interviews; newspapers need stories; *People* is about exactly that — people and events.

Publicity opportunities are a big bonus to event marketing and to sponsors. Not only does the sponsor or brand reap all the benefits, but also, what can the brand's competitors do to match this? Even with celebrity advertising endorsers, competitors will never reach the audience that an event's publicity will reach. They would have to pay a celebrity endorser as much as it would cost to pay for an entire event marketing program, spokespeople included.

An event promotion may also include a cause, charity, or fund-raising tie-in. This gives the sponsor other avenues to gain image, awareness, and a "good citizen" aura. The event itself can actually raise much needed money for charity at the same time. "Live Aid," "Hands Across America," and "Farm Aid" were events that raised millions of dollars for great causes while they also furthered their sponsors' objectives.

Event promotions are also *very* flexible and allow for quick reaction to situations. During the 1989 event "Procter & Gamble Presents Barry Manilow," Hurricane Hugo hit the South. Manilow and Procter & Gamble both wanted to help — and quickly. The tour was diverted to a building (that was still standing) in Columbia, South Carolina, and raised more than $100,000 dollars plus tons of food and clothing donations. Not only was it a nice thing to do, but also the public relations benefit was endless, and everyone came out smelling like a rose.

An event promotion allows sponsors to reach out and "shake hands" with their customers/consumers and public. It's said that the strongest form of advertising is "word of mouth," so let an event speak out!

There are several different ways to position each project, but there are also a few things that should be done for publicity's sake that are common to all projects:

1. Start with a national "kickoff" campaign.
2. Initiate a well-thought-out promotional plan aimed at the consumer audience in general, targeting the particular demographics for the event.
3. Work with local media outlets to augment their promotional objectives in individual markets.
4. Use phone interviews, live interviews, press releases, and feature stories. Use your event property in a way traditional media cannot equal.

EVENT PROMOTERS

Events have promoters. Every concert, play, or tennis tournament that comes to town has someone, somehow putting up money to be a part of that event in exchange for sharing in revenues (ticket sales, merchandise, concessions).

If revenues do not exceed the total cost of staging that event, a promoter loses money. Whether it's an individual company, a charity trying to raise money, or the local nightclub highlighting local talent, these entities are risking their money and time to make money. In a sense, event promoters make a living by rolling the dice every day, gambling that an event will be a success. Most people do not understand what it takes to bring a major show or event to town. Promoters do this without any guarantee of earning a profit but with the risk of losing a lot of money.

The important thing to remember is the money that brought the event to town and that advertised it is the promoter's. In the early days of music events, sponsors would contract directly with the artist to perform on their tours, and they paid the artist directly for that right. The promoters didn't see a dime, yet promoters were asked to give tickets to some sponsor's friend (tickets the promoter was counting on selling), hang banners, and advertise for nothing! Very often, sponsors and their representatives were met with resistance and received little cooperation from promoters.

Although promoters still do not directly share in sponsorship dollars per se, they are most cooperative when they, too, are included in an overall sponsorship.

How can a sponsor include them? Again, begin by considering their objectives. A promoter's number one objective is to sell tickets as quickly as possible (in order to cut advertising expenditures as quickly as possible). To do this, a promoter must let as many people as possible know that the event is coming, while also building some "hype" around the promotion. A sponsor's marketing plan and marketing power can help achieve the promoter's main objective.

The sponsor and promoter have some common ground — awareness. Awareness for the event is critical for ticket sales. Start there.

The sponsor needs to build its promotional and advertising plans and execution to include a means for the local promoter to also promote its shows. Whether you "tag" sponsor media or point-of-sale materials, remember the other common ground between sponsor and promoter — both want the event to succeed.

Keeping a promoter happy is something that helps ensure that the things a sponsor needs to achieve at the event will go smoothly — from getting the right number of tickets in the right locations at the right times, to inclusion in the promoter's advertising, event signage, and sampling, to the hospitality parties at the event's conclusion.

Always think of promoters from the start when putting sponsorships together. That way it won't be a "gamble" when dealing with them.

THE EVENT PROPERTY

Event marketing obviously deals with an event of some sort. Whether utilizing entertainers or sports celebrities, there is always an event "property."

In the early days of event marketing, especially in the entertainment and sports arenas, sponsors usually showered sponsor cash on the event property. This practice, however, can be detrimental to the event industry as a whole. The use of any medium must deliver a "payback" to the user, which is generally measured in overall sales. Ultimately, all sponsors are, of course, going to measure the success of their sponsorship by comparing overall sales results with total costs. In other words, did the promotion pay out? It is therefore important to keep event property fees in check, both for the success of the given event promotion and for the event industry as a whole.

Remember, early on in event marketing, many in the marketing business, especially advertising agencies who were starting to lose some of their advertising revenues to promotional events, were taking potshots at this new medium. Comparing effectiveness to cost is always an easy place to start looking for problems.

Event agencies that represent a corporate sponsor are responsible for protecting that sponsor and advocating that client's interests. The interest is obviously not in making the event property — those entertainers and celebrities pivotal to an event's success — any wealthier than necessary. Event agencies that represent the event property, as well as the corporate sponsor, face potential conflicting interests. A representative for an event property is interested in getting as much money out of a corporation as possible, and if he or she is also representing the corporation, the sponsor may not receive the best deal possible. Unfortunately, this goes on all the time.

If not excessive cash, is there something else that a sponsor can offer an event property to ensure cooperation? What are the event property's objectives? Usually, they are almost identical to the promoter's — ticket sales, ticket sales, ticket sales, plus merchandise sales — and all achieved at as little advertising and promotional costs as possible.

Unlike the promoter's objectives, an event property may also want to sell something else. Entertainers want to sell records. Sports celebrities may want to sell clothing, instructional videos, or autographs. Cultural events may want to raise additional charitable dollars or sell subscriptions to something. The key is to know the event properties well enough to find their "hot" buttons. These then represent a negotiating or leveraging position from which to deal.

While it is a lot easier to simply pay an event property's asking price, in the long run, it is far better to avoid this because an event promotion will be more profitable in the end.

What happens after identifying the event property's interests? It's time to get creative again. This time, let's do it by example.

When Procter & Gamble sponsored an event with Dolly Parton and Kenny Rogers ("Downy Presents Kenny Rogers/Dolly Parton," 1988), it was a fourth-quarter promotion, and both Kenny and Dolly were coming out with holiday record albums. This presented the perfect opportunity for using the event's clout to help achieve objectives mutually beneficial for the sponsor and the event property. In this case, the reach and marketing power of Downy was used to help sell records. In addition to making Kenny and Dolly offers that included marketing their concerts (ticket sales), there was also an offer to help them sell their new records. Every bottle of Downy carried a "hangtag" alerting the consumer that if they bought a certain size of Downy fabric softener *and* Kenny and/or Dolly's album, Downy would send them a two-dollar rebate. On all of the Downy in-store point-of-sale materials and displays that supported the in-market event (Kenny and Dolly's concert), the new albums were featured, furthering consumer awareness of Kenny and Dolly's new products. Conversely, inside all of Kenny's and Dolly's new albums was the information on how to receive the rebate. Furthermore, each album was flagged on the outside telling consumers they could buy this album and receive the rebate. This created a win-win situation. Kenny and Dolly received a lot of nontraditional advertising and awareness for their new albums, and Downy was featured in nontraditional marketing avenues as well — record stores and in and on the albums.

While Downy picked up the tab for the $2.00 redemptions, it was a better use of money than paying direct cash to Kenny and Dolly for the event sponsorship. Money that is thrown at an event property is "dead" money in that it is money that cannot be used to achieve the sponsor's objectives. The creative use of rebating in this case helped Kenny and Dolly gain cash through higher album sales, yet Downy also achieved its objectives simultaneously.

Scratching someone else's back will always get a positive

response. Creativity here can go a long way toward making an event more profitable all around. The saying that "Cash is king" is still true. However, when negotiating with event properties, it is better to think "Direct cash is not always king." Accomplishing other objectives for them can achieve royalty as well, or, in the record business, royalties!

THE CONSUMER

The almighty consumer. That's what marketing and promotion are all about, is it not? The goal is to get the consumer to buy or try a given product or service by creating brand image and brand loyalty which, along with a good product, will keep the consumer buying the product.

However, the majority of purchases today are impulse purchases, and that's the hard fact. In addition, consumers very often can be swayed from one brand to another through certain promotional inducements, such as coupons, rewards, and exclusives. These avenues are often strictly price-oriented and typically have no connection to brand imaging and awareness.

Event marketing allows marketers to reach consumers through multiple traditional and nontraditional means and to induce or reward them to buy or try products while simultaneously building brand image and awareness.

The importance of the trade in supporting and displaying a brand in the store has already been discussed. Trade support is especially important for impulse purchasing. Once trade support is forthcoming, including "loading up" on product stock, higher levels of consumer takeaway (sales) are possible than are accomplished through traditional trade support of displays, features, feature pricing, and other methods. Research has shown that consumers would buy or try a product to get a discount on tickets for an event or concert that they were interested in attending. Consumers claim also to buy or try a product if it allows for other special rewards or exclusives — for example, on-pack offers for exclusive tour merchandise, audiocassettes, or other event- or entertainment-oriented tie-ins or specials.

Several consumer and product purchase offers and rewards were tested in conjunction with Kellogg's 1991 "Kenmei Cereal Presents Barry Manilow in Concert" event. These included (1) a $7.50 discount off each Manilow concert ticket with two proofs-of-purchase for Kellogg's Kenmei cereal, (2) a free audiocassette of Barry Manilow with two proofs of Kellogg's Kenmei cereal redeemable right in the grocery store (instant gratification), (3) discounts on tour merchandise, and, of course, (4) special rewards of front row concert seats and backstage passes. The brand experienced a share increase of seven times its then-current position! Kellogg was also able to achieve an approximate share of four times its initial share position in the months following the promotion/event, meaning that consumers were repurchasing the brand in order to exchange product purchases for rewards (see Exhibit 11.3).

EXHIBIT 11.3

In addition to rewarding consumers for their purchases, event marketing also allows a marketer to build instant brand imaging and awareness through the close association with the event property (artist, sports figure) and its own inherent image. People, by and large, are very image-conscious and like to be associated with things that "tell" them or reinforce to them that they are, in fact, "cool."

The "Chivas Regal Presents Frank Sinatra's Diamond Jubilee" tour/event for the House of Seagram's premium scotch created an association which in itself said something instantly to the consumer and the trade. Sinatra is as premium as one gets in the entertainment industry and to consumer demographics that fit Chivas Regal targets. If Sinatra represents "the best," Chivas Regal must too.

However, do not make the mistake that lots of failed event marketing programs have. Remember it's not the event; it's how the event is leveraged to accomplish multiple goals! The Chivas Regal/Frank Sinatra program included retail display tie-ins, retail hospitality, media tie-ins and public relations, a special customized Chivas Regal audio-cassette of Frank Sinatra's greatest hits that was featured on-pack, plus more tie-ins to make sure the brand received trade support, media support, and, of course, consumer takeaway. The program was hailed as one of the most successful programs Seagram's has ever had and "raised the bar" for future House of Seagram promotions.

Consumers spend over $700 million a day on entertainment and recreation. Event marketing can uniquely reward both the consumer and the sponsor company by allowing all parties involved to get a little closer to something they already revere and enjoy. It definitely surpasses most sponsors' competitive promotions!

EXECUTING AN EVENT

Execution is the most important element in event marketing and probably in every other marketing venture. A big idea is just that, an idea. To bring it to life and to make it work takes flawless execution and implementation.

This following story typifies the problem of executing major event programs:

> A grandmother was walking her little grandson down a Miami beach one day, when all of a sudden a giant wave came out of the sea, grabbed the little boy, and took him away. Horrified, the elderly woman looked up to the sky and said, "I've never asked you for anything in my life! I've lived a decent, moral, and righteous life and I just do not deserve this." And so she said, "I'm asking now, please return my grandson to me, please!" With that, a giant wave appeared from the sea again, this time gently placing the little boy next to his grandmother, unharmed. The woman looked down to her beloved grandson, then she looked up to the sky and said, "HE HAD A HAT!"

To properly execute a successful event marketing program takes a lot of experience, much planning, proven systems for implementation, and the realization that it's not the obvious things that will get in the way of success. Rather, the small, almost unknown or unseen elements will cause an event to falter — like the hat in the story.

Consider a 70-city musical tour/event for a major sponsor. Everything is humming along — free media support, retail support, and sales surpassing the prior year's sales by 180 percent in a bad economy! The president of the sponsor company shows up totally unannounced with his teenage daughter and her friend, in a city where he has no ties. He did not bother to get concert tickets, nor did he show up to the event on time. Needless to say, there was some trouble accessing the talent backstage to impress his daughter and friend, and the star had already left by the time they did go backstage. Product sales were through the roof — but so was he. It didn't matter that his company was seeing sales results it hadn't seen in decades, or the fact that this was the most economical marketing program ever done. In his eyes, the program wasn't a success.

To be a successful event marketer, agency, or sponsor takes a talent for execution that cannot be taught anywhere. Successful execution takes experience, an unbelievable amount of diplomacy, and an ability to respond quickly to unforeseen problems when they occur. All the planning and focus on detail are critical, but so is the ability to react and to react quickly.

In the previous situation, a private rendezvous with the event's star for the president and his daughter was arranged by having the local sheriff stop the star's motorcade to explain the situation. Now local dealers and the president have agreed that this was an enormously successful event/promotion.

So, careful planning, realistic time and action tables, and being prepared to expect the unexpected are essential to an event's success. Face any problem or situation Honestly, and find the needed Answer in a very Timely manner. An event involves so many people, so many egos, so many elements. Always remember the H.A.T.!

MEASUREMENT

Not only can an event's success be measured, but also the results can be measured better and more accurately than with almost any other medium today. Since the exact promotional periods of the event promotion are known, event success can be directly measured:

By Account:
- Case sales
- Display penetration
- Shipments
- Features
- Price reductions
- Post-event surveys

By Intangibles:
- Image/awareness
- Product positioning
- Trade relationship building
- Field enthusiasm

By Media:
- PR (conversion)
- Leveraged (affidavits)

By Consumer:
- Scanner detail
- Redemption
- Nielsen (market share)
- Exit polls/intercepts

There also exist "bonuses" to event marketing that are harder to measure directly but are certainly part of its success. These bonuses/elements include:
- **Trade relationship building** — especially after a successful program with a fun personal backstage party visit
- **Sales force morale** — giving them the upper hand for once and making them feel good about their jobs
- **Brand imaging and awareness** — through the multitudes of media and promotions and the association with the event or star

One event can deliver all of the above; it is doubtful that a television commercial could do the same.

SUMMARY — IT'S NOT THE EVENT

By now it should be obvious how potentially powerful this medium of event marketing can be. Marketers have only just begun to experience the *surface* of what it can offer. It works because it addresses everyone's needs in today's marketplace. It is one of the most flexible means of marketing today because it permits adaptation not only to every individual market but also to every individual retailer, local medium, and consumer need.

The sales increases that event programs have generated are staggering, especially in today's economic climate. Event programs can gain four to eight weeks of retail and media support and obtain big consumer takeaway directly tied to special proof-of-purchase offers. Seldom do well-conceived events garner less than 85 percent retail support in any given market. In fact, cooperation is usually closer to 100 percent and lasts for extended weeks — without trade incentive dollars! Product sales typically range anywhere from 45 percent more than the prior year to 200–300 percent more than the prior year. And all of these event programs can, and should, be based on total payout, that is, the programs can and do pay for themselves while generating these levels of sales and profits. Does event marketing work? You bet!

The future of event marketing has only just begun. Event marketing is an innovative promotional technique and one that works very well. But the key to successful events is to remember that it's not the event itself, it's how you leverage it, add to it, evolve it, and use it that matters.

Richard G. Ebel is Director of Marketing Communications at Promotional Products Association International (PPAI), an Irving, Texas-based trade association representing manufacturers and distributors of ad specialties, premiums, business gifts, and awards. Affiliated with PPAI since 1969, he currently supervises the association's public relations, advertising, and marketing research activities.

Prior to joining PPAI, Ebel was on the editorial staff of The National Underwriter, *a leading insurance newspaper, and subsequently served as editor of membership publications for the National Association of Retail Druggists and the National Moving and Storage Association. He is a frequent contributor to advertising and marketing publications.*

Ebel is a graduate of the Medill School of Journalism at Northwestern University, and has an M.A. degree with a public relations emphasis from Northern Illinois University.

CHAPTER 12

SPECIALTY PROMOTIONS

Advertising specialties or specialty promotions is one of the oldest forms of producing a sale or advocating a cause, yet nobody seems to really understand it. In the United States, ad specialties have been around for a spell. In its extensive exhibit of antiques at its Irving, Texas, headquarters, Promotional Products Association International displays a *Farmers' Almanac* promoting a chemist (drugstore) in 1830. And that is not among the earliest of the promotional almanacs.

When Ohio newspaper publisher Jasper Meek found in 1880 that revenues from printing ads on schoolbook bags and horse blankets were enough to successfully operate a stand-alone business, he drew numerous imitators and, in effect, launched what has since become a $5.5 billion industry.

In the early days, the ad-imprinted merchandise — usually made of cloth, paper, wood, glass, or leather — was thought of as "reminder" or "goodwill" advertising. Those functions are still important. However, the inventory of applications has proliferated enormously.

This versatility is reflected in the diversity of users: manufacturers promoting to dealers, retailers trying to draw store traffic, trade associations and labor unions recruiting members, churches attempting to boost attendance, fund-raisers soliciting donors, and politicians chasing votes.

PROMOTIONAL PRODUCTS: COMPONENTS AND DISTINCTIONS

Under the "promotional products" umbrella we find ad specialties, business gifts, premiums, awards, prizes, and commemoratives. The fact that an item, such as a desk paperweight, can be used as any of these promotional products, tempts one to ignore some significant distinctions.

Ad specialties are always imprinted with an advertiser's identification or message, and they are given free.

Business gifts are also given free. They cost more than some ad specialties, and normally they don't carry an imprint. Nowadays, however, there seem to be more business gifts with the donor's logo subtly inscribed.

Premiums are the true incentives because the receiver needs to do something to get them. Sometimes imprinted, but usually not, premiums are distinguished from ad specialties by the fact that they are earned by making a purchase, a deposit (in a bank), or a financial contribution.

Awards, too, are earned by performance or simply by hanging onto the job long enough to be honored for retiring gracefully.

The point is, the items can be the same in all cases, and the only difference may be in their functions. Yet it is a difference that goes beyond mere hairsplitting.

TYPES OF PRODUCTS: WHEN TO USE WHICH PRODUCTS

Someone with apparently nothing better to do once added up the different types of merchandise used as ad specialties and calculated that number to be about 15,000. When one takes a type — for example, writing instruments — and multiplies it by model — ink pens, ballpoints, rollerballs — and by brands, figure on tens of thousands more.

In 1980, Jim Lindheim, then with the old Yankelovich, Skelly & White social research firm, told an audience of ad specialty practitioners that the desire of younger Americans for self-expression on the things they wore would have a considerable impact on the promotional products industry. His prophecy was right on the money. Today, one out of every five dollars spent on ad specialties goes for T-shirts, baseball caps, and other wearables.

Other top-five product categories are writing instruments, desk/office accessories, ceramics/glassware, and calendars.

For the most part, these are useful, conventional, everyday products. Where, then, are the unique, the novel, the one-of-a-kind? They serve a purpose, and thus they are out there, too.

If the objective is to be remembered and appreciated, a promotional product that the intended audience will want to keep is important — for example, an attractive, quality, personalized ballpoint or ink pen. On the other hand, if the objective is attention — not retention — and what is really wanted is a tangible exclamation point, a ballpoint that is contorted into a shape, from a heart to an outline of the state of Texas, may be more suitable.

The industry caters to differences in objectives and sizes of budgets. These differences include items that are kept and maybe even revered, as well as items that are thrown away after the objective has been accomplished.

STRENGTHS AND WEAKNESSES

Ad specialties are a perfect way to keep a company's name in front of its prospects, provided, of course, that an item has been selected that is useful to the prospect and is likely to be retained. The ability to give a company a continuous presence with buyers is an important attribute of ad specialties, but there are other advantages as well, such as the following:

- **Long-lasting exposure** that produces high recall.
- **Targetability.** Like some other forms of promotion, ad specialties can deliver impressions to narrowly defined audiences.
- **Budget flexibility.** With prices ranging from a few cents apiece to tens of dollars, there is a good choice of items for

even the leanest budget.

- **Goodwill.** People like to receive something for nothing. Their appreciation builds points for the giver.
- **Unobtrusiveness.** Impressions can be conveyed without becoming a nuisance — no doorbells to answer, no phone calls to disrupt dinner, no frequent commercial breaks to interrupt entertainment.
- **Compatibility with other media.** Promotional products work well with other forms of promotion and enhance their effectiveness. They boost response rates and increase traffic counts.

The following are some caveats to consider:

- **Small copy area.** Given the size of many promotional products, long messages are often out of the question. Sometimes space will accommodate only the corporate logo. Marketers who need to say more can surmount this problem by using advertising curls, tags, and other printed appendages.
- **Long lead times.** Lead times may be longer than what some marketers are accustomed to. Don't place an order and expect to get delivery next week. Figure on three to five weeks as a norm (or be prepared to pay rush charges) on catalog products. Custom work will take even longer.
- **Duplication.** Suppose an item is chosen and the recipient already has 10 of them. The gift may be ignored and pitched. The wastebasket can be avoided if the item is more attractive, more useful, more distinctive than similar promotional products the recipient might have. Or, why not personalize the item by imprinting the recipient's name or initials? People tend not to discard gifts with their names on them.
- **Sporadic accountability.** In many uses of ad specialties, it's difficult to say just what effect the items had on the promotion. As with some other forms of advertising and promotion they may be using, marketers may believe the imprinted "gifts" are having an impact but not really know if they are or not. Fortunately, the promotional products industry is developing measurement systems, generally associated with pre-test/post-test methodologies, and some are now available.

This brings up some options to ponder. Should one buy out of a specialty catalog or does one go to the expense of customizing the item given? Should one look for durability in a specialty product, or is there an advantage to wear-out? By supplying a company's sales force with desk note trays to give their prospects, as the notepaper is used up, salespeople will be particularly welcomed on subsequent visits when they bring refills.

If the goal is to thank or reward customers, but the budget prevents going top-of-the-line, then resort to stratified selection. The "A" customers or prospects — for instance, the heavy users — get first-quality items, while the "B" customers appropriately receive more modest gifts.

TYPICAL APPLICATIONS

As noted earlier, there is a multitude of objectives that can be successfully addressed with promotional products.

Creating Awareness. Creating awareness was the objective of IBM when it scheduled demonstrations of its PCs on campuses of three private universities in Texas. On one campus, the company announced the demonstration in the school newspaper. At the second school, imprinted combination ballpoint/highlighters were distributed in engineering and computer science classroom buildings. At the third campus, IBM split its promotion budget between the school newspaper and ad specialties. Surveys of the demonstration audiences showed that twice as many persons attributed their attendance and exposure to the demonstrations to the ad specialty than to the newspaper. In fact, exposure to the ad specialty alone was also more effective than the ad specialty-newspaper combination.

The point to be made here is that, like direct mail, promotional products represent a targeted form of promotion that is particularly effective among selective rather than mass audiences.

Generating Leads. When it comes to lead generation, direct mail often bogs down because of mailbox clutter. Promotional products, however, can make a difference in response rates.

A good illustration is furnished by Premier Bank, one of the largest in Louisiana. The Shreveport branch targeted 1,500 difficult-to-reach prospects — many of them doctors, attorneys, and accountants — with the intention of securing appointments for the bank's calling officers. A sales letter to one group drew a 1.8 percent response. Aided by inclusion of an inexpensive ad specialty (a digital clock), the mailing to the second group produced a 2.7 percent response. Even more effective was the offer to the third group of an incentive to return the enclosed business reply card. The incentive offer — a more expensive digital clock — produced a 7.3 percent response. It also achieved a per-appointment cost of $34.76 compared with the $100.24 cost of the sales letter alone.

Dimensional items are particularly effective in neutralizing gatekeepers such as secretaries and mailroom policies that shield executives from third-class mail. A bright-yellow package with the likeness of Einstein and the copy "Positively Brilliant" was mailed to 500 ad agencies and photo labs. The inference was that the mailer, Color Corporation of America, was capable of brilliant work. Inside the package was a pair of imprinted sunglasses for the recipient and vivid graphics on the interior depicting the famed genius wearing similar sunglasses (see Exhibit 12.1). An 80 percent response rate suggested that penetration was accomplished.

EXHIBIT 12.1

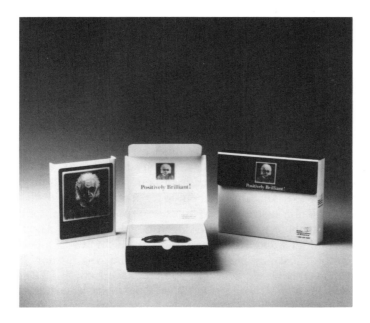

Obtaining Referrals and Recommendations. Referrals and recommendations from satisfied customers and influencers are coveted by almost every sales manager, but sometimes it takes more than just asking for them. A California insurance agency, Dodge, Warren & Peters, augmented its appeals to clients with an imprinted pocket telephone index. Then, when they referred a prospect, clients received an imprinted pocketknife, and later a desk diary.

To induce veterinary receptionists to recommend its brand of canine vitamins, the Upjohn Company mailed samples along with a mug for coffee breaks. Enclosed with the mugs and samples were a cassette tape and stickers for a sales log. Each sale was worth points, and receptionists could redeem their completed logs for prizes.

Building Traffic. Like premiums, ad specialties can be effective traffic builders. In a controlled field experiment involving trade show attendees, Hoechst Celanese Corporation found that mailing an ad specialty to advance registrants drew three times more traffic to its booth at the National Plastics Exposition than an invitation without a gift. Hoechst also experimented in a preshow mailing of an ad specialty coupled with an offer of an additional gift that could be picked up at the booth. The response, in terms of bringing the invitation coupon to the booth for redemption, was nearly twice as great (11.6% vs. 6.7%) when the preshow gift and the at-the-booth gift were companion items, in this case an imprinted coffee mug that went with the ceramic coaster that was mailed before the show.

As a traffic builder, promotional products work for retailers, too. Merchants at Burtonsville Crossing Shopping Center in Maryland banded together to draw commuters to the mall. On the second Tuesday of every month, hostesses at a bus stop greeted park-and-ride commuters with coffee, rolls, and coupons. After work, the commuters could redeem their coupons for ad specialty gifts, such as pocket flashlights and coffee mugs, at the store shown on the coupon. Redemption rates were impressive, ranging from 72 percent to 83 percent.

Introducing New Products or Services. Ad specialties are often used in introducing new products, services, and facilities and in reinforcing awareness of existing ones. As physical objects, ad specialties constitute a promotion form capable of being touched and inspected as well as being seen. That makes them ideal demonstration devices.

An Alabama distributor, Wholesale Wood Products, took advantage of this attribute when it introduced a new synthetic wood to lumber yards, builders, and architects. The item selected was a desk pencil caddy. But not just any pencil caddy. This one was fashioned from a block of the synthetic wood being promoted (see Exhibit 12.2).

Motivating Salespeople and Other Employees. A customary tactic for motivating salespeople and other employees is to stage a contest.

EXHIBIT 12.2

That is good thinking, but contests work so much better with promotional products, used either as a reward for performance or as a means of maintaining interest and excitement in pursuing the reward. Since enthusiasm tends to flag during a long-term contest, reinforcement with promotional products is advisable.

When Sparkletts Water Systems discovered that supermarket stockers were lax in replenishing shelves with the company's bottled water, marketing management was aghast at the sales being lost. The solution, the managers decided, was to get the broker salespeople to do the stocking. To announce the change, salespeople were mailed a brass dart and a walnut desk holder engraved "Stick it to the competition" (see Exhibit 12.3). Theme-imprinted decals were affixed inside the bottle cartons. Salespeople could redeem the decals for two cents each. To get them, of course, they'd have to unpack the cartons and stock the shelves. The salespeople were to bring their darts to the monthly sales meetings. Those who collected the most decals were eligible to fling the darts at a board on which were listed cash bonuses in various amounts. In this way, Sparkletts reduced out-of-stock averages by 30 percent.

Typical contests feature a start, sprints, and a finish. At its annual sales meeting, Sysco Frozen Foods launched a two-month contest. Doffing an Indiana Jones-style hat, the marketing vice president distributed foil-wrapped chocolate coins from a treasure chest. Salespeople

EXHIBIT 12.3

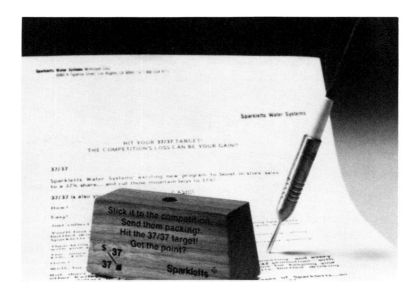

also received an ice scraper (copy: "Scrape up sales this winter. Relax in Bermuda this spring.") and a corked bottle containing half a treasure map. To sustain interest, midway through the contest period, pocket puzzles were mailed to the sales force. The first person to unscramble the puzzle was treated to a dinner for two. Once in Bermuda, members of sales teams making their goals were handed cardboard treasure chests. Inside was the other half of the treasure map that revealed a gift certificate which could be found when the goal-busters checked into their hotel rooms.

Creating Goodwill. The role of goodwill in marketing tends to be underemphasized, totally ignored, or relegated to the public relations department. Goodwill certainly isn't a concern of sales promotion. This is an attitude in need of adjusting, particularly as marketers contend with declining brand loyalty and recognize the economics of customer retention.

Beginning in the late 1980s, the marketing faculty at Baylor University executed a series of studies on the impact of specialty advertising on customer goodwill. The results of goodwill, researchers determined, are (a) customer loyalty, (b) willingness to make repeat purchases, and (c) willingness to recommend the company/brand to others.

In field experiments involving the Houghton-Mifflin Publishing Company and a Texas-based regional wholesale florist, researchers found the following:

- By using ad specialties as opposed to a thank you letter only, you can enhance your goodwill standing with customers significantly.
- By using ad specialties, you can increase your goodwill standing over competitors.
- The level of increase in goodwill is likely to depend somewhat on the perceived value of the ad specialty.

TACTICS

Skillful promotional products distributors are as much tacticians as they are purveyors of imprinted merchandise. They often use tactics related either to the product itself or to the psychology of consumer behavior. Designed to motivate or excite, these tactics are many and varied.

- **Contingent fulfillment.** Here the target audience receives part of an ad specialty — maybe a pair of sunglass lenses without the frames or a single glove. They get the other part — the one that makes the item work or completes a pair — only when they respond in the manner the marketer desires (see Exhibit 12.4).
- **Peer approval.** A helmet adorned with performance decals does more than give a football lineman an opportunity to crow about the number of running backs he's leveled. Such symbols motivate

EXHIBIT 12.4

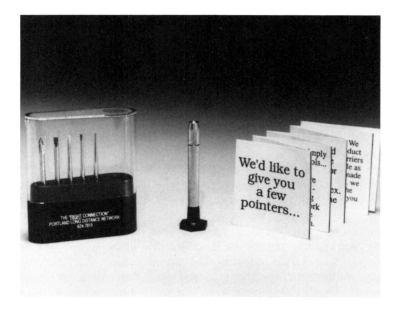

teammates to earn their own insignia that infer they belong in the company of star performers. So, too, awards and other recognition devices drive salespeople to either show them who's best or at least justify their position on the payroll.

• **Status conferral.** A riverfront restaurant in Virginia offers ID cards to its best customers, making them feel special, which they are. Flashing the cards to the maitre d', they get preferred seating and don't have to bother with long waiting lines. They also receive T-shirts, sunglasses, and other ad specialties from waiters serving their tables. Club privileges are much sweeter when they create envy.

• **Curiosity arousal.** Arousing curiosity goes beyond mere teasing. The target audience needs to ask, "What is it?," and be willing to find out. For instance, a bank in Spokane, Washington, scheduled a grand opening for a new branch. Prospective depositors were mailed an unrecognizable plastic disk and were told they could find out what it was — and get the part that made it a useful appliance — by attending the open house. Several hundred did, and they found out that the mailed enticement was the top to a tape dispenser.

• **Collector appeal.** From antiques to baseball cards, the pervasiveness of collector mania is evident in the number of newspaper columns, magazines, and trading shows devoted to this special interest. There is a marketing parallel, too. One National Basketball Association team provides an example. As an attendance builder, a set of coins was struck with likenesses of the team players. For many fans, the first one they were given was sufficient bait to draw them to the next dozen or so home games to acquire the complete set.

• **Influencing the influencers.** Perhaps no group influences purchase decisions more than children, a perception that led to placing the first premium in a cereal box. Promotional products formed the enticement of the "Kids Go HoJo Fan Club" campaign in which children, ages 3 to 12, of guests at any Howard Johnson property received free "fun packs." The contents included imprinted crayons, coloring/activity books, decals, and postcards. And tactics that work with children can also work with adults.

• **Authentication.** In this case, the specially crafted promotional product becomes attention-getting memorabilia because it is actually a piece of the real thing. For its "Dodger Diamond Dust" campaign tying into the 25th anniversary of Dodger Stadium, a cable TV service scooped up dirt from the L.A. team's infield and it authenticated, poly-bagged, and packaged the dirt in collectible cans. An accompanying romance curl described the inaugural day in 1962 when "the dust of a freshly groomed diamond was kicked up for the first time." To add excitement, genuine diamonds were inserted in randomly selected cans.

SOURCES AND SERVICE PROVIDERS

The 15,000 types of imprinted promotional products mentioned earlier are provided by 2,500 or so companies. They are called suppliers rather than manufacturers because many — assemblers, converters, or importers — don't manufacture anything. What they have in common, however, is an imprinting capability, which could be letterpress, silk screening, hot stamping, photo etching, laser engraving, embroidering, and a number of other processes. Since suppliers have no sales forces, they market their products through independent distributors. Some suppliers will sell directly to end users. But most, eager to avoid competing with their distributors, prefer not to. In that respect, promotional products differ little from other packaged goods industries.

The 12,000 distributors in the United States offer some diversity in services. Some are basically product sellers. Their customers are agencies and companies who rely on their own creative departments to provide what creativity, if any, is called for in integrating the promotional products into the campaign. At the other end of the scale are distributors — more aptly called promotion planners — that do it all. In addition to supplying the items, they do the creative and the execution, sometimes in conjunction with the clients' agencies.

Regardless of the services distributor firms may offer, what makes them indispensable to end users is the familiarity they have with their business environment. Their personnel are expected to know not only what products are available but also what suppliers are reliable in terms of quality production and imprinting and in making delivery schedules. Neglecting these considerations can result in a very stressful promotion experience.

ELEMENTS OF PROMOTION DEVELOPMENT

Promotions obviously differ from distribution, which can amount to no more than setting out a box of imprinted matchbooks on the cashier's counter. The architecture of promotions involving imprinted products has many of the same plinths and columns found in other types of campaigns. The planning elements to be dealt with are as follows:

- **Objective.** What is expected to be accomplished with the promotion?
- **Target audience.** With whom will the promotional products be communicating?
- **Budget.** How much can be spent on the promotion?
- **Distribution.** What is the most effective way of delivering the promotional products to the target audience? By direct mail? On sales calls? Through a related third party?
- **Theme.** Often no more than clichés on their billionth go-around, themes nevertheless give the promotion an identity and coherence that ties everything together.
- **Item selection.** Of those 15,000 imprintable items that exist, which will do the job best?
- **Evaluation.** Evaluation is often ignored, but without some sort of auditing, whether the promotion worked is unknown.

When laying out a plan, one of the first things to notice is how some elements will dictate others — budgets, for example. If there isn't enough money to reach an audience with anything but a very cheap item, it may be difficult to accomplish a particular goal. If the budget can't be increased, sending a more expensive and attractive incentive only to respondents may fit the bill better than sending a less attractive, less expensive item to the entire mailing list.

There are many trade-offs to be made, and the trick is to adjust and compromise without reducing the voltage.

James Kunze has 14 years of experience in providing marketing planning, advertising, and sales promotion services to clients, including his responsibilities at J. Brown Associates, Inc., a Grey Advertising subsidiary, where he currently is Executive Vice President and General Manager. He has worked with a wide range of clients, including AT&T, Procter & Gamble, United Airlines, Polaroid, Texaco, Philip Morris, R.J. Reynolds, and others.

Prior to joining J. Brown Associates in Chicago, Kunze was Executive Vice President for William A. Robinson, directing that agency's business development and strategic planning functions, in addition to managing clients. Also in his career he has worked in sales management at Procter & Gamble; directed consumer promotion and brand management activities at Warner-Lambert; and was responsible for advertising and sales promotion at Estech.

He is a graduate of the Krannert School of Management at Purdue University and attended law school at Indiana University.

CHAPTER 13

TRADE PROMOTION

OVERVIEW

The practice of offering rewards in order to induce specific kinds of actions by the distribution channel for a packaged goods product is generally known as trade marketing or trade promotion. The practice has evolved over the past quarter-century into an extremely important class of marketing tool. Most sources today agree that trade marketing expenditures are the largest segment of marketing spending, representing more than 40 percent of total marketing expenditures. A comparison of expenditures for major categories of marketing between now and 20 years ago shows the shift (see Table 13.1).

TABLE 13.1
PERCENT OF TOTAL MARKETING BUDGET

Spending Category	1971	1991
Consumer advertising	60	35
Consumer promotion	15	25
Trade promotion	25	40

What has fueled this growth? Basically, several factors have contributed:

1. **Initial success.** When marketers shift funds to reward retailers for the performance of specific objectives, such as extra display or new distribution, the result is usually very good initially. Display commitments happen, new sizes go into distribution, and extra sales result because an important distribution channel variable has been altered.

2. **Recessions.** When marketers have faced recession in the last 20 years, the response has been to emphasize price reduction through special allowances and price-oriented consumer inducements, such as rebates. Having placed so much emphasis on price in tough times, most marketers find that the road back to a more balanced marketing approach is exceedingly difficult, if not entirely impossible, without absorbing a large volume reduction in the short term.

3. **Shift in power.** An explosion in the number of new products, new forms, new sizes, and new flavors has resulted in higher demand for retailer services by marketers. The demand has enabled retailers to reap the benefits of ever higher trade spending.

If your responsibilities are in sales planning, sales promotion, or brand management, you'll want to know how to employ trade marketing for maximum effectiveness in both the short and long term. Your success will probably depend upon it. Because trade marketing has become such a large portion of most marketers' budgets, the amount of time spent planning, discussing, and defining trade marketing programs has mushroomed.

Today, in fact, most brand marketers find that it is extremely difficult to achieve management approval for brand advertising and/or consumer promotion plans, because every discussion of these subjects converts into a discussion about how the trade support necessary for volume achievement will be obtained and where the funding for the advertising and/or consumer promotion will fit into the overall budget, since trade promotion must be funded first.

You'll want to know the techniques of trade marketing and the objectives each is intended to accomplish. The next segment of this chapter will provide a review of these areas. Then, you'll want to know about the long-term implications for your overall marketing plan of employing trade marketing techniques. This discussion will follow the techniques review.

Finally, you'll be introduced to a trade marketing approach that is new and very promising and that illustrates the need to do effective trade marketing planning within the context of overall brand building, rather than within the short-term volume perspective exclusively.

THE TECHNIQUES OF TRADE MARKETING: PURCHASE INCENTIVES

There are two primary classes of trade marketing techniques: purchase incentives and performance allowances.

Purchase incentives are all of the forms of payment offered to the distributors of packaged goods products, which are designed to cause initial purchase, restocking, or increased inventory of the product. Within this class of trade marketing techniques, we'll look at the following:

1. Slotting allowances
2. Off-invoice purchase allowances
3. Dating
4. Free goods

This class of techniques has seen explosive growth in recent years. It's this class in which the shift in power from marketer to retailer has been so strongly reflected. Retailers collectively have been extremely successful in obtaining ever growing amounts and forms of purchase incentives.

To illustrate the dramatic shift, one of America's largest and most successful food marketers has seen an overall net shift in marketing spending from 30 percent trade/70 percent consumer focus 20 years ago, to 70 percent trade/30 percent consumer focus currently.

Technique at a glance

Type: Slotting/shelving

How it works: Usually expressed as a percent-of-invoice price of product, that is, 5–15 percent of nonpromotional invoice cost of merchandise.

Objective of the technique: To induce buyers to place the product into distribution and assign it warehouse, computer, and store shelf space.

Discussion: Slotting/shelving allowances are a relatively recent form of purchase incentive. The term has come into broad-scale use during the past 10–15 years. It is the result of a tidal wave of new products, sizes, flavors, and forms offered by product marketers to retailers in recent years. For example, the average supermarket today carries more than 16,000 items, which is 40 percent more than just six years ago.

Slotting allowances have come about for two main reasons: first, to fulfill a need for distributors to recoup their true costs of adding all of the new items on a constant basis and second, to recognize an opportunity to extract additional funds from marketers because of the increased demand for store and warehouse space. For many packaged goods marketers, slotting allowances have become a major barrier to the successful introduction of new items. The level of slotting allowance required frequently is greater than the budget for advertising the product to the consumer. *An example:* An entirely new beverage product was introduced by a mid-sized beverage marketer in the mid-1980s. The product had strong taste and health benefits to sell to the consumer. The product was positioned to an upscale audience and was premium priced. The product was successfully tested and the sales target for year one nationally was set at $100 million. This is the kind of product that performs best with high levels of consumer awareness, which requires significant advertising levels, perhaps in the $10–20 million range. However, since the brand was forced to introduce with an introductory plan that was top-heavy with slotting and promotion allowances, less than $6 million was left for advertising. The brand achieved year one sales goals on the strength of the strong trade merchandising support, but it could not sustain this volume longer term, since overall levels of consumer awareness were too low. The brand has now shrunk to less than $50 million annual volume.

Some marketers have resisted paying slotting by emphasizing the importance to the retailer of the new item and the high level of support that will be placed behind the item by the marketer. Generally, only a few of the largest and strongest consumer marketers have been able to make this approach work.

The good news: Slotting fees usually result in successful initial placement of a new item.

The bad news: Slotting fees frequently reduce the budget available for making the new item a success with consumers, thus contributing to the high failure rate of new items.

Technique at a glance

Type: Off-invoice

How it works: An amount, usually 5–25 percent of the nonpromotional case price of the product, is subtracted on the invoice, leaving a discounted case cost to the distributor for a specified time period or limited number of orders, usually one or two.

Objective of the technique: To induce purchase of inventory, which is significantly in excess of needs based on normal rate of sale.

Discussion: Off-invoice allowances represent the largest class of purchase inducement. The technique is direct, easy to understand, and effective in inducing the distribution channel to buy additional inventory. Off-invoice allowances have replaced many forms of performance allowances, which are paid only after performance has been confirmed. This has occurred because of retailers' objections to billback offers and their appreciation for direct off-invoice offers.

The technique is most effective when employed concurrently with an extra advertising or consumer promotion effort designed to sell through the additional product inventory to the consumer. Too often, however, the technique is used to stimulate a short-term increase in shipments without any accompanying consumer effort. The result is a period of significantly increased shipments followed by a period of significantly decreased shipments because the distributors' inventory is excessive. The off-invoice purchase inducement in this case has produced forward-buying and has done so at a major cost, primarily, the amount of the discount. Further, some distributors aggressively forward-buy when a product is offered at a large off-invoice discount, then reship the product to other distributors after the deal period ends and the manufacturer is then offering the product at normal price. This practice, called diverting, is very disruptive for the marketer. The sales force's local quota/shipment goals may be significantly distorted, leading a marketer to think that the product is enjoying a major growth pattern in a certain market when it is not, or that a product in a market where diverted merchandise is flowing in has a major decline occurring when no such problem exists.

Diverting can significantly alter promotion analysis and can be very difficult to control, and the level of difficulty increases as the level of off-invoice allowances increases. In some distributors, an off-invoice allowance will result in a temporary reduction in resale price to the consumer, with a resulting increase in rate of sale.

The good news: Off-invoice allowances are easy to execute, and they are a form of allowance that many distributors strongly favor.

The bad news: Off-invoices are a very tempting short-term "fix" for volume problems, which can result in forward-buying and little else.

Technique at a glance
Type: Dating
How it works: The extending of payment terms to the distributor which are lengthier than the marketer's normal invoice payment terms — usually expressed as a cash discount if paid within a stipulated number of days, for example 2 percent 10/net 61 days, which means 2 percent discount if paid in full within 10 days; full amount due within 61 days.

Objective of the technique: To induce distributors to buy sooner or to induce the purchase of extra inventory.

Discussion: The use of extended dating terms as a promotional tool is intended to enable the distributor to commit early to a new product or to a promotional or seasonal buying program. In all of the cases, the product may not have any significant rate of sale established until new-product advertising begins or until the season starts. In these situations, some distributors prefer to delay ordering until demand is established. Since this reduces availability of the product to the consumer, the marketer may utilize a tool such as dating to induce earlier distributor purchase.

Dating is usually effective in achieving the noted objectives, because it effectively allows the retailer to sell the product before having to pay for it. The true cost of this trade marketing tool is the cost of financing the order amount for the extended time period. In some cases, the opportunity cost for the funds is considered as well when attempting to assign a cost. Many corporate controllers are reluctant to permit the use of dating because of the effects on cash flow and the cost of the tool.

Another factor to be carefully considered before offering special dating terms is the precedent-setting nature of this offer. Future programs will be much tougher to sell without extended terms, once the practice has been utilized.

The good news: Retailers like it. Dating is simple and effective against limited objectives.

The bad news: It can be extremely expensive when precedents are considered. Dating can result in undesirable competitive reaction and in unwanted repetition.

Technique at a glance
Type: Free goods
How it works: Distributors receive additional cases of product at no cost, at a predetermined ratio to cases purchased, for example, one case free with 12 purchased.

Objective of the technique: To increase inventories of product in the distribution channel.

Discussion: Free goods are used in lieu of off-invoice allowances by some product marketers to induce purchase of additional inventory by distributors. Proponents argue that offers of free goods result in greater inventory increases than from comparable off-invoice offers. Their reasoning is that, in an example account, the sales representative with a 10 percent off-invoice allowance may suggest a promotional order of 1,000 cases to an account that normally sells 500 cases per month. The sales representative with a matching free goods offer, one case free with 10, will do likewise. But after selling the distributor on 1,000 cases, the additional "free" 100 cases will be added to the order, making the total order 1,100 cases.

Detractors say that free goods offers are more confusing to explain, and they don't really result in more inventory. This form of inducement is less frequently used in packaged goods than in some other industries, such as apparel. *The good news:* Offer of free goods may result in additional inventories when compared to off-invoice offers. *The bad news:* The offer does not provide for a temporary case price reduction by the distributor to the retail outlets and therefore may not provide any retail stimulus.

Purchase Incentives Wrap-Up.

The good news: The most frequently used type of trade marketing tools, purchase incentives are favored by retailers because they directly reduce the cost of goods, and they don't require any other special activity. Some sales managers like them because distributors will buy additional inventory and because sales presentations are simple and straightforward.

Marketers who rely heavily on this form of promotion cite lower training costs and higher sales calls per day as advantages. Purchase incentives generally are effective in achieving short-term tactical objectives.

The bad news: Purchase incentives are relatively less efficient in generating incremental sales to the consumer than performance allowances, which require distributors to perform consumer-influencing activities to earn. The use of purchase incentives on a regular basis has developed an inefficient distribution pattern for many marketers in which retailers forward-buy to capture an allowance then sell product at the regular rate, thus reducing orders for a following period.

The additional negative is that large purchase allowances result in the practice of diverting, further distorting the distribution picture. The marketer then has a shipment pattern that contains significant "peaks and valleys," causing plant inefficiency, shipping problems, and forecasting problems.

Most important, the too-heavy use of purchase allowances reduces funds available for consumer-influencing activities and consequently has an important negative effect on long-term brand vitality.

PERFORMANCE ALLOWANCES

Performance allowances are all of the forms of payment offered to distributors of a product, which are designed to induce an action by the distributor that increases the rate of sale of the product to the final consumer. Key activities that occur in the distribution channel and positively affect the rate of sale of a product to the consumer include the following:

1. Temporary price reduction
2. Second location or off-shelf display
3. Expanded shelf space
4. Demonstrating or sampling product in store
5. Advertising the product under the store's name to the consumer

Marketers typically offer performance allowances to induce some or all of these activities on their products. The next section will review these specific types of performance allowances:

1. Price reduction allowance
2. Display/merchandising allowance
3. Advertising allowance
4. Count/recount allowance

A marketer wishing to use performance allowances has many hurdles to overcome. First and foremost, retailers generally resist billback offers because too much administrative time is used qualifying and collecting and because they want additional flexibility. Second, retailers have the benefit of the balance of power to use to enforce more favorable terms, and that enables the request for less restrictive kinds of offers to have more clout. Third, the marketer's own sales force resists performance allowances because of the extra time it takes to administer the contracts and because of the retailer resistance, which limits their success.

The fact that marketers still do use performance allowance offers indicates how much value comes from giving them, in spite of all these difficulties. A general rule today is that the program for which performance allowances are offered should be an exceptionally strong one with obvious retailer benefits to offset the negatives of the offer.

Technique at a glance

Type: Price reduction allowance

How it works: An allowance per unit is paid to the retailer for a corresponding price reduction for a specified time period. The allowance may be an offer for purchases during a particular time period or an annual accrual on all case purchases.

Objective of the technique: To induce the retailer to reduce the price to the consumer for a product during a specified time period.

Discussion: This type of performance allowance is a major category of brand promotion spending. Many products today have a price reduction allowance that is accrued on an annual basis and that represents 10–15 percent of brand sales volume. The allowance may have any of several different names, including Brand Development Fund, Special Marketing Fund, Key Market Fund, or Customer Marketing Fund. An indication of the importance of this category of trade spending today is that, for many brands, price reduction allowances are the largest item on the brand marketing budget, larger than total advertising expenditures, for example. The use of periodic price reduction allowances continues but with less usage than that of the annual-fund type of price reduction format.

The good news: Price reduction allowances are very effective in generating strong trade promotion for a brand. This type of retailer effort on behalf of a brand generally is successful in producing incremental consumer sales for the brand.

The bad news: Price reduction allowances have grown to be the largest category of marketing spending on many brands, reducing the amount of consumer effort the brands can afford. This trend is therefore shifting the balance of brand consumer communication strongly toward "buy because it's cheap" and away from "buy because it's better."

Technique at a glance

Type: Display/merchandising allowance

How it works: An allowance is paid to the retailer in exchange for a specific kind of in-store merchandising performance, usually either a second location display or an enhancement to normal shelf space or position.

Objective of the technique: To obtain a visibility advantage for the product in-store or to secure year-round shelf space advantage.

Discussion: Merchandising/display allowances represent another form of allowance offered to packaged goods retailers. These allowances are aimed at a key sales-inducing variable: retail visibility. Since extra display and/or shelf space has been shown to be a major sales increase factor, it is not surprising that marketers seek to induce retailers to provide this advantage for their product.

A quick look at some typical results of studies of retail visibility variables shows the following:

1. Off-shelf, second location display of a product at the everyday price increased the sales of a beverage product by 104 percent.
2. A study of shelf space dynamics showed that sales increased by 32 percent for a product whose shelf space was increased by 50 percent.
3. A product whose shelf position was changed from a standard on-aisle location to a higher-traffic location near the front end of the stores saw sales increase by 57 percent.

Allowances offered for the achievement of a specific retail visibility variable may or may not be successful. Success factors include the effectiveness of the sales force in enforcing display requirements prior to the retailer's receiving payment, the appeal of the product to the trade as either a traffic-builder or a profit opportunity, and competitive reaction.

An additional factor in making the offering of display allowances less successful is a trend to pay display allowances off-invoice in exchange for intended performance. As a result, in recent years many marketers have moved away from offering display allowances in favor of price reduction allowances, with the hope that good sales force follow-through coupled with a retailer price feature will result in extra display.

The good news: Extra display for a brand at retail can be a major sales booster.

The bad news: Display allowances are tough to enforce and more difficult to administer if they are paid after performance via billback.

Technique at a glance

Type: Advertising allowance

How it works: An allowance is paid to the retailer for advertising the product in the retailer's ad.

Objective of the technique: To induce the retailer to advertise the product to the retailer's customers.

Discussion: Advertising by the retailer can increase the sales of a packaged goods product by as much as 50 percent for a weekly promotional period. Advertising by a retailer also frequently is the prerequisite for achieving extra merchandising or special pricing; so most marketers include some kind of advertising inducement in their retailer offers, along with a merchandising allowance, a price reduction allowance, or a special consumer offer to induce good retailer participation.

Advertising allowances from marketers represent an important revenue source to retailers. These moneys are frequently used to defray some or even all of the costs of the retailer's advertising program and department. The type of advertising generally achieved is brand name, package visual, and price, with size or length of ad being influenced by the requirements in the allowance agreement.

In most offerings of advertising allowances, retailers are given broad discretion to create any ad they choose, using perhaps a required package shot and allotting a prescribed amount of space or time to the product. Much less frequently, advertising allowances are accompanied by specially developed creative from the marketer that the retailer must utilize in order to collect the allowance. This is a particularly important area for future development, and one which will be discussed at the end of this chapter.

The good news: Advertising allowances usually are effective in achieving the goal of retailer advertising of the marketer's product.

The bad news: Significant administrative follow-up is frequently required. An ad allowance doesn't work well without also offering purchase or price reduction allowances.

Technique at a glance

Type: Count/recount allowance

How it works: Qualifying warehouse accounts receive a payment for each case of product shipped to retail stores during the promotional period.

Objective of the technique: To increase retail inventories.

Discussion: The count/recount allowance is so named because it requires the determination of warehouse inventory at the beginning and at the end of a promotional period. The difference, plus inbound shipments received during the period, determines the number of cases of product on which the count/recount allowance is paid. This form of allowance is less prevalent today than in years past, having been replaced by slotting and price reduction allowances in many cases.

The good news: The performance called for is measurable.

The bad news: The allowance frequently represents a second payment for the same product, after the slotting or initial purchase allowance, and it still doesn't require any activity that will increase the rate of sale to the consumer.

Performance Allowance Wrap-Up. Performance allowances generally are effective in achieving target objectives if the following can be achieved:

1. The trade resistance to being given a conditional offer can be overcome by a resourceful sales force.
2. A competitor's heavy use of off-invoice purchase allowances hasn't made a performance approach unattractive.
3. The marketer hasn't so overused nonperformance allowances that the offering of performance allowances is ineffective.

Because performance is required, the marketer must judiciously choose requirements that are measurable and that the marketer's sales force is capable and willing to enforce. In spite of the difficulties, a trade marketing plan that includes performance requirements generally produces a greater return for the marketer for each dollar invested.

The good news: Performance allowances enable marketers to focus on specific objectives that best suit their overall marketing efforts, resulting in better program payout.

The bad news: More selling time is required to explain, enforce, and follow up on performance allowance offers. The retailer does not like conditional offers and will resist their use.

THE DILEMMA

Here is the dilemma you will face if you're considering what type of trade marketing effort to propose for your products. Carefully constructed trade marketing efforts, which are executed with precision and discipline, usually meet or exceed objectives. That's good, right? Initially yes, but the dilemma is how to meet or exceed those results in the next quarter or annual period.

This dilemma exists and becomes increasingly bigger over time because of the following rationale. Since trade marketing by itself primarily attracts consumers by means of the positive effects of extra in-store merchandising and sale pricing, most marketers find it is impossible to meet or exceed the sales volume of the first trade marketing program without repeating the trade marketing offer that fueled the earlier success.

In fact, since most trade marketing efforts of equal value do slightly less well the second time around, the temptation is to enrich the program to achieve sales goals. At this point, the marketer is well along on a path to marketing that is increasingly weighted toward trade marketing. This is the exact path that most packaged goods marketers have followed over the past 15 years.

This continued growth in trade marketing expenditures has caused a major reduction in funding for consumer marketing initiatives. Reduced consumer marketing efforts produce less consumer demand for the product. To maintain sales volume, the marketer must increase trade inducements, thus repeating the cycle and further reducing consumer demand for the product.

Today, many packaged goods products do not have adequate funding to achieve high levels of consumer awareness and attention based on the benefits of the product. Marketers know that inflated trade marketing costs are the problem, but they don't know how to reduce those costs without a disastrous reduction in sales volume. Is there a better way? The answer is a qualified yes.

THE BETTER WAY

The better way is to utilize trade marketing as part of a balanced overall program of marketing, with sufficient funding for brand franchise-building activities — for example, brand-equity-focused advertising, trial-generating consumer promotion, product innovation. This is easy to say, but it's very hard to do, especially if you're already spending heavily on trade marketing.

A number of leading packaged goods marketers today are embarking on an effort to alter the balance to a more favorable consumer-to-trade ratio by significantly reducing the overall level of allowances and at the same time reducing the everyday cost of the product to the retailer and the consumer.

This effort has acquired a name: EDLP (everyday low pricing) or value-pricing. This effort has quickly drawn much media attention and significant retailer resistance. Retailers are very concerned about seeing a major revenue source reduced, and trade marketing funds are a major revenue source. In fact, the trade marketing expenditures of the top two packaged goods marketers, Kraft General Foods and Procter & Gamble, last year exceeded the total profits of the 40 largest food chains.

What will it take to make the reinvestment in brand-building consumer marketing — that marketers need — and at the same time, address the retailers' need for building customer loyalty and traffic and for maintaining high levels and advertising awareness of their stores? It will take a concerted effort by marketers to create and implement programs that:

1. Reach consumers with brand-building messages,
2. Identify individual retailers and their special merchandising,
3. Do both at the same time.

The best news is that this type of approach has been tried with major success by a few leading marketers. This is how it's been done.

First, the marketer decides how best to attract the consumer to his product with positioning and consumer benefits, traditional advertising tools. Then, the marketer creates and runs the advertising for the consumer to see. But rather than creating the advertising and then placing it in the traditional manner, the marketer goes to the retailer, shows the advertising and shows how it will look with each retailer integrated into the advertising. The marketer obtains the retailer's commitment to specially merchandise the product at a time of the retailer's choosing, and then the marketer schedules advertising to run that tells the consumer both about the product and about the retailer's special merchandising in the same ad.

The marketer does this for each retailer on a proportionately equal basis. The net result is a total amount of advertising that is effective in achieving share of voice for the product. In addition, all of the advertising directs the consumer to a specific retailer who has special merchandising on the product at that time; consequently advertising and merchandising work together to generate incremental results for both the marketer and the retailer.

Since the advertising is brand-benefit based, it attracts consumers who are interested in the product because of its benefits, not because it is cheap. Since the advertising is also retailer-specific, it attracts the consumer to a store with strong brand visibility for the product. So the retailer who provides special merchandising gets extra sales with less emphasis on deep-cut pricing.

For the marketer, the best news is that dollars previously deployed for wasteful levels of couponing and/or too-frequent trade deals can now be rechanneled to reward both the retailer and the marketer with significantly higher sales and better long-term prospects.

A major additional benefit is that marketers can create and implement brand-reinforcing consumer promotion programs, which will provide big sales volume increases at the same time. This is possible because the program is advertised with effective message, reach, and frequency to the target audience, and with the news of which specific retailer has special merchandising of the event.

Benefits scorecard

Benefits for the retailer:
1. Meaningful equity-building advertising for the store
2. Extra sales from each merchandising effort
3. Relief from deep-cut price total emphasis

Benefits for the marketer:
1. Significant incremental sales with brand equity focus
2. A net increase in consumer spending and strong retailer support at the same time
3. For the first time, a way to communicate value-added news and reward the retailer who merchandises it well

A few facts from some of the early uses of the program illustrate the potential:
1. Incremental sales of 182 percent against display without the advertising.
2. More than 400 retail accounts participated in the program, representing more than 70 percent ACV.
3. An average of 400 Gross Rating Points nationally on TV during the month of the program, totally funded by nonmedia funds.

Implementation of this program has limitations:
1. The program requires a specialized resource expert in the nuances of the program who is executionally equipped to handle 400–500 individual media buys and commercial customizations, in quick turnaround fashion, with 100 percent accuracy.
2. The approach works well only if the marketer has a meaningful investment in brand equity to leverage.
3. The program must be turnkey for retailers. That is, their participation must be no harder than buying and merchandising the product.
4. The program must work for all sizes and types of retailers. To do so, the program needs media choices and flexibility designed in.

This approach to trade marketing, reaching the consumer with brand-building programs that also leverage each individual retailer, is particularly well-suited to helping marketers restore long-term brand health in an uncertain economic environment. This approach also permits the marketer to reevaluate the elements of the overall marketing plan in order to be consistent with long-term brand building and shorter-term volume requirements at the same time.

TRADE MARKETING KEYS

For the person with trade marketing responsibilities, the following short list of keys is recommended to guide your efforts:
1. Use trade marketing wisely and carefully to achieve important

distribution channel objectives.

2. Fight to limit use. It's really tough to cut back.

3. Use it to support a consumer marketing approach/program rather than as a stand-alone effort.

4. Build an effective long-term trade marketing program by providing tools that help retailers and the brand at the same time.

INDEX

building, trade promotion of, 250–251
enhancement, in point-of-purchase
advertising, 104, 105e, 106e
P-O-P advertising and, 87, 94
putting power in, 207–208
television and, 208

Brand loyalty, frequency programs
and, 76

Broadcast sales management, co-op
advertising in, 164

Brown and Williamson Tobacco
Company, 37

Budget/budgeting
advertising, 164–165, 167
for cooperative advertising, 157
flexibility, specialty promotions and,
228–229
for frequency program, 77
marketing, 239, 239t
for point-of-purchase program, 96
for sweepstakes, contests and games,
49, 63–65

Business gifts, 39

Buying patterns, continuity promotions
and, 68, 69e

Buy One, Get One Free (BOGO), 21, 44

C

Cable television, 208

Campbell Soup, 81

Canada, couponing in, 32

Carolina Manufacturers Service (CMS), 17

Cash prizes, 64–65

Catalogs, co-op advertising in, 164

Celebrities. *See also specific celebrities*
product licensing of, 183

Central location handout couponing,
23–24

Cents-off coupons, 21, 195

Charity events, 215

Cher, 183

"Chivas Regal Presents Frank Sinatra's

Diamond Jubilee," 205, 221

Choices, accelerated, 123t

Clayton Act of 1914, 156

Clearinghouses, for coupon redemption, 27

Collect-and-Win Games, 57, 59e

Collector appeal, of specialty promotions,
235–236

Color Corporation of America, 230, 231e

Communications, technologic
advancements in, 150–151

Competition
co-op mailings and, 117
coupon usage and, 19
meeting through co-op advertising,
161
research on, 95

Consumers
acceptance of sweepstakes, 48
event marketing and, 219–221
incentives for, 35, 42
response to self-service, 86
"trading up," couponing for, 19
unplanned purchases of, 86

Container pack incentives, 39

Contests
advantages of, 49–50
budgeting for, 63–65
definition of, 49
planning for, 61–63
as specialty promotion, 232–234, 233e
types of, 57, 60e, 61
use in tie-ins, 195

Contingent fulfillment, 234, 235e

Continuity programs, 37–38, 70, 143.
See also Frequency programs

Contracts, product licensing, 192

Control of advertising, co-op plans and,
163–164

Co-op accrual system, 169

Co-op advertising
basic conflict of interest in, 157
benefits, for smaller retailers, 168
control of advertising and, 163–164

D

O

P